Digital Parenting

Digital Parenting
Raising Balanced Kids in a Screen-Filled World

Anika Vermeer

Mindful Pages

Published in 2025

ISBN: 9789371349666 (PB)
ISBN: 9789371343749 (eBook)

Published by

Mindful Pages
Imprint of Alpha Editions LLC
312 W. 2nd St #1834
Casper, WY 82601, USA

This book was developed using advanced writing tools to support the drafting and ideation process. All content has been thoughtfully curated, refined, and reviewed to ensure quality and relevance.

Content

Introduction

There is no analogue in the historical record for the breadth and velocity with which technology has upended the contours of everyday life. The digital revolution has not crept in quietly—it has arrived with a thundering permanence, reshaping how we speak, learn, unwind, labour, and build relationships. For today's children, screens aren't an accessory; they're the air they breathe. Touchscreens are swiped before shoelaces are tied, digital avatars slip seamlessly into the role once occupied by imaginary playmates, and the once-clear border between online and offline is now a blurred and shifting line. Of course, every generation has had to contend with technological change. But no generation—until now—has had to do so from the moment they could hold a toy or toddle across a room.

And so, modern parents face a puzzle that feels both urgent and entirely unfamiliar. How do you raise a child with emotional depth, intellectual rigour, and resilience in an age where the screen is omnipresent? How does one cultivate digital fluency without surrendering a child's attention to a thousand apps clamouring for it? The tools that promise to connect and educate can just as easily overwhelm or distort—so where does that leave the people tasked with guiding young minds?

Digital Parenting: Raising Balanced Kids in a Screen-Filled World sets out to wrestle with these questions—not by retreating into rose-tinted nostalgia, nor by casting technology as a villain, but through a lens that is both critical and compassionate. This isn't a manifesto against devices; it's a manual for how to use them wisely. It invites parents to take up the mantle not of digital gatekeeper, but of thoughtful guide—one who sees clearly that technology is neither miracle nor menace, but a tool, and one whose impact depends on how it is used. With intention and discernment, screens can become not a threat, but a companion in the raising of thoughtful, grounded, and capable young people.

The book opens by sketching the broad strokes of how childhood has transformed in the digital age. Where earlier generations might recall scraped knees, handwritten letters, and whispered secrets between friends, today's children are more apt to trade emojis, compete in multiplayer games, and absorb knowledge through animated touchpoints. These changes are not easily categorised. They carry both promise and peril, expanding horizons even as they introduce new stressors. This opening chapter takes stock of both—the opportunities and the landmines. And it doesn't forget the parents themselves, many of whom carry a gnawing sense of unease: Am I getting this right? What damage might I be doing—or failing to prevent? The chapter makes a pivotal argument early on: successful digital parenting cannot be reactive, driven by panic, nor restrictive to the point of futility. It must be purposeful, informed, and, above all, balanced.

To grasp what screens are truly doing to children, one must look beneath the surface—beyond behaviours, into the biology. The second chapter journeys into the realm of neuroscience, exploring how digital inputs affect a child's brain—attention mechanisms, dopamine patterns, emotional regulation. Social media, it turns out, is no mere distraction; it's often a cleverly engineered system, designed to hijack the brain's natural reward loops. Yet the picture isn't all bleak. When used with care, technology can bolster problem-solving abilities, stimulate creativity, and support learning. The key is nuance. Parents need to resist black-and-white thinking—this idea that all screen time is either virtuous or corrupting. A more sophisticated understanding allows for a middle path, where technology becomes a tool for growth rather than a source of depletion.

One of the more persistent myths in popular discourse is the obsession with screen *quantity* over screen *quality*. Chapter Three challenges this metric-based fixation. The amount of time spent with a device tells only a fraction of the story. After all, an hour building a digital model or producing music is vastly different from an hour passively watching loud cartoons. The chapter draws essential distinctions—between active and passive use, solitary scrolling and collaborative creation, intention and mindless drift. It also offers tangible strategies, including the widely useful 80/20 rule: that most screen time should be constructive, creative, or educational. Instead of imposing hard limits with an iron fist, the chapter encourages a more relational, collaborative method—one that recognises a child's agency while still establishing guardrails.

Of course, managing devices is only half the task. The other is preparing children to interpret the vast, messy world they encounter through those devices. Chapter Four zooms out to examine the landscape of digital information—its speed, scale, and frequent slipperiness. Media literacy is no longer a luxury but a necessity. Today's children must learn to ask questions: Who created this? Why does this story appear first? What's being left out? Shielding them from misinformation isn't a long-term solution. Instead, this chapter champions guided exposure, where curiosity is nurtured and critical thinking is modelled. Parents are invited to become conversation partners rather than content police, fostering discernment without descending into paranoia.

Then there's social media—that vast, shifting sea where many children now stake their self-worth. Chapter Five peers into its depths, with all its promise and peril. What begins as connection can quickly morph into comparison, into anxiety, into compulsive performance. Adolescents, in particular, are vulnerable to the quantification of worth: likes, shares, followers—these become stand-ins for self-esteem. The chapter explores how parents can help unhook their children's identity from digital metrics, encouraging instead a sense of self rooted in offline relationships, personal growth, and internal values. It also tackles cyberbullying, privacy, and the often-overlooked art of online empathy—skills children must learn not just for their own wellbeing, but for the sake of a humane digital culture.

And yet—to dwell only on the dangers would be a disservice. Technology holds within it immense potential. Chapter Six takes a brighter view, looking at the positive, even inspiring ways in which children are using digital tools: composing songs, launching small businesses, coding interactive games, creating animations. The chapter showcases how digital creativity can be a family affair, a space for bonding and shared exploration. Parents are encouraged not just to monitor, but to *join in*—to celebrate the projects, engage in the learning, and cultivate the skills that will help their children thrive in a fast-changing world.

Naturally, no matter how carefully one plans, resistance is part of the parenting territory—especially when it comes to limits. Chapter Seven addresses the art (and occasional chaos) of boundary-setting. Rules imposed by decree tend to backfire. This chapter offers a more collaborative approach, including the creation of a family digital agreement: a living document shaped by mutual respect, one that outlines expectations, responsibilities, and consequences. The chapter also explores screen-free zones, parental modelling (which, truth be told, often speaks louder than any rule), and how to navigate the inevitable moments when children test the limits. The aim isn't control—it's shared responsibility.

But raising a digitally healthy child involves more than rules; it requires inner resilience. Chapter Eight turns inward, focusing on self-awareness and the cultivation of mindfulness in digital life. Children must learn to recognise their own habits, to pause, to choose. The chapter doesn't call for rigid digital fasts, which can feel punitive and performative. Instead, it suggests gentle recalibrations: weaving in more analogue moments, restoring the balance between screen and soil, dialogue and silence. Technology should serve, not dominate—and this chapter offers tools to help children make that distinction for themselves.

Still, even with the best intentions, things will at times go awry. Chapter Nine grapples with the tough stuff: compulsive usage, dangerous interactions, and defiance. These aren't indictments of parental failure—they are, rather, signals that something deeper needs attention. The chapter offers a clear-eyed approach to crises, encouraging a return to connection rather than punishment. It introduces resources—therapists, educators, digital wellbeing experts—and reminds parents that the work is not to be perfect, but to persevere.

The final chapter peers ahead. Tomorrow's technologies—augmented reality, generative AI, omnipresent surveillance—will make today's digital dilemmas seem quaint. But retreat is not the answer. Instead, Chapter Ten makes a compelling case for future-ready parenting: cultivating habits of digital discernment, ethical awareness, and open dialogue. These are the tools that will carry children through the storms ahead. And the chapter invites parents to engage, not just with devices, but with the cultural and ethical frameworks that shape them: questions of data, autonomy, transparency. Not for the sake of theory, but because these things are becoming the fabric of daily life.

Ultimately, this book is a reframing. Digital parenting is not a chore, not a desperate reaction to a wave of change. It is a calling—a chance to raise children who are not just protected, but prepared. Who can think clearly in a noisy world. Who can choose substance over spectacle. Who can build relationships that mean something, even across fibre-optic cables.

The screens are not going anywhere. But neither is the steady, anchoring presence of a parent who chooses to lead with curiosity, conviction, and love. This book offers a path to navigate the one, without losing faith in the other.

Chapter 1
The Digital Landscape: Understanding Today's Tech-Driven World

It's often remarked that childhood mirrors the age in which it unfolds—and rarely has that reflection been more sharply refracted than in our digital era. The world children now inhabit scarcely resembles the one familiar to their parents. Gone are the days when play was anchored in scraped knees, whispered secrets passed in notes, and long conversations under open skies. In their place: glowing screens, real-time chats, and digital avatars. What were once luxury gadgets have now become near-constant companions, seamlessly woven into the rhythms of daily life. Online interaction, rather than a supplement to the real world, has become, for many, its very core. The shift has been swift—at times thrilling, often bewildering—and it presses us to ask: what, now, does it mean to grow up?

Comparing then and now lays bare just how radically the digital tide has redrawn the map of childhood. A generation ago, the clock governed a child's day: the school bell rang, dinner was served at six, and bedtime stories signalled lights out. Communication was tethered—geographically and socially—most often involving those nearby, perhaps extending to a friend on the other end of a corded phone. Entertainment was time-bound and shared: television adhered to a schedule, books came to a close, and outdoor games ended with dusk. Today, those boundaries have been blurred beyond recognition. Children are plugged into an ever-expanding world—content is endless, games evolve in real time, and conversations unfold across continents. They live not solely in the material world, but within a vast digital overlay—an environment as immersive as it is intangible, where identity is crafted as much as it is lived.

This revolution, for all its turbulence, brings a paradox of breathtaking proportions. The same tools that tether us to screens have thrown open doors that earlier generations couldn't have imagined. Children today can compose music with a fingertip, programme robots before they've mastered handwriting, and engage with peers across the globe in real time. Learning, once limited by geography or means, has been democratised. Digital resources have transformed literacy and numeracy acquisition, while children with learning differences or physical challenges can access tools that amplify their strengths rather than emphasise their struggles. Creativity, too, has found new frontiers—digital art, video production, interactive storytelling—all now possible from a bedroom desk. These are not trivial gains; they are transformative.

And yet. The very same technology that enables connection can fracture it just as easily. Screens compete, relentlessly, for attention—often winning at the cost of present-moment awareness, meaningful relationships, and even the body itself. Sleep patterns shift, exercise dwindles, and conversations, when they happen, are frequently punctuated by a glance downward. Social media in particular has cultivated a strange theatre of comparison—where curated perfection masquerades as reality, and self-worth too often hinges on numbers: likes, shares, views. Even play, once grounded in physicality and imagination, now risks becoming another feedback loop—engineered for retention rather than joy.

This duality—at once liberating and corrosive—demands that we approach technology not with blanket condemnation, nor with unthinking embrace, but with discernment. The question is not whether screens are good or bad. It is: how are they being used, and to what end? Just as a knife may carve or cut, so too can digital tools either enrich or erode. This perspective, admittedly less tidy than the simple pro/con binary, is also far more useful. It anchors digital parenting not in fear, but in purpose.

Still, one cannot ignore the fatigue many parents feel in trying to keep pace. The modern parenting landscape is littered with contradictory advice, ever-changing platforms, and ambiguous dangers. Unlike previous generations—where the hazards of childhood were largely physical and visible—today's risks often hide in plain sight, cloaked in pixels. Parents worry not just about screen time, but about screen content, about social pressures their children won't disclose, about cyberbullying they may never witness. And with no universal playbook, no clear consensus on best practices, decision fatigue sets in. Even the act of saying "no" can feel isolating, out of step with a world that equates tech-savviness with social currency.

And it's not just children who are ensnared. Adults, too, are caught in the same gravitational pull. One might intend to model good habits, but soon finds themselves scrolling during dinner or replying to emails long past bedtime. This digital dissonance—knowing better, doing otherwise—can quietly corrode confidence, breeding guilt and sparking friction in the family dynamic. The pressures mount from all directions: schools promote tech fluency, peers expect online interaction, and broader society seems to reward hyper-connectivity. Amidst all this, drawing the line feels less like setting a healthy boundary and more like swimming against the tide.

Knowing when screen use veers into unhealthy territory is a delicate art. Some signs shout—tantrums when devices are removed, skipped meals, homework undone. Others whisper—a quiet drift from offline friendships, an obsession with online affirmation, or a steady decline in spontaneous play. Even shifts in sleep or unexplained anxiety may trace back to digital roots, though they're easily misattributed to hormonal upheaval or "just a phase." The challenge lies not in spotting every red flag, but in noticing patterns—when the digital world begins to replace rather than complement the real one.

But caution: not every hour spent on a device signals a problem. The instinct to pathologise all screen use is both tempting and misleading. A child deep into a game may not be "addicted," but may simply find in it a sense of mastery or camaraderie they're not getting elsewhere. In such cases, screen time is a mirror—not the monster. What's needed, then, isn't a clampdown but a closer look: What's driving the behaviour? What's missing offline that the digital world is supplying?

From this place of observation and honesty, a more grounded philosophy of digital parenting begins to emerge. One that doesn't hinge on bans or blind trust, but on clarity. The goal isn't to fence children off from technology, nor to give them unrestricted reign. It's to help them build a relationship with it that's reflective, purposeful, and aligned with their development—not at odds with it.

This approach starts by accepting that families are not carbon copies. What works in one home may flounder in another. Children differ in temperament, resilience, and curiosity—and so must the boundaries we place. It also requires us to shift from policing to guiding. Surveillance, no matter how well-intentioned, rarely builds trust; conversation does. Censorship may silence, but it won't educate. Connection, honest and sustained, remains the bedrock of any effective parenting strategy—digital or otherwise.

Throughout this chapter—and indeed this book—you'll find strategies that are rooted in both principle and practicality. The intention is not to overwhelm, but to equip. From recognising signs of digital fatigue to crafting screen routines that flex rather than fracture, from de-escalating power struggles to nurturing tech-enabled creativity, these insights are drawn from the messiness of real family life. You'll find no moral purity tests here, just a call for progress. Progress towards a home life where devices serve human connection, not replace it.

Let's be clear: the digital age is not a phase our children will outgrow. It is the soil in which their identities are taking root. Learning to navigate it—its beauty, its traps, its endless noise—is part of growing up now. And for parents, understanding that landscape isn't a side project. It's the work. This chapter, then, offers a starting point: a path towards clarity in the face of chaos, and confidence in a realm that too often feels out of our grasp. If we lead with empathy, stay curious, and remember that wisdom needn't always come with certainty, we may just raise a generation who can thrive—both online and off.

The Evolution of Childhood in the Digital Age

Childhood has always reflected the cultural and technological context of its time. Yet, never before has that context shifted so rapidly, comprehensively, and irreversibly as it has with the advent of digital technology. The concept of a "digital native" has emerged to describe the child born into a world saturated with devices, networks, and screens—an environment in which digital interaction is not just common but foundational. Unlike previous technological leaps, such as the printing press or the television, the digital transformation is not limited to a single domain of life. It is ubiquitous, shaping the way children play, learn, socialise, and construct their sense of self. As such, understanding how technology has reshaped childhood is not simply an academic exercise—it is an urgent imperative for parents, educators, and society at large.

The most striking difference between childhood then and now lies in how children spend their time and what occupies their attention. A generation ago, play was predominantly physical, unstructured, and localised. Children built dens from sofa cushions, climbed trees, and rode bicycles until dusk. Their world was bounded by physical space and real-time interactions, punctuated by tangible feedback and sensory engagement. They learned through trial and error, often in outdoor or communal settings, where their actions had immediate and visible consequences. These activities supported not only physical development but also emotional resilience, social negotiation, and creativity.

Today's play, by contrast, is increasingly mediated by screens. Digital games, interactive apps, and online platforms have become the default leisure activity for many children. These tools offer levels of engagement and novelty that traditional toys cannot match. A tablet or smartphone provides access to a vast universe of games, videos, and social content, all curated to optimise retention and interaction. While these digital tools can foster fine motor skills, hand-eye coordination, and certain types of strategic thinking, they often lack the multisensory and interpersonal dimensions that define traditional play. The physicality of the playground has, for many children, been replaced by the virtual space of Minecraft, Roblox, or YouTube.

This shift is not inherently problematic. Digital play can be imaginative, collaborative, and deeply engaging. Platforms such as Minecraft, for example, enable children to construct complex worlds, simulate architectural models, and engage in cooperative tasks with peers across the globe. Educational games can reinforce mathematical reasoning, language development, and scientific inquiry in ways that are adaptive and personalised. The key distinction lies not in whether technology is involved, but in how it is used. Is it passive or active? Is it isolating or interactive? Does it promote reflection or merely distraction?

Another major transformation has occurred in the way children socialise. For much of human history, children formed friendships through proximity—neighbours, classmates, family gatherings. Social bonds were nurtured through shared activities and extended periods of face-to-face interaction. Emotional nuances were interpreted through tone of voice, facial expression, and body language, all of which are essential for developing empathy and emotional intelligence.

The digital age has introduced new modes of communication that are faster, broader, and often more superficial. Social media platforms, text messaging, and online forums allow children to maintain relationships across time zones and geographies. Yet these interactions are often filtered, abbreviated, and curated. A conversation conducted via emojis or TikTok duets lacks the complexity of in-person dialogue. Moreover, the performative nature of social media—where likes, shares, and followers serve as social currency—can distort a child's understanding of friendship, self-worth, and community.

Consider the experience of a twelve-year-old receiving their first smartphone. Previously, their social world would have been contained within school, family, and neighbourhood. With a device in hand, they are suddenly connected to thousands of voices, trends, and potential influences. While this connectivity can foster a sense of belonging, it can also expose children to online harassment, unrealistic body ideals, and peer pressure to present a curated version of themselves. The psychological pressure to remain "visible" online—through posting, commenting, or maintaining streaks—can become a source of chronic anxiety, particularly during adolescence when self-image is in flux.

The educational landscape has also undergone a digital metamorphosis. Where once children depended on encyclopaedias, textbooks, and direct teacher instruction, they now have access to an ocean of information at their fingertips. Search engines, video tutorials, interactive simulations, and learning apps have revolutionised how knowledge is acquired. Children can explore the solar system through virtual reality, dissect a frog in 3D on a tablet, or learn algebra from gamified platforms that adapt to their learning pace. For the inquisitive mind, these tools offer unprecedented opportunities for enrichment and discovery.

However, the abundance of information has its drawbacks. Not all sources are reliable, and the ability to discern credible content from misinformation is a skill that must be taught, not assumed. Additionally, the sheer volume of digital input can fragment attention, reducing the capacity for deep focus and sustained engagement. Children accustomed to switching between tabs, notifications, and apps may struggle with traditional forms of concentration required for reading, problem-solving, or reflective writing. This cognitive fragmentation has implications not only for academic achievement but for emotional regulation and self-awareness.

Moreover, the physical consequences of increased screen time are becoming more apparent. Children today are more sedentary than any generation before them, with rising rates of childhood obesity, myopia, and sleep disturbances linked to excessive screen exposure. Blue light emitted from devices disrupts circadian rhythms, making it harder for children to fall asleep and reducing the quality of rest. The reduction in outdoor play also limits exposure to sunlight, which is essential for bone development and mood regulation. While these effects are not uniform across all children, they signal a broader pattern of lifestyle change that demands careful attention.

It is also important to consider the changing role of the parent within this digital landscape. In previous generations, parenting largely focused on physical safety—making sure children wore helmets, avoided strangers, and came home before dark. Today, the threats are more psychological and less visible. Parents must worry about screen addiction, exposure to harmful content, online predators, and the long-term impact of digital overstimulation. The absence of a clear societal consensus on how much screen time is too much, or what constitutes healthy online behaviour, leaves many parents feeling uncertain and anxious.

The omnipresence of technology in children's lives also creates a new form of generational divide. Many parents did not grow up with smartphones or social media and are therefore less equipped to understand the digital habits of their children. This gap can lead to miscommunication, mistrust, or overly simplistic responses such as blanket bans or unrestricted access—neither of which are effective long-term strategies. Digital literacy is no longer optional for parents; it is a critical component of effective guidance and connection.

Amidst these profound changes, it is tempting to yearn for a return to a "simpler time." However, nostalgia can obscure the opportunities that technology presents. It is not feasible—or desirable—to raise children in a digital vacuum. The goal is not to reject technology, but to integrate it thoughtfully into childhood in ways that preserve its benefits while mitigating its risks. This requires a shift in perspective: from viewing screens as threats to seeing them as tools that can either enrich or erode development depending on their use.

Practical steps toward this integration include co-viewing and co-playing with children, using digital content as a springboard for discussion, and setting collaborative boundaries that evolve with age and maturity. Encouraging offline activities—sports, reading, unstructured play—remains essential, not as punishment for screen use, but as vital components of a balanced life. Most importantly, children must be taught to reflect on their own digital habits: how they feel after scrolling, what content they trust, and why they gravitate towards certain platforms. These conversations build the foundation for self-regulation, critical thinking, and digital citizenship.

The evolution of childhood in the digital age is neither a dystopian decline nor a utopian advance. It is a transformation—multifaceted, ongoing, and deeply influential. Technology has reshaped the landscape of childhood, but it has not rewritten its essence. Children still need love, boundaries, challenge, and play. They still thrive on meaningful relationships, exploration, and the freedom to fail and try again. What has changed is the context in which these needs are met. Our task, then, is not to lament the past or fear the future, but to understand the present with nuance and respond with wisdom.

To raise children in a screen-filled world is to navigate complexity with courage, curiosity, and care. It is to accept that while we cannot return to a pre-digital childhood, we can shape a future in which technology coexists with humanity—where screens illuminate but do not dominate, and where children learn not only to use technology, but to understand, question, and ultimately master it. This is the challenge—and the promise—of parenting in the digital age.

The Double-Edged Sword of Technology

Few innovations have transformed the human experience as profoundly and swiftly as digital technology. For children growing up today, the digital world is not a novel or separate dimension—it is seamlessly interwoven into the fabric of everyday life. From smart toys and tablets to educational apps and social media, digital engagement has become a defining feature of modern childhood. Yet for all its promise and potential, technology also presents a complex web of risks. Its impact is neither singular nor static; it is multifaceted, dynamic, and deeply context-dependent. Understanding this duality—the promise and the peril—requires a careful, honest, and nuanced appraisal.

Digital technology offers remarkable benefits to children, particularly when harnessed with intention and oversight. Educational platforms have revolutionised access to knowledge, democratising learning in unprecedented ways. No longer confined to the content of a single textbook, children can now explore the cosmos through virtual simulations, experiment with physics concepts in gamified formats, or engage with historical events via immersive storytelling apps. These tools cater to diverse learning styles and enable self-paced study, particularly beneficial for children who may struggle in traditional classroom settings. Adaptive learning technologies, for instance, adjust in real-time to a child's progress, offering tailored challenges that neither bore nor overwhelm.

Moreover, the internet has vastly expanded children's capacity to explore the world beyond their immediate environment. A child in a rural village can now interact with peers across continents, gain insight into different cultures, and witness global events as they unfold. This exposure can foster empathy, curiosity, and a more inclusive worldview—traits that are increasingly essential in an interconnected global society. Digital tools also allow children to express themselves creatively in ways that were once out of reach. A ten-year-old today can compose music, animate a short film, or design a video game with nothing more than a tablet and an internet connection. Technology, in this sense, has become a powerful enabler of creative agency.

Communication is another domain in which digital platforms have redefined the parameters of connection. Messaging apps, video calls, and collaborative platforms such as Google Workspace have allowed children to sustain friendships, collaborate on schoolwork, and maintain social ties during periods of disruption, such as the global pandemic. For children with communication challenges or social anxiety, asynchronous or text-based interactions may offer a less intimidating mode of engagement, fostering confidence and inclusion.

Yet these undeniable benefits exist alongside equally significant risks, many of which are subtle, cumulative, and not always immediately visible. One of the most pressing concerns is the impact of screen-based activity on attention and self-regulation. Many digital experiences—particularly those designed for entertainment—are built around rapid stimuli, frequent rewards, and constant novelty. Video games, social media feeds, and short-form video platforms like TikTok are engineered to captivate the brain's reward circuits, releasing dopamine in response to likes, wins, and new content. While this may enhance engagement in the short term, prolonged exposure can alter children's ability to sustain attention, tolerate boredom, or engage in tasks that require delayed gratification.

The implications for learning and development are considerable. Teachers increasingly report that students struggle to concentrate on tasks that are not mediated by screens or punctuated by digital incentives. Parents observe children becoming irritable when asked to disengage from devices, or disinterested in activities that lack the immediate stimulation of digital media. This habituation to high-intensity input can reshape neural pathways, privileging short bursts of satisfaction over long-term effort and reflection. Such a shift may undermine not only academic performance but also emotional resilience, which depends in part on the ability to cope with discomfort, ambiguity, and delayed rewards.

Another area of concern lies in the social and emotional effects of digital engagement. While online interaction can broaden social horizons, it can also distort the nature of relationships. Social media platforms, in particular, encourage performance over authenticity, visibility over depth. Children are drawn into cycles of comparison, seeking validation through metrics such as likes, comments, and followers. These external measures of approval can become internalised, leading children to equate their worth with their online popularity or perceived attractiveness. For adolescents especially, whose identity is still in formation, this pressure can be deeply destabilising. The curated nature of digital content—where everyone seems happier, more successful, and more admired—can exacerbate feelings of inadequacy, anxiety, or exclusion.

Cyberbullying presents another serious hazard. Unlike traditional bullying, which is often confined to specific settings and times, online harassment is relentless, anonymous, and difficult to escape. A hurtful comment posted on a social feed, a rumour spread via a private chat, or a doctored image shared without consent can have devastating psychological consequences. Victims often suffer in silence, ashamed or afraid to tell their parents, and the digital footprint of such incidents means they can be revisited again and again, compounding the trauma. Furthermore, the perceived distance and anonymity of online communication can lead children to say things they would never utter face-to-face, blurring moral boundaries and weakening the development of empathy.

The addictive nature of digital platforms must also be considered. While the term "addiction" should be used cautiously in a clinical context, many children exhibit behaviours that align with dependency: compulsive use, irritability when access is restricted, and neglect of other responsibilities or interests. The mechanisms behind these behaviours are often deliberate. Tech companies deploy sophisticated psychological and behavioural science to maximise time-on-device, using techniques such as variable reward schedules, autoplay, and endless scrolling to reduce user agency. Children, whose executive functioning and impulse control are still developing, are particularly vulnerable to these manipulative design strategies.

Sleep disruption is another well-documented effect of excessive digital engagement. Exposure to blue light from screens interferes with melatonin production, delaying the onset of sleep and reducing its quality. Notifications, messages, and late-night scrolling further fragment sleep cycles, leading to fatigue, irritability, and impaired cognitive performance. These effects can ripple outward, affecting mood regulation, academic focus, and family dynamics. A tired child is more prone to tantrums, less resilient to stress, and more likely to seek refuge in passive digital consumption—thus perpetuating the cycle.

Despite these risks, the solution is not to ban technology outright or romanticise a pre-digital past. Such approaches are both unrealistic and counterproductive. Technology is neither inherently good nor bad; its impact depends on how it is used, and by whom. A balanced approach begins with acknowledging the legitimacy of both the benefits and the drawbacks. This enables parents to make informed decisions that are context-sensitive and developmentally appropriate, rather than reactive or fear-driven.

One practical strategy is to differentiate between types of digital engagement. Passive consumption, such as binge-watching videos or endlessly scrolling through feeds, has very different effects from active creation, problem-solving, or skill development. A child editing a short film or building a digital model is engaging in cognitively demanding tasks that foster perseverance and innovation. By contrast, compulsive scrolling or gaming sessions that replace meals, sleep, or social interaction are cause for concern. Helping children become aware of this distinction empowers them to use technology more consciously and purposefully.

Equally important is the cultivation of open dialogue within families about digital habits, emotions, and experiences. Rather than policing screen time with rigid rules, parents can co-create boundaries with their children, grounded in mutual respect and shared understanding. This collaborative approach not only builds trust but also models the very self-regulation that children must ultimately develop for themselves. Regular check-ins about how certain apps make them feel, what they're learning online, or which platforms they find meaningful can transform technology from a battleground into a bridge for connection.

Schools also have a crucial role to play in guiding digital engagement. Digital citizenship programmes, which teach children about online safety, empathy, critical thinking, and digital ethics, are becoming increasingly essential. Encouraging media literacy—teaching students to question sources, identify bias, and reflect on digital content—can offset some of the distortions of the online world. These skills will not only protect children from immediate harms but equip them for thoughtful, responsible participation in an information-saturated society.

It is also essential to acknowledge the broader ecosystem in which children's digital behaviours are formed. Parents, educators, policymakers, and tech companies all share responsibility. Ethical design practices—such as removing autoplay features for children's content, limiting intrusive advertising, or incorporating natural stopping cues—can mitigate some of the most exploitative aspects of digital platforms. Advocacy for child-centred tech development, grounded in developmental science and pedagogical insight, is gaining momentum and deserves sustained support.

Ultimately, the double-edged nature of technology is not a problem to be solved, but a reality to be navigated. It demands that we move beyond simplistic narratives of screen time good or bad, and instead embrace complexity, context, and care. By recognising both the potential and the pitfalls of digital engagement, we can help children develop the skills they need not only to survive but to flourish in a tech-driven world. This means equipping them with the ability to focus amidst distraction, to connect authentically in digital spaces, to think critically about the information they consume, and to take meaningful breaks from screens when needed.

Digital technology will continue to evolve, bringing with it new tools, platforms, and paradigms of interaction. Our response, then, must evolve with equal sophistication and integrity. By fostering awareness, balance, and intentionality, we can ensure that technology remains a tool that serves human development—not the other way around. And in doing so, we give children the greatest gift of all: not just access to the digital world, but the wisdom to use it well.

Parental Challenges in a Hyper-Connected World

Parenting has never been a task for the faint-hearted. It has always demanded intuition, patience, and a capacity for both firmness and warmth. Yet, in today's hyper-connected world, the complexities of raising children have escalated in ways few could have anticipated. The digital revolution has not only reshaped childhood but has also introduced a new and often invisible layer of stress and uncertainty for parents. Where previous generations worried about curfews, playground injuries, or television habits, today's parents must contend with screen addiction, online predators, digital peer pressure, and the sheer omnipresence of devices in family life. These concerns are not occasional disruptions but ongoing realities that demand daily negotiation and deep emotional investment.

One of the most pressing and visible challenges for modern parents is managing screen addiction—or what appears to be it—in their children. Many parents report that once a child becomes immersed in a screen-based activity, extracting them from it can provoke extreme resistance, tantrums, or emotional withdrawal. This behaviour is often interpreted as disobedience or laziness, yet it is more accurately understood as a response to carefully engineered digital environments designed to capture and hold attention. Platforms such as YouTube, TikTok, and various online games are structured around mechanisms of intermittent reinforcement, rewarding continued use with new content, upgrades, or social validation. These mechanisms trigger the release of dopamine, a neurotransmitter linked to pleasure and reward, thereby creating behavioural loops that are difficult to break—especially for children whose impulse control and executive function are still developing.

Parents often find themselves locked in a battle over screen time limits, unsure of where to draw the line between healthy engagement and harmful dependence. Attempts to restrict access are frequently met with emotional backlash, creating friction that can damage the parent-child relationship. Some parents, fatigued by constant arguments, concede more screen time than they believe is appropriate. Others resort to authoritarian tactics—confiscating devices, enforcing harsh time restrictions—only to find that such measures can lead to secrecy, resentment, or even the development of guilt and shame around technology use. Neither extreme fosters the open, trust-based environment that is necessary for effective digital parenting.

Beyond addiction-like behaviours, the pressure to keep up with rapidly shifting digital trends poses another significant challenge. Children and teenagers are immersed in a culture of perpetual novelty, where new apps, memes, influencers, and social platforms emerge almost weekly. The landscape is not only unfamiliar to many parents but also deliberately opaque. For example, the way Snapchat erases messages or TikTok's algorithm personalises content makes it difficult for adults to monitor or even comprehend what their children are consuming. As a result, many parents experience a profound sense of disorientation and helplessness. They worry about what they cannot see, struggle to relate to experiences they do not share, and feel as though they are perpetually behind the curve.

This disconnection is compounded by digital peer pressure—an often underestimated force that can profoundly influence children's behaviours and parents' decisions alike. Children today do not merely want a smartphone; they want the same apps, devices, and digital privileges that their friends have. They compare screen time limits, game access, social media followers, and even the speed of their internet connections. For parents trying to establish healthy boundaries, this creates a dilemma. Say no, and the child may feel excluded or resentful. Say yes, and the parent may worry they are compromising their values or exposing their child to risks they are not prepared to handle. The weight of these decisions is compounded by the fact that children often lack the maturity to understand long-term consequences, while parents are held responsible for outcomes that may not fully manifest for years.

Furthermore, parents themselves are not immune to the pull of the digital world. Many adults struggle with their own screen habits—whether it is compulsively checking emails, scrolling through social media, or binge-watching series late into the night. Children, highly observant by nature, quickly notice inconsistencies between what their parents say and what they do. A mother who tells her child to put away the tablet during dinner but answers work messages at the table sends a confusing message about priorities. A father who criticises social media obsession while posting daily status updates undermines the credibility of his concerns. These inconsistencies erode parental authority and make it harder to enforce digital rules with authenticity and fairness.

Another less frequently discussed but equally important challenge is the emotional labour of digital parenting. The constant vigilance required to stay informed about potential risks, monitor screen time, check device histories, and navigate conflicts is exhausting. Many parents report feeling mentally depleted and emotionally disconnected, unsure of whether their interventions are effective or even appropriate. This uncertainty is exacerbated by conflicting advice from experts, media outlets, schools, and other parents. Some advocate for tight controls and limited access; others promote digital literacy and self-regulation. With no clear consensus, parents are left to chart their own course through a landscape that feels both urgent and uncharted.

This ambiguity extends to schools, which increasingly integrate technology into learning without always equipping families with the tools to manage its use at home. A child may be assigned homework on a tablet, encouraged to research online, or required to join class discussion forums. While these practices can enhance engagement and access to information, they blur the boundaries between educational and recreational screen time. Parents attempting to limit device use may find themselves at odds with academic requirements, creating confusion and frustration for all involved. Moreover, not all families have equal access to devices, high-speed internet, or digital fluency, leading to disparities that can affect both educational outcomes and parental confidence.

Cultural expectations also play a role in complicating the digital parenting landscape. In some communities, high levels of screen engagement are normalised or even celebrated as signs of modernity, intelligence, or global connectedness. In others, there may be strong resistance to digital tools, leading to polarised views within families or between parents and educators. Multigenerational households may include grandparents who see digital play as laziness, while younger parents may view it as a developmental opportunity. These differing perspectives can create tension and inconsistency, which children are quick to exploit or internalise.

Despite these multifaceted challenges, it is important to recognise that parents are not powerless. While the digital environment is indeed complex, the fundamental principles of effective parenting remain relevant. Children still need guidance, boundaries, empathy, and above all, connection. The key difference lies in how these principles are applied. Rather than simply restricting access, parents must engage with their children's digital lives—ask questions about their favourite games, watch videos together, discuss online dilemmas, and explore how technology makes them feel. These conversations not only build trust but also teach children to think critically about their own behaviour.

Practical strategies can also help mitigate daily stress. Establishing consistent digital routines—such as screen-free dinners, shared tech activities, or device curfews—can create structure and reduce conflict. Modelling balanced digital habits reinforces expectations more effectively than verbal admonitions. Parents might also consider creating a family digital agreement, where rules are co-created and periodically reviewed. This encourages children to take ownership of their digital conduct and feel respected as participants in the process.

Seeking community support can be another powerful tool. Parenting groups, online forums, school partnerships, and digital wellbeing workshops can provide both practical advice and emotional validation. It is reassuring to hear that others share similar struggles, and that there is no perfect formula—only ongoing adjustment and informed decision-making. Educators, paediatricians, and mental health professionals can also offer tailored guidance when specific issues such as gaming addiction, cyberbullying, or screen-related anxiety arise.

Above all, parents need to extend compassion to themselves. The demands of digital parenting are vast and often invisible, yet they are carried out with little recognition or systemic support. Feeling overwhelmed is not a sign of failure but a reflection of genuine care. The willingness to reflect, learn, and adapt is in itself a mark of conscientious parenting. There is no universal script for raising children in a hyper-connected world, but there are principles—honesty, curiosity, empathy, boundaries—that remain constant even as the context shifts.

Digital technology has brought with it extraordinary benefits and equally daunting challenges. For parents, the task is not simply to manage devices but to cultivate discernment, resilience, and meaningful connection in the face of relentless digital stimuli. This requires not just rules but relationships—relationships in which children feel seen, heard, and guided with integrity. In a world of constant connection, it is this human connection that matters most. And it is through this connection that parents can reclaim their rightful place—not as digital gatekeepers, but as compassionate mentors helping their children navigate both the promises and the pressures of a wired world.

Recognising Digital Red Flags

As digital technology becomes more embedded in the daily lives of children, the boundaries between healthy engagement and unhealthy dependence have become increasingly difficult to delineate. Screens are no longer just tools or toys—they are social arenas, learning platforms, and entertainment hubs all rolled into one. Because of their ubiquity and functionality, it is not always obvious when a child's use of technology shifts from beneficial to problematic. Yet this line, though blurry, is critical to identify. Recognising early signs that a child's digital habits are becoming unhealthy is a vital skill for any parent, educator, or caregiver striving to foster balanced development in a tech-saturated world.

One of the first and most telling signs that something may be amiss is when screen use begins to displace essential life activities. Children need sleep, exercise, face-to-face interaction, and unstructured play in order to thrive physically, emotionally, and cognitively. When screen-based activities begin to crowd out these foundational experiences, it should prompt a closer look. A child who consistently skips meals, delays bedtime, or avoids going outdoors in order to remain online may not simply be enthusiastic—they may be exhibiting early signs of digital over-dependence. These behaviours often start subtly: an extra half hour of gaming after dinner, a reluctance to put away the tablet when asked, or a growing disinterest in non-digital pastimes. Over time, these patterns can solidify into routines that are difficult to reverse without deliberate intervention.

Emotional reactivity around devices is another significant red flag. If a child becomes disproportionately upset, irritable, or withdrawn when asked to stop using a device, it may indicate an overreliance on screens for emotional regulation. Parents frequently describe scenarios in which simply turning off the Wi-Fi or confiscating a device triggers an emotional meltdown. While some frustration is expected—after all, children enjoy what they're doing—extreme reactions often signal a deeper entanglement, where digital engagement has become a coping mechanism for boredom, stress, or low mood. This is particularly concerning because it suggests the child has not developed alternative strategies for emotional self-regulation, relying instead on screens to distract or soothe.

Changes in mood and behaviour that correlate with screen use can also provide important insights. A child who is consistently more anxious, moody, or agitated after extended time online may be experiencing cognitive or emotional overload. The content they consume, the pace of information, or the social dynamics of online platforms may be overstimulating their developing nervous system. This is especially common with fast-paced video content, competitive gaming environments, or social media interactions that provoke comparison, conflict, or exclusion. When a child's temperament shifts noticeably around digital activity—either during use or afterwards—it is worth exploring what they are engaging with and how it is affecting them.

Academic performance and motivation are other areas where digital red flags often appear. A child who was once curious and engaged may begin to struggle with schoolwork, show signs of fatigue in class, or express a disinterest in learning. While many factors can contribute to academic changes, excessive or poorly managed screen time is frequently involved. Children who stay up late using devices often experience reduced concentration and memory retention during the day. Furthermore, if screen-based entertainment is heavily prioritised over reading, problem-solving, or critical thinking tasks, the brain adapts accordingly, becoming less attuned to activities that require sustained focus and mental effort. The lure of instant gratification offered by digital media can make traditional educational tasks feel unrewarding by comparison.

Social withdrawal, particularly from offline friendships and family interaction, is another key indicator. It is natural for children, especially adolescents, to value peer relationships and seek independence from parents. However, when digital interaction replaces most or all face-to-face engagement, it can hinder the development of crucial interpersonal skills. Some children begin to favour online friendships exclusively, finding comfort in the anonymity or curated nature of digital communication. Others may avoid social settings altogether, preferring the predictability of screen-based experiences to the messiness of real-world interaction. Over time, this can erode empathy, communication skills, and emotional resilience—traits that are not easily cultivated in digital isolation.

There are also cognitive indicators of digital overload that may go unnoticed but are equally significant. These include reduced attention span, poor memory retention, and difficulty transitioning between tasks. A child who cannot focus on a single activity without checking a screen, who becomes restless when not being entertained, or who struggles to follow multi-step instructions may be experiencing digital-induced cognitive fatigue. This often occurs in children who regularly multitask—such as watching videos while doing homework or messaging friends during class. Although the brain can technically switch between tasks, this rapid shifting reduces processing depth, leading to surface-level understanding and diminished learning outcomes.

In some cases, digital red flags take the form of secrecy or defensiveness. A child who consistently hides their screen from view, quickly closes tabs when someone walks by, or becomes evasive when asked about their online activity may be engaging with inappropriate or potentially harmful content. This might include exposure to violent or sexual material, interaction with strangers, or participation in risky online behaviours such as dares, challenges, or unmoderated forums. While a degree of privacy is developmentally appropriate, persistent secrecy—especially when coupled with mood changes or sleep disturbances—should not be ignored. Open, non-punitive dialogue is essential in these situations to understand what the child is experiencing and to re-establish trust.

Parents must also be alert to signs of digital comparison and performance anxiety, particularly linked to social media. Children and teens are increasingly exposed to carefully curated images of peers who appear happier, more attractive, more popular, or more successful. This often leads to internalised self-judgement, dissatisfaction, and even depression. If a child begins to express a persistent sense of inadequacy, obsessively checks their social media status, or seeks reassurance based on likes or comments, it may reflect a growing dependence on external validation through digital metrics. These patterns can be psychologically corrosive and are associated with lower self-esteem and greater vulnerability to mental health challenges.

Importantly, many of these red flags do not operate in isolation. They often appear in clusters and accumulate gradually, making them easy to dismiss as passing phases or normal behaviour. The key is to observe patterns over time rather than reacting to isolated incidents. A single meltdown over screen time is unlikely to indicate a serious problem—but repeated meltdowns, coupled with reduced sleep, increased secrecy, and diminished offline engagement, paint a different picture. Parents should trust their instincts and consider the holistic context of their child's wellbeing.

Responding to these warning signs effectively requires a combination of empathy, boundaries, and active engagement. Blaming or shaming a child for their screen habits is counterproductive and may drive the behaviour underground. Instead, parents should seek to understand what emotional or psychological needs the digital activity is meeting. Is the child bored, lonely, anxious, or trying to fit in? By addressing the underlying causes rather than merely the symptoms, interventions become more compassionate and more likely to succeed.

For example, if a child uses gaming as an escape from academic stress, support might involve rebalancing their workload or exploring learning strategies that reduce frustration. If a teenager is obsessed with a particular influencer, discussing what they admire about that person can open the door to conversations about identity, values, and self-expression. When screen time is used to soothe difficult emotions, parents can model and teach alternative coping strategies—mindfulness, journaling, physical activity—that gradually become more appealing or effective than scrolling through content.

Professional support may also be necessary when red flags persist despite parental intervention. Digital addiction, depression, anxiety, and self-harm are increasingly intertwined in adolescent cases, and early engagement with mental health professionals can prevent long-term consequences. Likewise, schools and community organisations can provide workshops, counselling, or peer mentorship programmes that normalise discussions around digital wellbeing and help children feel less alone in their struggles.

As the digital environment continues to evolve, so too must our understanding of its impact on young people. Recognising digital red flags is not about moral panic or controlling behaviour—it is about protecting the developmental foundations that enable children to grow into emotionally healthy, intellectually curious, and socially connected adults. It means cultivating awareness, both in ourselves and in our children, so that screen use becomes a conscious choice rather than a compulsive default.

Technology is here to stay, and in many ways, that is a gift. But like any gift, it must be used wisely, with discernment and care. The first step in that direction is to notice—really notice—when something doesn't feel quite right. By paying attention to these signals, asking the right questions, and responding with compassion and consistency, parents can intervene before minor issues become major problems. In doing so, they offer their children not just guidance, but the tools to eventually guide themselves.

Setting the Stage for Balanced Digital Parenting

In today's hyperconnected world, the role of a parent is increasingly intertwined with the digital lives of their children. From toddlers swiping through story apps to teenagers navigating the complex terrain of social media, screens have become an integral part of daily life. Digital technology offers unprecedented access to information, learning, entertainment, and connection—but with that access comes responsibility, and for parents, a profound sense of uncertainty. It is no longer sufficient to merely restrict screen time or monitor device use. The real challenge lies in fostering a healthy relationship between children and technology—one rooted not in control, but in awareness, purpose, and mutual understanding. This is the essence of balanced digital parenting.

At the core of this book is the philosophy of *mindful, intentional tech use.* This approach recognises that technology, like any powerful tool, can be either constructive or corrosive depending on how it is employed. It rejects both the naive optimism that all tech is progress and the fear-driven tendency to treat all screens as harmful. Instead, it calls for conscious engagement—by parents and children alike—with the digital world. This means asking not only *how much* screen time is occurring, but *why* it is happening, *what* it is replacing, and *how* it is affecting the child's overall wellbeing.

Mindful tech use begins with presence. In many homes, digital devices function as background noise—always on, always within reach, always demanding attention. Children eat meals while watching videos, complete homework with notifications pinging in the background, and relax by scrolling endlessly through curated content. Such a digital environment fragments attention and displaces the quiet moments necessary for creativity, self-reflection, and emotional growth. Parents, too, are often caught in the same loop—checking work emails at the dinner table, scrolling social media during family outings, or replying to messages late into the night. The result is not only overstimulation but a subtle erosion of relational quality. A conversation cut short by a notification, eye contact replaced by a glance at a screen—these moments accumulate and send powerful, if unintended, messages to children about the value of human connection.

Adopting a mindful approach requires us to pause and consider the intentions behind our digital behaviours. Are we reaching for our phones out of habit, anxiety, or boredom? Are our children using screens to explore, to connect, or simply to escape? These are not questions of morality, but of clarity. Intentional tech use involves cultivating this clarity and making choices that align with our values and priorities. It encourages parents to define what a healthy digital life looks like for their family, and to model those principles in everyday interactions.

This philosophy is not about achieving a flawless digital balance, but about striving for alignment. A family might decide that screen time is acceptable after homework and chores are completed, or that devices stay outside bedrooms overnight. Another household might focus on co-viewing content, discussing online experiences openly, or prioritising creative over passive screen use. The point is not to impose uniform rules but to develop shared expectations based on open dialogue, empathy, and mutual respect.

Such intentionality also invites a shift from fear-based control to trust-based guidance. Many parents, overwhelmed by media headlines and anecdotal horror stories, respond by trying to eliminate risk through bans, restrictions, or surveillance. While boundaries are certainly necessary—especially for younger children—excessive control can backfire. It may breed secrecy, resentment, or dependence on external authority rather than fostering the internal self-regulation children need to thrive in a digital world. A mindful approach, by contrast, helps children understand *why* certain boundaries exist and encourages them to participate in setting those limits. This empowers them to make responsible choices not because they are being watched, but because they have internalised values and developed discernment.

Real-world examples illustrate how this philosophy can be applied. Consider a nine-year-old who enjoys video games but often becomes frustrated and agitated after playing for long periods. A mindful parent might observe this pattern and initiate a conversation: "I notice you seem upset after gaming. Have you noticed that too?" Together, they might agree on a time limit and brainstorm alternative activities to wind down in the evening. Rather than imposing rules unilaterally, the parent includes the child in problem-solving, modelling emotional intelligence and promoting autonomy. The goal is not to eliminate gaming, but to help the child become more aware of its impact and make informed choices.

Or take the case of a teenager using social media to stay connected with friends, but who begins expressing insecurity about their appearance. An intentional response might involve exploring the curated nature of online content, discussing the difference between self-worth and digital validation, and reinforcing offline sources of confidence. This approach fosters critical thinking and emotional resilience, rather than shame or restriction. It also creates a space where the teenager feels seen and heard—a crucial element in building trust.

Balanced digital parenting also recognises the evolving nature of childhood and adolescence. What works for a seven-year-old will not be suitable for a fourteen-year-old. As children mature, so must the strategies we use to support them. Younger children benefit from clear structure and close supervision, but older children require increasing freedom to make decisions, learn from missteps, and develop their own sense of digital identity. A mindful parent adjusts not only the rules, but also the conversations—shifting from directives to dialogue, from control to coaching. This gradual handover of responsibility mirrors other aspects of development, from managing money to navigating friendships, and is essential for building lifelong digital literacy.

Intentional tech use also involves being attuned to context. Not all screen time is created equal, and what may be beneficial in one situation could be harmful in another. A child using a tablet to research a school project is engaging very differently than one passively watching a video for three hours. Similarly, using a messaging app to support a friend through a difficult time has a different impact than endlessly scrolling through viral memes. A mindful approach examines not just the activity, but its timing, purpose, and emotional consequences. It also considers broader lifestyle balance—ensuring that screen time does not crowd out sleep, movement, family connection, or unstructured play.

Technology, for all its risks, also offers tremendous opportunities for growth and connection. A child interested in wildlife might explore virtual safaris, participate in citizen science projects, or join online forums with fellow enthusiasts. A teenager passionate about coding can access free courses, contribute to open-source projects, or even develop their own apps. These are not trivial pursuits—they represent the digital equivalent of hobbies, apprenticeships, and creative endeavours. Supporting these positive uses of technology requires an open mind and a willingness to engage. Parents who learn about their child's digital interests, ask curious questions, and even participate occasionally build bridges of understanding that pay dividends over time.

To cultivate this engagement, parents may need to reflect on their own relationship with technology. It is difficult to promote balance when our own habits are skewed. Many adults feel tethered to their devices—checking emails late at night, scrolling during family time, or reaching for a phone in every idle moment. Children notice these behaviours and internalise them. By modelling mindful use—putting devices away during meals, creating screen-free rituals, or discussing our own challenges with digital balance—parents can demonstrate that tech habits are not about perfection, but about awareness and intention.

Educational institutions and broader communities also have a role to play in reinforcing the principles of balanced digital parenting. Schools can offer media literacy curricula, digital wellbeing workshops, and guidance on online ethics. Communities can host dialogues, provide resources, and create spaces for families to connect offline. When children see consistent messages across their environments, it strengthens the foundation of mindful engagement. It also reminds parents that they are not alone—digital parenting is a shared endeavour, not an individual struggle.

At its heart, this philosophy is not about controlling technology—it is about elevating human development. It is about using technology as a tool, not a crutch; as a medium for connection, not a substitute for presence; and as a source of learning, not escape. It calls for an approach that is thoughtful, compassionate, and grounded in values. One that acknowledges complexity, embraces dialogue, and prioritises relationships over rigid rules.

Setting the stage for balanced digital parenting is not a one-time task—it is a continuous, evolving process. It requires us to listen deeply, reflect honestly, and act with intention. But it is also profoundly rewarding. When parents and children work together to navigate the digital world with clarity and care, they create more than just healthy tech habits—they cultivate trust, resilience, and mutual respect. And those qualities, unlike apps or devices, never go out of date.

Chapter 2
The Science of Screens: How Technology Affects Kids' Brains

In recent years, neuroscience has begun to illuminate the complex interplay between experience and brain development—offering a particularly urgent lens through which to examine childhood in an age defined by screens. The world today's children inhabit is not merely digitally enhanced; it is digitally embedded. Where older media like radio or print offered passive content, today's digital environments are responsive, immersive, and algorithmically tailored to individual users. They are not just consumed—they adapt, interact, and react in real time. For anyone concerned with the growth of young minds—parents, teachers, policymakers—grappling with the neurological implications of this shift is not an academic exercise but an immediate necessity.

One of the central mechanisms in this story is dopamine—the neurotransmitter that shapes motivation, learning, and reward. In traditional contexts, dopamine is released when effort leads to accomplishment: a completed puzzle, a problem solved, or praise earned. Digital media, by contrast, often short-circuits this process. It offers dopamine spikes without the delay—notifications, achievements, endless new content, algorithmically designed to keep users engaged. A child playing a game may be rewarded not once, but continually, with lights, sounds, points, and status upgrades. Social platforms drip-feed approval in the form of likes, emojis, or comments. In these environments, gratification isn't earned—it's manufactured.

And so begins a loop. The young brain, hungry for pleasure and novelty, finds in screens a source of immediate and repeatable stimulation. Over time, the cost becomes evident. The subtle pleasures of reading a chapter, waiting for the paint to dry on a drawing, or sitting with boredom—these begin to pale. Real-world activities, which unfold more slowly and require greater effort, can start to seem less rewarding. The brain begins to tilt its expectations.

Attention, that essential capacity for depth and sustained focus, starts to fragment.

It's no wonder many parents speak of the battle to "pull their child back" after screen time. Post-device, children may be irritable or sluggish, unfocused or impatient. They're not just being obstinate. These behaviours often reflect neurobiological shifts. The prefrontal cortex—the part of the brain responsible for planning, regulation, and impulse control—is still under development in children and adolescents. When it is repeatedly overwhelmed by rapid-fire digital input, it struggles to mature in the way it should. Skills that depend on slowness—reflection, emotional modulation, patience—begin to atrophy.

Social media magnifies these dynamics in uniquely potent ways. Platforms like TikTok, Instagram, and Snapchat create ecosystems of performance, where children are both audience and spectacle. Here, identity becomes a function of feedback. One post receives dozens of likes—validation. Another falls flat—doubt creeps in. Adolescents, already attuned to social cues and peer judgment, become especially vulnerable. Their developing sense of self is mirrored back to them through algorithms and metrics.

The pressure isn't just to be seen—it's to be seen in a certain light. Influencers, peers, celebrities—these curated digital selves set the bar. The images children consume are often filtered, staged, or edited, but that doesn't make them feel any less real. A teenage girl might measure herself against a stranger's perfected image and come up short. A boy may internalise unrealistic standards of success or masculinity, based on what others choose to highlight online. This quiet, constant comparison wears at self-esteem. And because it's embedded in daily interaction, it's rarely noticed until the effects become acute.

More insidiously, the performance of happiness itself becomes a demand. Children are encouraged—implicitly and sometimes explicitly—to present as always cheerful, accomplished, socially engaged. Authenticity gives way to curation. Vulnerability becomes risky. And behind the gloss of perpetual connectivity, many children report feeling increasingly alone. Even when the phone is off, the anxiety lingers: What did I miss? Who's out without me? The fear of exclusion, of falling behind socially, doesn't stop at the screen's edge.

Sleep is another quiet casualty in all this. The body's natural rhythms—its circadian clock—depend on cues like darkness to release melatonin and prepare for rest. Blue light from screens disrupts this, delaying sleep onset and reducing sleep quality. Children who use devices before bed may struggle to wind down, waking groggy and unfocused. But it's not just about the light. It's also the mental activity—scrolling, messaging, anticipating responses—that keeps the mind in a state of partial alert. Many children sleep with their devices nearby, waking to check notifications or falling asleep mid-scroll. The result is fractured rest and a brain that never quite powers down.

Gaming presents a more nuanced picture. Games often blend achievement, storytelling, social interaction, and competition in ways that feel deeply meaningful to children. For some, gaming is not merely entertainment—it's a space of mastery, belonging, and narrative engagement. A child who feels marginalised at school might find a team online. A teenager struggling with anxiety may discover a sense of control and competence within a game's structured world. These experiences can be profoundly validating.

Indeed, when gaming is balanced, it offers cognitive and social benefits. Strategy games sharpen executive function; cooperative formats teach communication and leadership. Educational games can reinforce learning through dynamic feedback loops. But these same elements—rewards, immersion, social validation—also make games intensely compelling, and therefore difficult to moderate. Games with no natural endpoint, or those tied to monetised incentives, blur the line between engagement and compulsion. Children may find themselves slipping into marathon sessions, drawn by the promise of the next reward, and resistant to the real world's slower tempo.

Of course, not all screen use is harmful. In fact, some digital tools enhance learning and creativity in ways few analogue methods could. Coding apps teach logic. Virtual science labs simulate experiments too dangerous or costly for the classroom. Children can compose music, create animations, build digital worlds. Augmented reality can animate a biology lesson; visual tools can bring abstract maths to life. And for children with learning differences, these tools aren't just beneficial—they're transformative.

Speech-to-text software can support a child with dyslexia. Time-management apps can help a child with ADHD stay on task. Gamified content can motivate learners who feel defeated by traditional instruction. For children with physical disabilities, digital platforms can provide a means of expression and connection that transcends physical limits.

So, the question isn't *whether* children should use screens, but *how* and *why*. Passive scrolling is not the same as intentional creation. Compulsive engagement differs profoundly from curiosity-driven exploration. The context, content, and emotional state of the child—all matter. Are they energised or exhausted afterward? Are they more open or withdrawn? More curious, or simply numbed? These are the metrics that count, far more than total hours tracked.

Helping children use technology well requires more than rule-setting. It demands presence. Parents and educators must become careful observers and open collaborators. Screen-free zones, digital curfews, and co-viewing are helpful structures—but equally vital is the willingness to talk. What do children *feel* when they're online? What excites them? What unsettles them? These conversations foster trust, and with it, self-awareness—something no parental control app can provide.

We are only beginning to understand the full neurological and psychological ramifications of digital immersion during childhood. But the stakes are plain. These are the years when the brain is building foundations for everything that follows: how we learn, how we relate, who we believe ourselves to be. Digital tools can either scaffold that growth or derail it. The difference lies in intention and awareness.

This chapter lays the groundwork for that awareness, drawing together research across neuroscience, psychology, and education to chart both the promise and the peril of screen-based life. It explores the inner workings of reward circuitry, the emotional architecture of social media, the neurological cost of overstimulation, and the surprising upsides of thoughtful tech integration. More than anything, it offers a framework—a way of thinking that parents and carers can carry into the daily, imperfect, deeply human work of raising children in a digital world. Not with fear, but with insight. Not with control, but with connection.

Digital Dopamine: How Screens Hook the Mind

Every parent has witnessed it: the child who, eyes locked onto a tablet, refuses to look up when called; the tantrum that erupts the moment the television is turned off; the teenager who insists they'll get off the phone "in five minutes," only to be scrolling an hour later. These behaviours, increasingly common, can baffle and frustrate caregivers. But they are not simply matters of poor discipline or modern laziness. At their core lies a powerful neurochemical process—one that shapes not only how children engage with technology, but how they learn, focus, and regulate their emotions. This is the world of *digital dopamine.*

Dopamine is a neurotransmitter crucial to the brain's reward system. It plays a key role in motivation, pleasure, learning, and habit formation. When we experience something enjoyable—a tasty meal, a compliment, a successful challenge—dopamine is released in the brain, reinforcing that behaviour and increasing the likelihood that we will repeat it. In evolutionary terms, this system has helped humans pursue beneficial actions, such as social bonding, exploration, and problem-solving. However, modern technology has learned to exploit this system with unprecedented precision.

Digital platforms—from social media to video games to video streaming—are meticulously engineered to stimulate dopamine release. Unlike traditional forms of play or interaction, which typically offer delayed or infrequent rewards, screen-based environments provide constant and instant feedback. A child taps a button and a cartoon character jumps; they win a game and are showered with visual effects and triumphant music; they post a photo and receive a flurry of likes within minutes. Each of these actions, small though they may seem, activates the brain's reward circuitry. Over time, the brain learns to associate screens with pleasure, control, and accomplishment—and craves more.

This craving is not addiction in the clinical sense, but it shares many of the same neurological pathways. The dopamine system is especially active in children and adolescents, whose brains are still developing and are more sensitive to reward. The prefrontal cortex, responsible for impulse control, planning, and long-term decision-making, is not fully matured until the mid-twenties. As a result, younger individuals are more susceptible to instant gratification and less equipped to moderate their own screen use. This developmental mismatch creates the perfect conditions for compulsive digital behaviour.

One key mechanism at play is what psychologists refer to as *intermittent reinforcement.* This occurs when rewards are delivered unpredictably, rather than on a fixed schedule. Slot machines are the classic example, and many digital platforms mimic this model. A child playing an online game may not know when the next prize, power-up, or level-up will occur, which keeps them engaged for longer. Similarly, social media notifications arrive at irregular intervals, making users check their phones compulsively in anticipation of new updates. This unpredictability keeps the dopamine system on high alert, reinforcing habitual checking and prolonged engagement.

The consequences of chronic digital stimulation are significant, particularly for attention. Attention is not merely about the ability to concentrate—it is a fundamental cognitive skill that underpins memory, learning, problem-solving, and self-regulation. When attention is constantly fragmented by screen-based activities, it becomes harder for children to engage with tasks that require sustained effort. Traditional classroom activities, such as reading a book, solving complex maths problems, or writing essays, may feel dull by comparison. The brain, accustomed to the rapid rewards of digital engagement, struggles to tolerate boredom or delayed gratification.

This neurological shift is observable in behavioural patterns. Children who spend extensive time on fast-paced digital content often show signs of restlessness, reduced patience, and difficulty completing non-digital tasks. They may interrupt conversations, lose interest quickly, or avoid challenges that do not offer immediate feedback. These behaviours are sometimes mistaken for attention-deficit disorders, but they may in fact be symptoms of overstimulated reward systems. While not all screen use leads to these effects, chronic and unregulated exposure increases the risk considerably.

Moreover, the impact of digital dopamine is not confined to cognitive function—it also affects emotional regulation. Because screens can serve as a quick fix for discomfort—whether it's boredom, sadness, or anxiety—children may begin to rely on devices to manage their emotions. A child upset after school may instinctively reach for a tablet rather than talking about their feelings or engaging in restorative play. Over time, this pattern can hinder the development of internal coping strategies. The device becomes a pacifier, offering distraction rather than resolution.

Real-world parenting scenarios reflect these challenges daily. A father might notice his ten-year-old becoming increasingly irritable when asked to stop playing a game, despite clear rules about screen time. A mother may find her daughter sneaking her phone under the covers at night, unable to resist checking for new messages. Teachers report that students are more distractible, less reflective, and more prone to emotional outbursts than in previous decades. While many factors contribute to these changes, the neurological impact of screen-driven dopamine release is a major piece of the puzzle.

Importantly, none of this means that technology is inherently harmful. The same mechanisms that create compulsive patterns can also be harnessed for learning, creativity, and skill-building—if guided appropriately. Educational apps that use gamified feedback can help children master difficult concepts. Mindfulness platforms can teach breathing and focus techniques. Music and art applications can stimulate creativity and persistence. The challenge lies in using these tools with intention, awareness, and balance.

One effective approach is to help children become aware of how digital experiences make them feel—both during and after use. A parent might ask, "Do you feel more calm or more restless after watching that video?" or "What did you enjoy about that game, and what didn't you like?" These questions encourage self-reflection and metacognition, helping the child to develop insight into their own patterns of behaviour. Over time, this awareness can lead to greater self-regulation and healthier choices.

Creating digital routines that include natural stopping points also helps to retrain the brain. For example, choosing games or videos with defined endpoints, rather than endless scrolling or open-ended play, allows for smoother transitions and less friction. Introducing screen-free times—particularly before bed, during meals, and in the early morning—gives the brain time to recalibrate. Sleep, nutrition, exercise, and unstructured play remain essential counterbalances to digital engagement and support the development of neural networks that govern attention and regulation.

The role of parents as digital role models cannot be overstated. Children are keen observers, and they learn not only from what adults say but from what they do. If a parent is constantly checking their phone, interrupting conversations to respond to messages, or using screens to unwind after stress, children will internalise these behaviours. Conversely, when parents demonstrate mindful tech use—such as putting devices away during meals, choosing screen-free leisure activities, or expressing curiosity about digital habits—they lay the groundwork for thoughtful, intentional engagement.

Educational systems must also respond to these neurocognitive dynamics. Classrooms that rely heavily on screens without balancing them with analogue tasks risk compounding attention issues. Schools can play a vital role in modelling balanced tech use, promoting media literacy, and integrating digital tools that reinforce focus rather than fragmentation. Collaborations between educators and families are essential in aligning messages and strategies to support children's cognitive and emotional development.

Dopamine is not the enemy. It is a natural part of our neurological landscape, one that motivates and rewards us for engaging with the world. But like any powerful force, it requires balance. When digital environments continually overstimulate this system without periods of rest or reflection, the brain adapts in ways that can be counterproductive. The result is a mind conditioned to seek constant novelty, react impulsively, and resist discomfort.

Recognising this dynamic allows parents to approach screen management not as a battle, but as a developmental task—one that involves teaching children to understand their own minds, regulate their own impulses, and choose activities that align with their values and long-term wellbeing. By bringing attention to the neuroscience of digital engagement, we move beyond moral judgements and into the realm of empowerment. Children are not simply passive victims of technology; they are active participants who, with the right guidance, can learn to use it wisely.

In a world where screens are omnipresent, the goal is not abstinence but awareness. Helping children navigate the allure of digital dopamine requires knowledge, empathy, and consistency. It asks parents to engage not just with rules and restrictions, but with relationships, routines, and reflection. When we understand how screens hook the mind, we are better equipped to unhook them—not by force, but by fostering the very qualities that make young minds flourish: curiosity, focus, emotional insight, and the capacity to choose wisely.

Social Media and Self-Esteem

For today's generation of children and adolescents, social media is more than just a form of entertainment—it is a cultural environment in which identity is shaped, value is assessed, and relationships are negotiated. Platforms such as Instagram, TikTok, Snapchat, and increasingly even YouTube have become digital mirrors, reflecting and refracting how young people see themselves and others. They offer instant access to peer feedback, endless content curation, and a platform for self-expression. Yet beneath this apparent empowerment lies a growing concern among psychologists, educators, and parents: how these platforms influence self-worth and perpetuate a culture of comparison that can erode self-esteem.

At the heart of this influence is the way social media turns identity into a performative act. Adolescents, by nature, are in the midst of an intense developmental phase where they are experimenting with self-image, values, and social roles. Historically, this process was navigated through direct interpersonal experiences—at school, during extracurricular activities, and within family and friendship circles. Today, much of that identity formation unfolds online, shaped by likes, follows, and filtered aesthetics. Social media invites young users to curate their lives into highlight reels—moments of happiness, achievement, beauty, and social acceptance—which are then measured against a global and highly selective peer standard.

This performative dynamic creates an environment where self-worth becomes closely tied to digital approval. A well-lit selfie that earns dozens of likes can trigger a surge of validation, while a post that receives little engagement can provoke self-doubt. These interactions are not inconsequential; they activate the brain's reward system, releasing dopamine and reinforcing behaviour. Over time, young people can become conditioned to equate their value with their visibility. The adolescent who receives consistent online affirmation may develop a fragile sense of self that depends on external validation, while one who is ignored or criticised online may internalise rejection as a reflection of their worth.

Comparison is an inevitable feature of social media, and it operates on both conscious and subconscious levels. Scrolling through a feed filled with polished images of peers on holiday, attending parties, achieving success, or displaying physical attractiveness can make one's own life feel dull, inadequate, or incomplete by comparison. The psychological phenomenon of *social comparison theory*—which suggests individuals determine their self-worth based on comparisons to others—is exacerbated in digital environments where everyone seems to be performing at their best. Children and teens may begin to believe that others are inherently happier, more attractive, more popular, or more talented, fostering a sense of deficit that undermines their confidence.

This distorted perception of reality is intensified by algorithmic design. Social media platforms are not passive tools; they are engineered to maximise engagement by showing users content that aligns with their interests, interactions, and browsing patterns. While this can create an appealingly personalised experience, it can also reinforce narrow ideals. A teenager who frequently engages with fitness content may be shown increasingly extreme portrayals of thinness or muscle definition. A child interested in beauty may encounter a stream of filtered, edited images that portray unrealistic aesthetic standards. These algorithmic feedback loops can limit exposure to diverse representations of success, beauty, and identity—trapping young users in a curated echo chamber of perfection.

The emotional consequences of these dynamics are evident in both qualitative studies and lived experiences. Psychologists are reporting rising levels of anxiety, depression, and body image dissatisfaction among children and adolescents who are heavy users of social media. Girls, in particular, are vulnerable to developing negative body image due to constant exposure to unattainable beauty ideals. Boys, though less often discussed, also face pressures—particularly around strength, status, and material success. What is perhaps most troubling is how early these patterns begin. Children as young as nine or ten are already posting content, seeking validation, and worrying about their online appearance.

Real-world stories reflect these concerns vividly. Consider a 13-year-old who deletes a post if it doesn't receive a certain number of likes within an hour, fearing social embarrassment. Or a teenager who spends hours retaking and editing selfies to achieve a look that meets peer expectations. Another child might feel excluded and inferior after viewing photos of a party they weren't invited to, even if they had been perfectly content before seeing the post. These experiences may seem minor to adults but can be deeply destabilising to young users still developing their sense of self.

Despite these challenges, it is important not to demonise social media. These platforms also offer opportunities for connection, creativity, and activism. For marginalised youth, in particular, online spaces can provide a sense of community and visibility not available in their immediate environment. Young people can use social media to share their art, express their views, and learn about the world. The issue is not the presence of social media, but the lack of critical tools with which to navigate it.

Developing those tools starts with fostering media literacy and emotional awareness. Children must be taught to question what they see online—recognising that posts are curated, edited, and often strategically constructed. They need help understanding that a filtered image or a viral video represents a fraction of someone's life, not the full reality. Encouraging children to ask, "What's not shown here?" or "How does this make me feel and why?" helps to break the automatic loop of comparison and invites reflection. These habits build resilience and reduce the risk of internalising unrealistic standards.

Equally important is the cultivation of offline sources of self-worth. Children who have strong relationships, meaningful hobbies, and a sense of purpose beyond the digital world are better equipped to resist the lure of social media validation. Activities that promote mastery, creativity, and contribution—such as sport, music, volunteering, or art—reinforce a stable sense of identity that is not easily shaken by fluctuating online feedback. Parents can support this by prioritising family time, encouraging diverse interests, and celebrating effort and character rather than appearance or popularity.

Open dialogue is essential. Rather than lecturing or criticising, parents can approach conversations about social media with curiosity and empathy. Asking children how they feel about what they see online, what they enjoy, what stresses them, and how they navigate digital friendships builds trust and invites honesty. These discussions provide a foundation for guidance that is collaborative rather than authoritarian. When young people feel heard and respected, they are more likely to internalise values and boundaries around digital behaviour.

Schools also have a role to play. Programmes that teach digital citizenship, self-esteem, and critical thinking can counteract some of the harmful effects of social media. Teachers can incorporate discussions of online identity into subjects such as English, PSHE, or even art and media studies. Role-playing scenarios, analysing online content, and reflecting on peer dynamics can help students understand the mechanisms of digital influence and develop healthier patterns of engagement.

Ultimately, the goal is not to shield children from social media, but to equip them to engage with it on their own terms. This involves recognising that self-esteem is not a static trait, but a dynamic process influenced by daily experiences and internal narratives. Social media is one of many inputs that shape this process, and with the right support, it can be one that children learn to navigate with confidence and integrity.

To achieve this, parents and educators must be proactive, present, and willing to evolve alongside the digital landscape. Platforms will continue to innovate, trends will shift, and pressures will morph. But the core developmental needs of children—for belonging, affirmation, authenticity, and self-understanding—remain constant. When these needs are met through real relationships, meaningful engagement, and reflective practices, the grip of social media on self-esteem can be loosened.

We cannot control every algorithm or eliminate every comparison, but we can create environments in which children learn that their value is not dependent on digital applause. We can help them build identities grounded in more than appearances, identities that are resilient to external judgement and enriched by self-awareness. In doing so, we offer them something far more enduring than likes or follows—we offer them the belief that they are enough, as they are, both online and off.

The Impact on Sleep and Mental Health

The digital revolution has transformed nearly every facet of daily life, and for children and adolescents, this transformation is perhaps most pronounced in the quiet hours meant for rest. What was once a time for mental and physical restoration is now often compromised by the presence of screens, pings, and constant cognitive engagement. The very tools that connect, entertain, and inform have also introduced a new set of challenges—chief among them, their disruptive impact on sleep quality and mental well-being. While the allure of devices is understandable, the neurological and psychological consequences of their unchecked use are becoming impossible to ignore.

Sleep is foundational to a child's development. It plays a critical role in memory consolidation, emotional regulation, immune function, and cognitive performance. During sleep, the brain is far from inactive; it undergoes complex processes that allow for learning, growth, and repair. Yet across households and age groups, sleep is increasingly under threat—not from traditional external demands, but from the devices children bring with them into their bedrooms and, more alarmingly, into their beds.

One of the primary culprits is blue light. Emitted by screens on smartphones, tablets, laptops, and televisions, blue light disrupts the body's circadian rhythm by suppressing melatonin production. Melatonin, often referred to as the "sleep hormone," is crucial for signalling to the brain that it is time to rest. Exposure to blue light in the evening hours effectively confuses the brain, tricking it into believing it is still daytime. As a result, children who use screens in the hour or two before bed may find it harder to fall asleep, experience lighter and more fragmented sleep, and wake up feeling less refreshed.

This effect is not trivial. Chronic sleep disruption can accumulate quickly, leading to a deficit that affects nearly every domain of functioning. A child who routinely goes to bed later because of digital engagement, even by just an hour, may experience diminished concentration, irritability, and slower cognitive processing the next day. Over weeks and months, this sleep loss can impact academic performance, mood stability, and physical health. Research consistently shows that insufficient sleep in children is linked to increased risks of anxiety, depression, obesity, and weakened immune responses.

Yet blue light is only part of the story. The content consumed before bed also has a profound influence on the mind's ability to wind down. Watching fast-paced videos, playing competitive games, or engaging in emotionally charged conversations on social media can all raise arousal levels—mentally and physiologically. The brain, when stimulated by such inputs, remains in a heightened state of alertness. Even when the device is finally turned off, the mental residue lingers. Children may lie awake rehashing a gaming loss, worrying about a text message left unanswered, or reliving the highlight reel of someone else's seemingly perfect life. The mind does not transition seamlessly from digital intensity to restful slumber; it needs time to recalibrate.

The issue is compounded by the design of many digital platforms, which are not built for completion but for continuation. Autoplay features, infinite scrolling, and algorithm-driven content delivery ensure that there is always one more video, one more update, one more notification to check. This design creates a sense of urgency and compulsiveness. Children may intend to spend just ten minutes on a device, only to realise they've lost an hour or more. This erosion of boundaries not only delays bedtime but contributes to a fragmented experience of time and attention throughout the day.

Notifications, often viewed as minor distractions, carry disproportionate weight in disrupting rest and mental clarity. The mere anticipation of a message or update can be enough to trigger anxiety and restlessness. When phones are kept within arm's reach at night, children may wake to the sound of alerts, feel compelled to respond, or simply sleep more lightly in anticipation. This state of perpetual connectivity prevents the brain from entering deep, restorative sleep cycles. Over time, it fosters what psychologists refer to as "hypervigilance"—a low-level stress response in which the body remains semi-alert to potential social or informational stimuli, even during rest.

These sleep disruptions have a cascading effect on mental health. Sleep and emotional well-being are deeply intertwined; one cannot be compromised without affecting the other. Children who sleep poorly are more likely to experience mood swings, difficulty managing frustration, and decreased resilience to stress. They may also be more prone to social withdrawal, lowered self-esteem, and cognitive distortions—negative thought patterns that reinforce feelings of hopelessness or inadequacy. For adolescents, who are already navigating complex hormonal and emotional shifts, poor sleep can exacerbate feelings of alienation and contribute to the onset of depressive or anxious symptoms.

The mental health implications of digital overstimulation extend beyond sleep. Constant connectivity and exposure to online content create a psychological environment characterised by comparison, judgment, and information overload. Children are bombarded with idealised images, peer interactions, and world events at a volume and speed that the human brain is not evolutionarily equipped to process. This continuous exposure can lead to what researchers call "digital fatigue"—a state of mental exhaustion resulting from excessive screen time and cognitive input. Symptoms may include irritability, apathy, difficulty concentrating, and a sense of being emotionally overwhelmed.

Social media, in particular, contributes to these effects by introducing performance anxiety and a need for perpetual social monitoring. Children feel pressured to respond quickly, maintain their digital persona, and stay updated on the activities of friends and influencers. This creates a chronic sense of urgency and inadequacy, as well as a reluctance to disconnect for fear of missing out. Even seemingly benign activities, like liking a post or responding to a message, become emotionally loaded. The cumulative stress of this digital vigilance can silently corrode mental well-being, even when it appears that a child is simply "relaxing" with a device.

Real-world examples bring these dynamics into sharp focus. Consider a twelve-year-old who reports headaches and poor focus at school, only for the underlying issue to be traced to late-night gaming sessions. Or a teenager who becomes increasingly withdrawn and anxious after months of fragmented sleep and excessive social media use, struggling to articulate why she feels so overwhelmed. These stories are increasingly common and echo the concerns voiced by parents, teachers, and mental health professionals alike. The impact is not limited to individual children—it influences family dynamics, academic environments, and long-term health outcomes.

So what can be done? Addressing the impact of digital overstimulation on sleep and mental health requires both awareness and action. It begins with recognising the interconnectedness of these domains—how overstimulation compromises rest, how poor rest affects mood, and how both shape a child's experience of the world. Establishing consistent routines, particularly around bedtime, can restore some of the lost rhythm. Limiting screen use in the hour before sleep, removing devices from bedrooms, and engaging in calming activities such as reading, journaling, or mindfulness exercises can help prepare the brain for rest.

Equally important is modelling balanced digital behaviour. When parents prioritise their own sleep, set boundaries around device use, and speak openly about the importance of rest, they send powerful messages that children absorb. Conversations that frame sleep not as a chore but as a form of self-care can shift attitudes and foster healthier habits. Similarly, teaching children to identify the signs of digital fatigue—mental fog, irritability, lack of interest in offline activities—can empower them to take breaks and seek restorative alternatives.

Mental health support must also be part of the solution. Schools, healthcare providers, and community organisations can play a crucial role in screening for sleep-related issues, offering psychoeducation, and promoting digital literacy. When children understand how their brains respond to light, stimulation, and connectivity, they are better equipped to make informed decisions. Supportive environments that validate their experiences, rather than simply imposing rules, create the trust necessary for lasting change.

Technology is not inherently the enemy of sleep or well-being. In fact, many digital tools—such as guided meditation apps, blue light filters, or sleep trackers—can support healthier habits when used thoughtfully. The goal is not to eliminate screens, but to create intentional boundaries that protect the brain's natural rhythms and allow for recovery. This is not only essential for cognitive functioning, but for cultivating the emotional resilience, creativity, and self-awareness that underpin lifelong mental health.

Ultimately, the conversation about sleep and digital wellbeing is a conversation about how we value rest, connection, and inner balance in a world that prizes stimulation and speed. For children to thrive, they need more than information and access—they need protection for the quiet spaces of their minds. When we restore those spaces, we offer them not just better sleep, but a more stable foundation from which to explore, engage, and grow with clarity and confidence.

Gaming and the Reward System

Video games are now a dominant feature of children's digital lives. No longer confined to arcade machines or weekend leisure, gaming has become an ever-present activity woven into the fabric of childhood and adolescence. With the rise of online multiplayer environments, mobile gaming apps, and immersive open-world titles, the gaming experience is more engaging, social, and accessible than ever before. But with this growth has come increasing concern—about excessive use, disrupted routines, and behavioural changes in young players. To understand the pull of video games and to foster healthy engagement, one must first examine the psychological mechanisms that underpin their design, particularly the reward systems that make them so captivating.

At their core, video games are sophisticated feedback loops. They present a challenge, offer the tools to overcome it, and then reward success with progress, points, status, or aesthetic upgrades. This cycle of effort and reward mirrors fundamental principles of behavioural psychology. Just as laboratory animals learn to press a lever for food pellets, human brains—especially those in development—respond powerfully to reinforcement. What distinguishes video games from most other childhood experiences, however, is the precision and immediacy with which they deliver that reinforcement.

Game designers use a range of reward strategies to maintain player engagement. The most basic is the fixed reward: complete a level, earn a badge. But far more compelling are variable rewards—prizes or progress delivered unpredictably, much like a slot machine. The uncertainty of these outcomes makes them more psychologically stimulating, activating the brain's dopamine pathways more intensely. This neurochemical reaction is especially potent in children and adolescents, whose prefrontal cortex—the region responsible for impulse control, foresight, and decision-making—is still under construction.

Games also offer layered forms of gratification. There are short-term rewards, such as coins, skins, or XP (experience points), and long-term goals, such as unlocking new maps or completing quests. Some games incorporate social reinforcement, allowing players to team up, share achievements, or climb leaderboards. These features activate not only the pleasure centres of the brain but also the social ones. A child may return to a game not just for its content, but for the community it fosters—peers who play together, exchange strategies, and validate one another's status in the gaming world.

The immersive nature of games amplifies their psychological grip. With dynamic graphics, compelling narratives, and responsive environments, children become absorbed in alternate worlds where their actions have immediate and visible consequences. These experiences offer a sense of agency and mastery that is often harder to achieve in offline life. For a child struggling socially or academically, a game can become a refuge—one in which they feel competent, in control, and rewarded for their effort. The stakes may be virtual, but the emotional impact is real.

Not all engagement with games is cause for concern. In fact, many games offer cognitive and educational benefits. Strategy games require planning, spatial reasoning, and adaptability. Role-playing games often involve storytelling, problem-solving, and ethical decision-making. Even fast-paced action games can enhance visual attention and hand-eye coordination. Collaborative games can strengthen teamwork and communication skills. The challenge, then, is not in eradicating gaming but in discerning when it is contributing to development—and when it is beginning to interfere.

Problems arise when the balance between gaming and other aspects of life becomes skewed. Children who play compulsively may neglect schoolwork, avoid physical activity, or withdraw from offline relationships. They may experience mood fluctuations, irritability when interrupted, or insomnia due to late-night sessions. These issues are often signs that gaming has moved from recreational to regulatory—that is, from being a source of joy to a means of escaping stress, boredom, or negative emotions.

Real-world examples reveal the complexities of this dynamic. A 10-year-old may begin playing a popular game to bond with school friends, only to find himself preoccupied with levelling up and anxious when disconnected. A teenager might use gaming to decompress after school, but gradually extend playtime into the early hours, affecting sleep and academic performance. These are not moral failings or character flaws. They are behavioural adaptations to digital environments that are expertly designed to sustain attention and evoke commitment.

Parents often feel unsure about how to manage gaming in the home. Some default to rigid restrictions, hoping that tight limits will curb the allure. Others, feeling out of their depth, adopt a hands-off approach. Neither extreme is ideal. Healthy gaming habits are best cultivated through guidance, dialogue, and structure—approaches that respect a child's interest while ensuring their digital lives do not eclipse their broader development.

One starting point is to understand the games themselves. Rather than dismissing all gaming as a waste of time, parents can take an interest in what their children play, why they enjoy it, and what skills they are using. This not only opens up communication but allows for nuanced decision-making about which games are appropriate and how they should be integrated into daily routines. For example, a parent might learn that their child's favourite game involves complex team strategies and time-limited challenges, making it easier to negotiate suitable windows for play that accommodate both digital and offline responsibilities.

Creating a framework around gaming is essential. This involves setting reasonable time limits, establishing device-free zones and hours (particularly before bed), and encouraging regular breaks during extended play. These boundaries help reinforce the importance of balance and signal that while gaming is a valued activity, it must coexist with sleep, study, physical activity, and social engagement. When these routines are developed collaboratively—with the child's input—they are more likely to be respected and maintained.

Crucially, children should be taught to reflect on their own gaming habits. Helping them identify when they are playing for enjoyment versus when they are playing to avoid something else fosters self-awareness. Questions such as "How do you feel after gaming?" or "What else would you like to do with your free time this week?" can guide children towards more intentional use. Over time, these conversations can help them develop the self-regulation needed to make good decisions independently—skills that will serve them well into adulthood.

Mental health professionals emphasise the importance of looking not just at the quantity of screen time, but at its *quality*. A child who plays for an hour each day but maintains good sleep, emotional balance, and social connections is likely using games healthily. By contrast, a child who spends similar time gaming but shows signs of emotional volatility, social withdrawal, or academic decline may need support in reassessing their digital routines. Context, in other words, is everything.

Some families benefit from creating a gaming agreement—a written or verbal set of shared expectations that clarify when and how gaming is allowed, what the consequences of overuse are, and how rewards can be earned through responsible behaviour. This transforms gaming from a source of tension into a platform for mutual understanding and accountability.

Educators and community leaders also have a role to play. Schools can incorporate discussions about digital wellbeing into the curriculum, highlighting the psychological design of games and helping students recognise their own patterns of use. Peer-led workshops or assemblies that explore gaming in an open, non-judgemental way can reduce stigma and encourage honest reflection. When children are invited to think critically about their digital environments, they are more likely to engage with them thoughtfully.

The gaming industry, too, must be part of the conversation. While many developers create age-appropriate, educational, or ethically designed games, others continue to rely on monetisation models that prioritise user retention over wellbeing. In-app purchases, loot boxes, and endless content loops can exploit young users' psychological vulnerabilities. Advocating for greater transparency, child-safe design, and regulatory standards is an important step toward a healthier digital landscape.

Ultimately, the psychology of video games is neither entirely problematic nor entirely benign. It reflects a deep understanding of human motivation—our desire for mastery, connection, challenge, and reward. These desires are not flaws to be corrected but opportunities to be redirected. When harnessed with insight and care, gaming can be a meaningful part of childhood. But left unchecked, it can encroach upon the very capacities—focus, creativity, empathy—that it has the potential to enhance.

Parents, educators, and policymakers must move beyond fear and towards fluency. By understanding the reward mechanisms that power games, by recognising the signs of overuse, and by engaging children in thoughtful, age-appropriate conversations, we can shift gaming from a source of conflict to one of growth. The objective is not to eliminate gaming, but to ensure that it is a component—rather than the centre—of a well-rounded, emotionally healthy life.

By guiding children to enjoy games without becoming ruled by them, we teach them not just how to play, but how to live with balance. In a world designed for distraction, this is a lesson of lasting value.

Cognitive Benefits of Technology

In the discourse around children and digital technology, much of the attention has focused understandably on the risks—screen addiction, social media pressures, sleep disruption, and declining attention spans. However, to engage with the subject responsibly, it is essential to acknowledge the other side of the equation. Technology, when used with intention and discernment, has the potential not only to entertain or distract but to enrich and extend human cognition. For young minds in particular, certain digital tools can be profoundly stimulating—enhancing problem-solving ability, unlocking creative potential, and supporting a dynamic, personalised approach to learning.

The cognitive appeal of technology lies in its interactivity. Unlike passive media such as television, many digital platforms require active engagement. Whether it's manipulating shapes in a geometry app, coding a short animation, or collaborating on a virtual science experiment, children are encouraged to make choices, test outcomes, and refine their understanding through direct experience. This interactive model mirrors the cognitive processes involved in critical thinking: hypothesising, experimenting, reflecting, and adapting.

Problem-solving, for instance, is at the heart of countless digital experiences. Puzzle games, logic-based apps, coding challenges, and simulation environments all require children to think sequentially, identify patterns, and evaluate multiple pathways to a solution. These activities cultivate flexible thinking, resilience, and persistence—core components of what psychologists term executive function. Even popular games with educational overlays, such as those that integrate mathematics into gameplay or require the coordination of multiple variables to progress, reinforce planning, forecasting, and goal-oriented behaviour.

Digital learning platforms can also tailor content to the user's current level of understanding, offering differentiated instruction that adapts to performance in real time. This form of personalised learning is difficult to achieve in traditional classrooms, where one teacher may be responsible for a diverse group of learners. Technology can provide immediate feedback, offer new challenges when a concept is mastered, and revisit topics when a learner struggles. This responsiveness creates an environment where frustration is minimised, and momentum is sustained—an important condition for developing cognitive confidence.

Consider the example of a child learning to code through a gamified platform. Unlike traditional instruction, where feedback is delayed and abstract, digital environments allow for immediate cause-and-effect responses. If a line of code doesn't work, the programme fails to run; if it does, the child sees their creation come to life. This real-time feedback loop encourages experimentation and iterative learning—qualities central to scientific inquiry and innovation. Over time, these small moments of success accumulate, reinforcing a mindset of competence and curiosity.

Creativity, too, flourishes in well-designed digital spaces. Technology has dramatically expanded the palette with which young people can express themselves. Through digital art programmes, children can explore form, colour, and composition without the constraints of materials or cleanup. Music apps allow for layering sounds, experimenting with rhythm, and composing original pieces without needing access to instruments or lessons. Storytelling platforms support the development of narrative skills, voice recording, and visual sequencing, empowering children to become both authors and illustrators of their own digital books.

What is especially powerful about digital creativity is its democratisation. Children who may not consider themselves "artistic" in traditional terms often find confidence in the accessibility of digital tools. A child who struggles with fine motor control might find joy in creating detailed illustrations using a tablet stylus. Another who is self-conscious about their handwriting may thrive when crafting stories with audio narration and animated scenes. Technology offers alternate pathways to creative expression, validating diverse intelligences and bridging gaps in traditional pedagogy.

The social dimension of creativity is also amplified. Children can collaborate on digital projects across geographical boundaries, engage in creative challenges with their peers, or share their work with real audiences. These interactions add meaning to the creative process, fostering not only cognitive growth but also a sense of purpose and connectedness. For example, a group of students designing a virtual city in a simulation game must coordinate ideas, delegate responsibilities, and negotiate differing visions—developing not only spatial reasoning and planning but also empathy and communication.

Learning, broadly defined, is another domain where technology has made considerable inroads. Beyond the classroom, digital platforms offer encyclopaedic access to knowledge, tutorials, simulations, and experiential learning environments. A child curious about astronomy can explore planets in three dimensions, zoom in on the rings of Saturn, or watch time-lapse footage of the Earth's rotation. A budding historian can take virtual tours of ancient cities, examine digitised primary documents, or construct timelines to better understand cause and effect. These multimodal experiences enhance comprehension by appealing to multiple senses and learning styles.

Furthermore, technology can support metacognition—the ability to reflect on one's own thinking. Digital learning dashboards, for instance, allow students to track their progress over time, identify areas for improvement, and set goals. Gamified platforms may use badges, levels, and challenges to make growth visible and motivating. When children understand how they learn, they become more strategic in their approach to problems, more resilient in the face of failure, and more proactive in seeking help or resources. This self-directed mindset is a critical feature of lifelong learning.

Real-world applications abound. A 10-year-old using a digital drawing app learns not only about shape and symmetry but about iteration and revision. A group of students designing a solar-powered vehicle using virtual prototyping tools internalise scientific principles through application, not memorisation. A child following a cooking tutorial online is exposed to measurement, sequencing, and cultural diversity—all while engaging in a hands-on task that promotes autonomy. These are not trivial gains. They represent the transfer of cognitive skills from digital play to real-world competence.

Technology also supports learners who might otherwise struggle in conventional settings. For children with learning differences, such as dyslexia, ADHD, or auditory processing challenges, digital tools can level the playing field. Speech-to-text software, audiobooks, visual schedules, and interactive reading programmes offer tailored supports that reduce frustration and enhance engagement. When these children experience success, their confidence grows, and their willingness to persevere increases. This shift in self-perception is as important as any academic gain—it lays the groundwork for sustained cognitive development.

That said, the cognitive benefits of technology do not arise automatically. They depend on thoughtful design, purposeful use, and appropriate scaffolding. Not all apps that claim to be educational are genuinely beneficial, and not all screen time is created equal.

Passive consumption, repetitive tasks, or poorly designed content can be cognitively numbing rather than enriching. What matters is how technology is used—whether it invites active engagement, challenges the user to think, and supports meaningful interaction with concepts and ideas.

Parents and educators play a crucial role in mediating this use. By curating high-quality tools, modelling reflective engagement, and contextualising digital activities within broader learning goals, adults can maximise the benefits while mitigating the drawbacks. Encouraging children to articulate what they are doing, why it matters, and how it connects to other knowledge deepens cognitive processing and builds a bridge between digital and offline learning.

Moreover, conversations about technology should not be limited to restrictions and screen time limits. They should include dialogue about the content, purpose, and impact of digital engagement. Questions such as "What did you learn today on that app?", "How did you solve that challenge?", or "What might you do differently next time?" invite children to think more deeply about their actions and choices. These reflective habits support metacognitive growth and promote an internal locus of control—key predictors of academic and life success.

The cognitive benefits of technology are not hypothetical—they are observable, measurable, and increasingly well-documented in educational research. But they are not inevitable. They require the intentional alignment of design, pedagogy, and parenting. When technology is used as a tool for exploration rather than distraction, for creation rather than consumption, it becomes a catalyst for intellectual development.

In a world where digital literacy is as fundamental as reading and numeracy, equipping children with the ability to think critically, solve problems creatively, and learn independently through technology is not an optional enrichment—it is a core component of modern education. By embracing the cognitive potential of digital tools, while maintaining a vigilant eye on quality, balance, and purpose, we can ensure that our children are not merely users of technology, but empowered learners who use it to deepen their thinking, expand their imagination, and engage with the world in informed, meaningful ways.

Chapter 3
Rethinking Screen Time: Beyond Time Limits

For quite some time now, the discourse surrounding children and screen time has hung over us like a stubborn fog—thick, omnipresent, and difficult to penetrate. The usual refrain has been familiar: parents, teachers, and health professionals alike defaulting to a tried-and-tested formula—limit the time, and you limit the harm. Simpler times called for simple solutions. But as screens quietly thread their way through the fabric of daily life—education, friendships, imagination, even family rituals—that tidy prescription begins to feel, well, insufficient. A timer may offer structure, but it tells us little about what truly matters: not merely how long, but how meaningfully, and in what company.

The phrase "less screen time" comes wrapped in a kind of moral shorthand, doesn't it? The implication is that screens are innately suspect, and any reduction is an unequivocal good. It's a convenient narrative, yet woefully reductive. Consider, for instance, a child and parent watching a stirring short film together, maybe even tearing up or laughing side by side. Now set that against a lonely hour spent trawling through random, forgettable clips online. Same screen, vastly different outcome. Or compare the focus required to compose a digital song or design a virtual city to the numbing repetition of yet another prank compilation. The disparity in cognitive and emotional impact is stark. Time alone tells us almost nothing.

We would do well, then, to shift our lens—from quantity to quality. From "how much?" to "what kind?" That begins with drawing a clear, if sometimes blurry, line between passive and active screen engagement. Passive use is what happens when attention dissolves into background noise—when the screen is merely a conveyor belt for stimulus. Scroll, click, repeat. Active use, by contrast, demands thought, energy, intention. It might mean solving a puzzle, drafting a narrative, learning to animate, or researching how a volcano erupts. And though the line can blur—some activities straddle both realms—recognising the distinction helps us shape more thoughtful habits.

The effect on the developing brain? Predictably divergent. Passive screen time, especially when it becomes a default state, can dull focus and chip away at motivation. Children emerge from it bored, not satisfied. Active engagement, meanwhile, often leaves them energised, curious, even proud of what they've accomplished. That's why the more insightful question for a parent isn't "How many hours?" but "What did that time contain?" The shift in emphasis is subtle, but it opens space for curiosity, not just control.

This reframe has ripple effects. Instead of standing on guard like digital sentinels, adults can move into a more participatory role. Watching a video together, joining a game, collaborating on a creative project—these aren't chores; they're invitations. They transform screen time from a solitary diversion into something shared, relational. Imagine a parent pausing a video mid-way to unpack a character's motives, or turning a science app into a discussion about climate change. These are not just teachable moments—they're connective ones.

And they do something else, quietly but profoundly: they help cultivate digital literacy. Not just in the technical sense, though that's part of it. But in the deeper, more critical sense—learning to interrogate what one consumes, to understand how design choices affect behaviour, to spot manipulation dressed up as entertainment. When a child reflects on what hooks them, or why they trust one site over another, they're learning to navigate a world saturated with digital influence. These are essential skills, not optional extras.

Some families find it useful to orient their screen use with the so-called 80/20 rule. Roughly speaking, 80 per cent of screen time should aim to nourish—educate, connect, create—while the other 20 per cent can be pure fun. Not a hard rule, more a sensibility. A guideline that says, "Yes, you can watch that cartoon—after you finish your project." It encourages moderation without dampening enjoyment. Done well, it teaches children to approach their screen choices with intention, not just instinct.

This philosophy also accounts for a rather plain fact: screens are now intrinsic to education. Research, homework, online discussions—it's all part of the academic landscape. To label all screen time as suspect is to risk conflating learning with laziness. We should be careful not to imply that all digital engagement is equal, or equally frivolous. If anything, teaching children to distinguish between productive and idle screen use is a far more empowering message than simply setting a timer and walking away.

That said, structure still matters. Children—especially the younger ones—need frameworks. Not so much iron-clad rules as gently imposed rhythms that help them balance competing needs: rest, activity, focus, play. But these should feel reasonable, not arbitrary. A teenager prepping for exams might justifiably need hours online. A primary-age child? Likely not. Including children in these conversations—"What's a fair amount of time for this game?" or "How will we make sure this doesn't interfere with dinner or sleep?"—invites agency, not just obedience.

It's also important to remember that children don't all arrive at self-regulation in the same way—or at the same pace. Younger kids, still learning the ropes of impulse control, might benefit from timers, visible schedules, or consistent routines. Older ones, edging into adolescence, will need more room to think things through. For them, it's less about rules and more about reflection. "Why do you think you felt so tired after that?" can open doors a rule never will.

Personalisation is key. One family might decide that Tuesday nights are for puzzles and board games, screens off. Another might keep devices in the living room only, to protect sleep. Yet another might make a habit of watching a new documentary together every weekend. These aren't rigid systems—they're living frameworks, responsive to family dynamics and values.

Naturally, none of this remains fixed. Children change. Technologies evolve. What makes sense for a child at seven may not fit at seventeen. A platform that's ubiquitous today might vanish tomorrow. What matters is adaptability—a willingness to revisit the conversation, to update the rules, to learn alongside your child rather than staying one step ahead of them. Parenting in a digital world isn't about mastery; it's about elasticity.

Support from outside the home helps, too. Schools can incorporate media literacy into the curriculum—not just how to use tools, but how to question them. Doctors and therapists can ask about screen content, not just time, when checking in on wellbeing. Community organisations can normalise these conversations, offer workshops, host parent circles. There's strength in shared wisdom.

Ultimately, reconceiving screen time is not an act of restriction but of reclamation. It's about moving past the language of fear and into a space of thoughtful engagement. Screens aren't going anywhere—nor should they. They offer a wealth of possibilities that were unimaginable a generation ago. But they require stewardship. Left to their own devices, both literally and figuratively, children can drift. Guided wisely, they can flourish.

By anchoring our parenting in values rather than suspicion, by showing up instead of simply shutting down, we help children build a digital life that is intentional, rich, and deeply human. The goal isn't zero screen time. The goal is meaningful screen time. That, perhaps more than anything, is how we prepare them—not just for the world as it is, but for the world they will help shape.

Why 'Less Screen Time' Isn't Always the Answer

For years, the dominant discourse around children and digital technology has hinged on one prevailing question: how much is too much? Screen time, often presented as a monolithic concept, has been monitored, timed, restricted, and punished in households across the world. Many well-meaning parents have felt an almost moral obligation to minimise their children's time on screens, equating less exposure with better outcomes. Yet as our understanding of technology's multifaceted role in children's lives deepens, it is becoming increasingly clear that this binary approach—less is good, more is bad—fails to capture the nuances of digital engagement. In reality, not all screen time is created equal, and a fixation on quantity alone may overlook more critical aspects of how screens affect development, learning, and well-being.

To understand the limitations of a purely time-based model, it helps to consider the diverse functions that screens serve. They are not simply tools for entertainment, although entertainment is certainly a large component. They are also platforms for learning, creative expression, communication, exploration, and problem-solving. A child might spend an hour on a video call with a grandparent, another hour completing a science project using a digital simulation, and a third watching nature documentaries or learning how to draw through a YouTube tutorial. While that total may exceed a recommended daily limit, the value of each of those activities is substantial. Conversely, a child who spends fifteen minutes endlessly flicking through social media or watching algorithmically generated videos may meet the screen time "quota" yet derive little to no developmental benefit.

The issue, therefore, is not merely how long a child spends in front of a screen, but what they are doing and why. Quality must take precedence over quantity. This shift in perspective aligns with a broader understanding of how children learn and grow. Engagement, curiosity, agency, and relevance are far more predictive of positive developmental outcomes than strict adherence to arbitrary time limits. A child who is engaged in meaningful digital activities—whether learning a new language through an app, producing digital art, or collaborating on a coding project—is activating key cognitive and emotional faculties. These experiences can be rich, rewarding, and educational, provided they are intentional and balanced.

Real-world examples offer insight into this complexity. A twelve-year-old spends ninety minutes each evening designing and programming a simple mobile game. While this may sound excessive on the surface, the child is learning logic, problem-solving, and iterative thinking. They're also expressing creativity and building technical literacy that could serve them well academically and professionally. Another child spends a similar amount of time scrolling through short-form videos, repeatedly exposed to fragmented content that demands little attention and offers few moments of meaningful reflection. Both are using screens, yet the cognitive and emotional outcomes are vastly different.

This disparity raises the question: why does the time-based model persist? One reason is that it offers a simple metric for a complicated issue. Counting hours is easier than assessing quality, particularly for parents who are overwhelmed by the pace of technological change or unsure how to evaluate digital content. Time limits feel like a form of control in a context where many adults feel powerless. However, this illusion of control can backfire. Children may feel unfairly restricted, leading to conflict, secrecy, or bingeing when unsupervised. Moreover, excessive focus on time can obscure more important conversations about content, values, and emotional responses to digital experiences.

Another factor is the fear-driven narrative surrounding technology. Headlines about addiction, developmental delays, and attention problems create anxiety and encourage reactive decision-making. While there are legitimate concerns—particularly around compulsive use, exposure to harmful content, or sleep disruption—these issues are better addressed through education and dialogue than blanket restrictions. A child who understands how screens affect their brain, mood, and relationships is more likely to self-regulate than one who is simply told "enough."

The alternative to rigid limits is a more nuanced, collaborative approach grounded in awareness, communication, and shared values. Parents can begin by asking not how much, but *what kind* of screen use is happening. Is it passive or active? Creative or consumptive? Solitary or social? Is it aligned with the child's developmental stage and personal interests? These questions provide a richer understanding of how digital habits fit within the broader tapestry of a child's life. They also open the door to conversations about purpose and intentionality. Why do we use screens? What do we enjoy about them? What do we find draining? These reflective questions promote metacognition and emotional intelligence.

Crucially, this approach also recognises that screen use is not separate from life but embedded within it. It intersects with education, social development, mental health, and family dynamics. Children use screens to connect with friends, complete schoolwork, explore hobbies, and unwind. Rather than drawing a hard line between "screen time" and "real life," parents can help children integrate technology into a balanced routine—one that also includes sleep, physical activity, face-to-face interaction, and unstructured downtime. When screens are seen as part of a holistic daily rhythm, their role becomes easier to manage and less polarising.

Practical strategies can support this shift. Parents might consider co-creating media use plans with their children, tailored to individual interests, needs, and values. This collaborative process fosters responsibility and mutual respect. It also allows for flexibility: more screen time might be appropriate during school holidays or for specific projects, while tighter boundaries might be needed during exam preparation or if digital use begins to interfere with well-being. The emphasis should be on balance and reflection, not punishment or perfection.

Participating in children's digital lives is another powerful tool. When parents take the time to understand and occasionally join their children in games, apps, or online communities, they gain valuable insight into what their children value and how they think. This shared experience can strengthen relationships and provide natural opportunities for guidance. It also helps parents move beyond stereotypes and assumptions about what digital engagement looks like. Not every game is violent, not every video is mindless, and not every online interaction is superficial. The digital world, like the real one, is full of nuance.

Educators and mental health professionals are increasingly adopting this more nuanced framework. Many now focus less on blanket restrictions and more on promoting digital literacy, resilience, and intentionality. This includes teaching children to evaluate content, manage online emotions, and recognise when screen use is affecting their mood, sleep, or relationships. These are not one-time lessons but ongoing skills, cultivated through repeated exposure and open dialogue. When adults model reflective, mindful tech use themselves—pausing to notice their own habits, acknowledging when they've spent too long on a device, and showing how they recalibrate—they demonstrate that these skills are part of a lifelong process.

The conversation must also expand beyond what screens take away to what they can give. Technology can be a powerful ally in learning, creativity, accessibility, and even social justice. It can offer platforms for marginalised voices, tools for children with learning differences, and avenues for exploration that were unimaginable a generation ago. To focus exclusively on restriction is to miss these possibilities. Instead, we must cultivate discernment—an ability to choose wisely, to know when to engage and when to step back, and to understand the difference between stimulation and nourishment.

There will, of course, be times when screen use does need to be curtailed. If a child is chronically tired, avoiding responsibilities, or showing signs of irritability or isolation linked to screen habits, boundaries are necessary. But even then, the goal should be to understand the underlying needs the screen is meeting. Is the child bored? Lonely? Anxious? Unchallenged? Addressing those root causes will be far more effective than simply removing the device.

Ultimately, the issue is not about control but about connection—connection to ourselves, to each other, and to the values that underpin our choices. When parents move from a fear-based to a values-based approach, they open up space for growth, trust, and mutual respect. Children are not passive recipients of technology;

they are active participants who, given the right tools and support, can learn to use it with wisdom and integrity.

Reframing the question of screen time is not an abandonment of boundaries. Rather, it is an invitation to create boundaries that are informed, flexible, and grounded in what truly matters. By focusing on content, context, and conversation, we move beyond the stopwatch and into a more meaningful understanding of how children live, learn, and thrive in a digital world.

Passive vs. Active Screen Time

Not all screen time is created equal. In the current discourse surrounding children and technology, there is a tendency to treat screen use as a homogenous activity—something to be quantified, timed, and restricted. However, this perspective overlooks one of the most important distinctions in how screens are actually used: the difference between passive and active engagement. Understanding this distinction is not just academic—it is crucial for parents, educators, and caregivers seeking to promote healthy digital habits in an age where screens are embedded into nearly every aspect of daily life.

Passive screen time refers to activities that require minimal cognitive effort, interaction, or emotional investment. This includes activities such as watching autoplay videos, scrolling endlessly through social media feeds, or flicking through short-form video platforms. These behaviours are largely consumptive. The user is a recipient rather than a participant, absorbing content without being required to respond, reflect, or create. While such activities can offer temporary distraction or relaxation, they often leave the individual feeling disengaged or fatigued, particularly when consumed in excess.

In contrast, active screen time involves purposeful engagement. It includes activities where the user is required to think, create, problem-solve, or interact meaningfully with others. Examples include coding, designing digital art, editing a video project, researching a topic for school, engaging in an educational game, or participating in a thoughtful online discussion. These activities often stimulate critical thinking, nurture creativity, and support skill development. Rather than zoning out, the user is mentally present and intellectually stimulated.

This distinction is particularly relevant for children and adolescents, whose brains are still developing and who are highly sensitive to both the content and the context of digital experiences. Passive screen time, especially when prolonged or unmoderated, has been linked to reduced attention spans, sleep disturbances, and increased feelings of boredom or anxiety. These effects are not simply a result of screen exposure itself, but of the way in which content is consumed. A child watching YouTube videos for hours without a clear purpose is engaging in a fundamentally different activity than one who is using a digital platform to learn animation techniques or solve mathematical puzzles.

Real-world examples illustrate this contrast vividly. Take, for instance, a ten-year-old who spends an hour scrolling through random videos on a mobile device, clicking from one clip to the next with little retention or thematic continuity. At the end of the session, the child may struggle to recall what they've watched, may feel overstimulated yet unsatisfied, and may exhibit signs of irritability when asked to stop. Now contrast this with another child who spends the same hour building a virtual model of a sustainable city using an educational simulation tool. That child is actively applying knowledge of geography, infrastructure, and environmental science, while also exercising creativity and decision-making. The screen is the same—but the experience is entirely different.

This isn't to say that all passive screen time is inherently negative or should be eliminated. Just as adults enjoy watching a television show or browsing social media to unwind, children too deserve downtime and light entertainment. The problem arises when passive use dominates a child's digital habits to the exclusion of more enriching experiences. Over-reliance on passive consumption can lead to decreased motivation for offline activities, social withdrawal, or an inability to focus on tasks that require sustained attention.

Moreover, passive consumption is often designed to be addictive. Algorithms on social media and video platforms are engineered to deliver an endless stream of highly engaging, emotionally charged, or novel content, tapping into the brain's reward system and encouraging prolonged use. For children who have not yet developed robust self-regulatory skills, these platforms can easily override internal cues of boredom, fatigue, or overstimulation. The result is not just lost time, but a disconnection from internal states and external responsibilities.

This is where the role of intentionality becomes central. Helping children differentiate between passive and active screen time is the first step towards building healthier digital habits. Conversations can be framed not around whether screen use is "good" or "bad," but around how it makes them feel, what they've gained from the experience, and how it fits within their broader goals and interests. A simple question such as, "What did you make, learn, or share today on your device?" invites reflection and fosters awareness.

Parents can also model this distinction by demonstrating their own engagement with screens in purposeful ways. For example, showing a child how to research a recipe, design a presentation, or use a digital map involves screens, but in a context that is constructive, intentional, and relational. When children see adults using technology as a tool for creation and communication, rather than a passive escape, they are more likely to internalise those values.

The education sector offers another domain where active screen use can be meaningfully integrated. Well-designed digital learning platforms support student-agency, adapt to individual learning styles, and provide immediate feedback that promotes metacognition. However, not all educational apps are created equal. Some merely digitise worksheets and reinforce rote learning, while others engage students in meaningful exploration and problem-solving. The key is to assess whether the tool fosters interaction, creativity, and critical thinking. A child using a maths app that allows them to build and manipulate problems engages differently from one who is passively watching tutorial videos without applying the concepts.

This distinction is also evident in the gaming world. While gaming often receives criticism for encouraging excessive screen time, many games actually involve highly active engagement. Strategy games require planning, memory, and logical reasoning. Sandbox games like Minecraft encourage construction, storytelling, and spatial reasoning. When played mindfully and in moderation, these games can provide a platform for collaboration, creativity, and even academic learning. The issue is not whether a child plays games, but which games, how often, and with what degree of thought and reflection.

Families can support more active engagement by creating a balanced digital environment that encourages curiosity, exploration, and creativity. This includes making time for collaborative digital projects, such as editing a family video, building a blog, or creating digital artwork. It also involves setting expectations around screen use that are clear but flexible—focusing not just on time limits, but on the nature and purpose of each session.

It is also important to recognise that active screen time does not always look serious or academic. A child experimenting with animation tools or composing a digital beat may appear to be "just playing," yet these experiences are rich with cognitive and creative potential. The challenge for adults is to look beyond appearances and ask deeper questions about what is happening cognitively and emotionally during screen use. Is the child building something new? Solving a problem? Exploring an interest? Reflecting on feedback? These are the signs of meaningful engagement.

Conversely, signs that screen time is becoming unbalanced or overly passive might include restlessness, irritability after use, reluctance to disengage, or declining interest in offline activities. In such cases, the goal is not to eliminate screens entirely, but to recalibrate how they are being used. Replacing or supplementing passive activities with more interactive ones can gradually shift habits and restore a sense of agency.

It is also essential to remember that children differ in their interests, temperament, and developmental stage. What constitutes active engagement for one child may not resonate with another. Some may thrive on visually rich, fast-paced games, while others prefer methodical design tasks or text-based research. The task of the parent or educator is not to prescribe one "correct" form of engagement, but to support children in discovering what kinds of digital activities help them feel focused, stimulated, and fulfilled.

Ultimately, the question is not whether children should use screens, but how they can use them in ways that enrich their lives rather than diminish them. By moving beyond time limits and instead focusing on the quality and intentionality of screen use, we empower children to build a relationship with technology that is thoughtful, balanced, and meaningful. This does not require perfect monitoring or total control—it requires presence, dialogue, and a willingness to see screens not as enemies, but as tools whose value depends entirely on how they are used.

Co-Viewing and Co-Playing: Engaging with Kids in the Digital Space

The digital lives of children today are no longer peripheral to their upbringing—they are central to it. From gaming platforms and video content to educational apps and social networks, young people are immersed in a world of screens that is rich with stimulation, interaction, and influence. As this landscape evolves, the challenge for parents is not merely to supervise or restrict their child's screen time, but to *engage* with it meaningfully. Co-viewing and co-playing—where parents actively participate in their child's digital experiences—offers a powerful alternative to surveillance or detachment. Rather than standing on the periphery of a child's digital world, these practices invite parents into it, creating opportunities for connection, guidance, and shared understanding.

Historically, co-viewing was associated with television—parents sitting with their children to watch a film or a favourite programme, perhaps discussing themes or laughing at shared jokes. The digital era expands this concept significantly. Co-viewing today might involve watching YouTube videos together, exploring an educational documentary, or even participating in livestreamed tutorials. Co-playing, meanwhile, refers to parents joining their children in interactive digital activities—whether that means navigating the challenges of a platform game, building virtual structures in a sandbox environment, or completing quests in a story-based adventure. These interactions are far more than leisure—they are relational touchpoints that help bridge generational divides and build digital literacy within the family.

For many parents, the idea of entering their child's digital world can feel daunting. The pace of change is relentless, and platforms that were unknown yesterday are central to a child's social life today. But this uncertainty should not deter participation. In fact, it's precisely this complexity that makes co-engagement so valuable. When parents take the time to ask, "What game are you playing?" or "What do you like about this video?", they signal interest and respect for their child's experiences. This curiosity lays the groundwork for open dialogue and mutual trust—two ingredients essential for healthy digital development.

One of the most immediate benefits of co-viewing and co-playing is the opportunity it provides to model critical thinking and digital discernment. Children, particularly younger ones, are still developing the capacity to evaluate content, distinguish between fiction and reality, and interpret messages embedded in media. A parent watching alongside can ask reflective questions: "What do you think that character was feeling?", "Does this video seem realistic to you?", or "What would you have done differently in that situation?" These conversations, while informal, cultivate analytical thinking and emotional literacy. They teach children that screen content is not to be passively absorbed, but actively interpreted.

Participation also enables parents to contextualise digital content within family values. For example, a parent might watch a series of TikTok videos with their teen and use the moment to discuss body image, peer influence, or consumerism. Or a family might play an online game together and use it to explore themes of cooperation, fairness, and perseverance. These are not lectures, but shared experiences that organically bring values to life. Rather than demonising screens or attempting to shield children from all online risks, co-engagement empowers parents to guide their children through them with nuance and empathy.

Another key advantage of co-playing is its potential to shift the dynamic from authority to allyship. Children and adolescents are often more receptive to guidance when they feel understood. When a parent plays a game alongside their child, they not only gain insight into the mechanics and appeal of that game, but they also demonstrate a willingness to meet their child on their terms. This positions the parent not as a distant enforcer of rules, but as a trusted partner. This shift is particularly valuable during adolescence, when young people are seeking autonomy but still need scaffolding to navigate complex digital spaces.

Consider the example of a father who regularly joins his daughter in a popular open-world game. Initially, he is sceptical of the time she spends online, but by playing together, he begins to see the strategic thinking, collaboration, and creativity involved. Their shared activity becomes a springboard for conversation—not just about the game, but about friendships, online etiquette, and managing screen time. This experience fosters understanding on both sides. The daughter feels seen and supported, while the father gains a clearer sense of how to guide without alienating.

Co-viewing and co-playing also create opportunities for digital mentorship. In a world where children are exposed to an overwhelming volume of media messages, they need adult role models who can help them navigate. By co-engaging, parents can demonstrate how to pause and reflect before clicking, how to respond to online conflict, or how to balance entertainment with educational content. These are not abstract lessons—they are lived practices, taught not through lectures but through example. A parent who says, "Let's take a break and go outside for a bit" models self-regulation. One who reflects aloud about feeling distracted after watching too many short videos models digital self-awareness.

Of course, the benefits of co-engagement extend beyond teaching and mentoring—they also strengthen emotional bonds. Shared digital experiences can be deeply meaningful, particularly when they align with a child's interests. A parent who celebrates a child's virtual achievement, who laughs at a shared video, or who learns a new game skill from their child builds a sense of connection that transcends the screen. These interactions affirm that the child's world matters, and that the parent values being a part of it.

Practical considerations can help families incorporate co-viewing and co-playing into their routines. Scheduling regular digital time together—perhaps a family game night or a shared video viewing session—can make these practices sustainable. Flexibility is key; not every moment needs to be a teaching opportunity. Sometimes, simply being present is enough. The goal is not to control the experience, but to participate in it in ways that foster trust, learning, and mutual enjoyment.

It's also important to acknowledge that not every parent will feel naturally comfortable in digital spaces, particularly if their own screen habits differ greatly from those of their children. Yet engagement does not require technical expertise. It requires presence, curiosity, and a willingness to learn. Parents who admit, "I don't know how this works—can you show me?" invite their children into a teaching role, reversing traditional hierarchies and empowering the child's confidence. This role reversal can be particularly affirming for children, who often feel more competent in digital environments than their parents do.

Co-viewing and co-playing also serve a protective function. When parents are familiar with the content their children consume, they are better positioned to recognise red flags—whether that's exposure to inappropriate material, signs of online bullying, or emerging patterns of compulsive use. More importantly, children who are used to discussing their digital lives openly are more likely to approach their parents when problems arise. Trust, once established, becomes a buffer against the isolation and secrecy that can characterise problematic digital use.

Schools and community organisations can reinforce these principles by offering digital literacy workshops that include parent–child activities, by recommending high-quality content for co-viewing, or by encouraging family digital projects. Educators can invite parents to collaborate on school-based tech assignments, bridging the gap between home and classroom digital experiences. When families and schools work together, children receive consistent messages about thoughtful and balanced tech engagement.

The broader cultural narrative must also evolve. Too often, parental engagement with screens is portrayed as either permissiveness or control. Rarely is it framed as a relationship-building strategy or a developmental opportunity. Yet the evidence is clear: when parents enter the digital world with their children—not as gatekeepers, but as guides—they foster digital resilience, emotional connection, and ethical awareness. These outcomes matter far more than how many hours are spent on a screen.

Ultimately, co-viewing and co-playing are about presence—being there, not just physically, but emotionally and intellectually. They are about listening, learning, and laughing together. They are about recognising that the digital world is not an intrusion on childhood, but a feature of it, and that parenting in a screen-saturated society requires engagement, not avoidance. Through these shared experiences, screens become not just sources of distraction or contention, but windows into the minds and hearts of our children. And from that vantage point, parenting becomes not a battle over screen time, but a partnership in digital life.

The 80/20 Rule for Digital Consumption

As digital technology becomes increasingly integrated into every aspect of children's lives, from learning and social interaction to leisure and creativity, parents and educators are faced with the complex challenge of helping young people develop a healthy relationship with screens. The traditional model of setting rigid time limits has often proven inadequate, failing to account for the quality and purpose of screen-based activities. A more flexible, values-driven approach is emerging as a compelling alternative—one that draws from a familiar principle in behavioural economics and productivity theory: the 80/20 rule.

Applied to digital consumption, the 80/20 rule proposes a broad framework in which approximately 80 per cent of a child's screen time is devoted to educational, creative, or enriching activities, while the remaining 20 per cent is reserved for entertainment and passive leisure. This balance is not a rigid formula but a guiding philosophy—one that shifts the focus away from the stopwatch and toward intentional, meaningful engagement with technology.

What makes this model particularly effective is its adaptability. Children differ in age, temperament, interests, and developmental stage, and the digital activities that stimulate growth in one child might bore or frustrate another. The 80/20 rule respects these differences by allowing for variation and negotiation. It doesn't demonise entertainment, nor does it elevate education to the point of joylessness. Instead, it affirms that pleasure and play have a rightful place in digital life, so long as they are balanced with opportunities for learning, expression, and cognitive development.

To apply this framework meaningfully, it is necessary to define what constitutes educational or creative screen use. Educational use includes not only formal learning platforms—maths apps, language-learning tools, or research for schoolwork—but also content that fosters curiosity, critical thinking, or practical skill development. A child watching a science documentary, experimenting with digital painting, or building structures in a physics-based simulation game is engaging with screens in ways that stimulate higher-order thinking and extend their understanding of the world.

Creative use, while often overlapping with education, focuses on self-expression and innovation. This could take the form of composing music with digital tools, designing levels in a game engine, or collaborating with peers on a digital storytelling project. These activities cultivate agency, patience, and imaginative thinking—skills that are not only valuable in school but essential for navigating a world increasingly shaped by technology and innovation.

Entertainment, which occupies the remaining 20 per cent in this model, encompasses games, videos, and other media consumed primarily for relaxation or enjoyment. Importantly, this category is not without merit. Passive media, when used in moderation, can help children unwind, manage stress, and connect with cultural narratives that form part of their peer socialisation. What the 80/20 rule cautions against is not entertainment per se, but its dominance—when screen time is overwhelmingly spent in passive or repetitive consumption, the opportunities for growth, exploration, and deeper engagement are diminished.

Real-world examples highlight how this framework can be applied within families. Consider a twelve-year-old who spends an hour after school editing a short film using digital video software. They storyboard the plot, adjust audio tracks, and learn basic editing techniques. This activity is cognitively demanding, requires sustained focus, and results in a tangible creative product. After finishing their project, they spend fifteen minutes watching a humorous video on their favourite platform—a light-hearted transition from effort to ease. In this example, the balance is clearly skewed toward enrichment, with a small portion reserved for entertainment.

Contrast this with a child who spends two hours scrolling through social media, watching gaming streams, and clicking from one short video to the next. This time may pass quickly, but the effects tend to include fragmented attention, emotional numbness, and decreased motivation for offline activities. The difference lies not only in content but in cognitive engagement. The 80/20 rule provides a lens through which parents and children can evaluate their digital habits and make adjustments that support their long-term well-being.

The practicality of this model lies in its customisability. It can be adjusted based on age and context. For younger children, the structure might involve more explicit scheduling and parental guidance. For older adolescents, it can evolve into a self-regulated goal, supported by reflective conversations and mutual accountability. Parents can ask, "How do you feel after using that app?" or "What did you learn or create today with your screen time?" These questions shift the conversation from control to consciousness, encouraging children to assess the impact of their own habits.

The 80/20 rule can also be visualised to help children understand and apply it. Some families use media logs or digital planners, allowing children to track their screen use and see how much of it aligns with their personal and educational goals. This approach reinforces the idea that screen time is not inherently negative, but rather a tool to be used wisely. When children recognise that their favourite game or show is part of a broader digital diet, they are more likely to accept boundaries without resistance or guilt.

Educators, too, can benefit from adopting this framework. By incorporating engaging, purposeful technology in classrooms—coding exercises, virtual field trips, or collaborative research projects—schools can demonstrate the value of active digital learning. When children see that screens are not just a form of escape but a means of exploration, they develop more sophisticated digital identities. Teachers can also share this framework with families during school meetings or through newsletters, creating consistency between home and school approaches to screen use.

Mental health professionals increasingly advocate for balanced digital engagement, especially as they see rising cases of digital fatigue and emotional dysregulation linked to excessive passive media use. The 80/20 rule aligns with this research, promoting a lifestyle where screens are used to enrich rather than drain. It acknowledges that dopamine-driven content—short videos, algorithmic feeds, or instant-reward games—has its place, but should not be the default mode of engagement. Encouraging children to build, inquire, and reflect through digital means fosters resilience, focus, and a deeper connection to their interests.

It's important to note that the 80/20 ratio is not a strict requirement but a directional guide. Some days may tip more toward entertainment, particularly during holidays or after a difficult week. Others may be highly structured and learning-focused, especially when deadlines loom or projects inspire deep engagement. What matters is the overall pattern. Just as we do not evaluate nutrition based on a single meal but on broader dietary habits, so too should we assess screen time in terms of its cumulative impact.

There is also value in applying this framework to adults, especially within the family context. Children learn not just from what we tell them but from what we model. A parent who uses their own devices primarily for scrolling or gaming but insists their child only use screens for homework sends a contradictory message. By sharing digital experiences, co-creating content, and discussing online articles or documentaries, adults can exemplify the kind of balance they wish to instil. This shared approach fosters empathy, reduces hypocrisy, and builds stronger intergenerational relationships.

The 80/20 rule for digital consumption offers a powerful alternative to restrictive or punitive models of screen management. It replaces conflict with collaboration, and guilt with intentionality. By focusing on what screens *do* rather than simply how long they are used, this framework supports a richer, more human approach to digital parenting—one that honours both the educational promise and the recreational appeal of technology.

More than a ratio, it is a philosophy: that screens are not to be feared or blindly indulged, but navigated with purpose. When children learn to balance entertainment with exploration, to alternate consumption with creation, they develop not just better digital habits, but stronger, more reflective selves. The 80/20 rule empowers families to create digital cultures rooted in curiosity, connection, and thoughtful engagement—preparing children not only to use technology, but to thrive within it.

Practical Tips for Setting Healthy Screen Boundaries

Setting healthy screen boundaries in a tech-saturated world is one of the most pressing, yet nuanced, responsibilities modern parents face. It is no longer enough to simply enforce time-based rules or remove devices as a form of discipline. The digital world is not a separate realm—it is woven into every aspect of children's lives, from learning and friendships to entertainment and creativity. As such, boundaries must evolve from blanket restrictions to thoughtful, responsive strategies tailored to a child's developmental stage, temperament, and family context.

Effective boundary-setting begins with the recognition that not all children engage with screens in the same way. Some are naturally self-regulating and can transition easily from devices to offline tasks without protest. Others struggle with compulsive usage, emotional reactivity when disconnected, or difficulty returning to non-digital activities. Understanding a child's unique relationship with technology provides a foundation for boundaries that support—not suppress—their growth.

For younger children, structure and consistency are especially important. At this age, routines offer a sense of security and predictability. Rather than focusing on daily time quotas, families can integrate screen use into a rhythm that complements other essential activities. For example, screens might be allowed after outdoor play or shared reading, but not before school or close to bedtime. These rhythms make it easier for children to accept limits because they are part of a larger routine, rather than arbitrary interruptions.

Young children also benefit from physical cues that help manage transitions. A visual timer, for instance, can help a five-year-old understand when screen time is ending. Saying "Five more minutes, and then it's time to wash up for dinner" gives them time to adjust and reduces the likelihood of conflict. Crucially, boundaries must be consistent but not inflexible. If a child is deeply engaged in a creative app or is near the end of a story-based game, allowing them to finish can reinforce the value of commitment and focus.

As children grow, so too must the boundaries. Pre-teens often seek more autonomy and may begin to negotiate—or challenge—the rules. Rather than tightening control, this is an ideal time to involve them in the boundary-setting process. Asking them what they think is a fair amount of screen time, what activities they want to prioritise, and how they can ensure digital life doesn't interfere with responsibilities encourages ownership and accountability. When children help create the rules, they are more likely to respect them.

Real-world examples show how effective this participatory approach can be. One family, noticing their ten-year-old son was struggling to sleep after late gaming sessions, sat down with him to review his evening routine. Together, they agreed on a wind-down period, with screens turned off an hour before bed. The boy, involved in the decision, complied more willingly than when his parents had imposed earlier restrictions. He also learned to recognise how screen use was affecting his own body and mood—a vital step in developing self-regulation.

Teenagers present a different set of challenges. Their digital lives are often tightly intertwined with social dynamics, academic obligations, and emerging identity formation. For teens, boundaries must be negotiated with respect and framed around values rather than rules alone. Discussions might focus on how screen use supports—or undermines—their goals, whether it's maintaining friendships, staying on top of schoolwork, or improving sleep and mental clarity. Parents can ask reflective questions: "How does that app make you feel after using it?" or "What would you like to spend more time doing if you had fewer digital distractions?"

It is also helpful for families to establish screen-free zones and times that apply to everyone—not just children. Common areas like the dining table, bedrooms, or the car can be designated as tech-free to encourage presence, conversation, and rest. These shared commitments prevent children from feeling singled out and reinforce that screen balance is a lifelong skill, not just a childhood rule. When children see adults putting their phones away during meals or choosing books over devices at bedtime, they are more likely to internalise these behaviours.

For children with particular sensitivities—such as those with ADHD, autism spectrum conditions, or anxiety—boundaries may require more precision and support. Some may become hyperfocused on digital content and find it difficult to disengage. Others may use screens to self-soothe, making transitions away from devices especially difficult. In these cases, a tailored plan that includes sensory breaks, gradual transitions, and visual schedules can help. Parents might say, "After this video, we'll stretch together and then you can choose your next activity," thereby providing a soft landing rather than a hard stop.

Regardless of age, boundary-setting should be anchored in communication and empathy. If a child reacts with anger or defiance when asked to turn off a device, it's important to explore what's driving the reaction. Are they in the middle of something important? Are they using the screen to escape a stressor? Are they tired, hungry, or overwhelmed? Addressing the emotional context, rather than just the behaviour, leads to more constructive outcomes and preserves the parent–child relationship.

Some families find success using digital agreements—written or verbal contracts that outline expectations around screen use. These can include daily time limits, content guidelines, and consequences for overuse, but also rewards for balanced habits and acknowledgements of effort. Rather than being punitive, these agreements are collaborative tools that promote clarity and fairness. They also provide a framework for revisiting the rules as needs change, whether due to school holidays, exam periods, or evolving interests.

Technology itself can assist in boundary-setting. Many devices and apps now include built-in parental controls that allow limits on usage, access times, and content types. While these tools should never replace conversations, they can serve as helpful scaffolding. For example, a parent might set a device to lock automatically at bedtime, signalling that screen use has ended for the day. Combined with an open dialogue, these tools can reduce conflict by shifting the burden of enforcement from parent to platform.

At the heart of effective screen boundaries is the principle of balance. Children, like adults, need time for rest, movement, imagination, social connection, and solitude. Screens can support or detract from these needs depending on how they are used. Rather than aiming for perfection, families can strive for patterns that reflect their values and support their overall well-being. Some days may be more screen-heavy, especially during bad weather or after illness. Others may be more active, social, or creative. What matters is the overall rhythm, not the occasional deviation.

It is also worth remembering that screen boundaries are not just about managing risk—they are about cultivating capacity. When children learn to navigate digital tools mindfully, to pause and reflect before clicking, and to balance consumption with creation, they are developing lifelong skills. Boundaries are not walls; they are guides—helping children move through the digital world with awareness, autonomy, and care.

In the end, setting healthy screen boundaries is not about controlling children but about supporting them. It is about creating an environment in which screens are a part of life, but not the centre of it. It is about recognising that digital engagement can be positive, even powerful, when it is purposeful and in proportion. And it is about building a family culture where screen use is aligned with the values, rhythms, and relationships that matter most. When boundaries are rooted in empathy, adaptability, and mutual respect, they become not just rules to follow, but skills to carry forward—equipping children not only to manage technology, but to flourish within it.

Chapter 4
Raising Critical Thinkers in a Digital World

In an age where information pours in without pause, the need to raise critical thinkers has never felt more pressing. It's no longer a luxury—it's a necessity. The digital world, for all its boundless educational promise, throws up challenges that previous generations simply didn't face. Today's children are growing up with unprecedented access to global knowledge, competing narratives, and conflicting worldviews. Such access can be thrilling, even empowering—but only if young minds are equipped with the tools to sift through it. Discernment doesn't come baked in. It must be taught, nurtured, and practised.

The real work, then, lies not merely in shielding children from the internet's darker corners but in arming them with the skills to probe, to analyse, and, ultimately, to decide for themselves. What follows is a closer look at how adults—parents, teachers, mentors—can help children develop digital literacy and media scepticism. These aren't just skills for online survival; they shape how young people think, how they understand the world, and how they find their voice within it.

The sheer glut of information that bombards a child the moment they pick up a device can be dizzying. Within the span of a few minutes, they might stumble across a dubious scientific 'fact', a polarising meme, an influencer's endorsement, or a bizarre conspiracy theory. Lacking the tools to critically evaluate what's being presented, they become easy prey—not just to misinformation, but to the subtle influence of repetition and emotional suggestion. Teaching children to pause and interrogate what they're seeing is the first meaningful defence. It also marks the shift from passive reception to active engagement with digital content.

Importantly, cultivating media scepticism doesn't mean raising cynics. It's not about knee-jerk dismissal but about developing a reflex to question and verify. When a child comes across an emotionally charged video or a wildly confident claim online, we want them to pause and ask: Who produced this? What are they trying to convey? What's backing it up? What other angles might exist? These small, habitual questions are the foundation stones of critical thinking. And once embedded, they can reshape a child's entire digital posture—from reactive to reflective.

Take a familiar scenario: a teenager stumbles upon a slickly edited video warning of a so-called "dangerous" ingredient in everyday foods. The visuals are dramatic, the tone urgent. Rather than forwarding it in alarm, a more critically minded viewer might consider who published it, what their motives might be, and whether reputable sources support the claim. This kind of cognitive approach doesn't happen by accident. It must be shown, encouraged, and revisited—again and again.

Detecting misinformation, as we know, is a major part of this equation. The internet teems with distorted headlines, misleading graphics, and carefully crafted videos that tug at our fears rather than appeal to our reason. Children must learn to look beneath the surface gloss. Tools like reverse image search, fact-checking platforms, and browser extensions that flag questionable content can be introduced gradually. But tools are just that—useless without the mindset to wield them properly. Children need to grasp why fake news spreads—how it exploits emotional triggers and existing biases—and how to spot when they're being nudged or nudged too far.

Here, adults have a particularly powerful teaching tool at their disposal: their own habits. Narrating one's thought process in real time—"That's quite a bold statement; I wonder if there's any data behind it. Let's have a look together"—offers children a window into how thinking works. It transforms scepticism from a private, internal function into a shared practice. It shows that asking questions isn't impolite or combative—it's how understanding begins.

Another dimension, often overlooked but hugely consequential, is the role of algorithms in shaping a child's digital experience. The content children see is anything but neutral. Algorithms serve up material based on previous clicks, shares, searches, and scrolls. The result? A feedback loop that reinforces existing preferences, creating a kind of invisible narrowing of perspective. What begins as a curious click can evolve into an echo chamber where only certain views are echoed back, again and again.

This narrowing has consequences. When a child repeatedly encounters the same kind of message—whether political, cultural, or personal—they're less inclined to question its validity and more likely to accept it as common sense. That's where algorithmic literacy comes in. Children need to grasp that what they see is curated, not comprehensive. Teaching them how these invisible mechanisms operate—what they amplify, what they obscure—introduces a layer of media awareness that few adults ever received themselves.

You don't need to lecture to make the point. If a child notices an influx of cooking videos after watching a few, that's the opening: "Interesting how the app's showing you more of those. Why do you think that is? And what kinds of videos might it be leaving out?" These kinds of conversations don't just raise awareness—they prompt children to think like investigators in their own media worlds.

Of course, digital engagement shouldn't be reduced to vigilance alone. The real opportunity lies in moving from mere consumption to meaningful creation. Instead of scrolling aimlessly or watching passively, children can be encouraged to make something. A website about marine life, a podcast on their favourite book series, or even participating in an online community with substance and respect—these are all forms of active engagement. They instil agency and a sense of digital authorship, which is quite different from the default role of viewer.

The bridge between online exploration and offline action is especially powerful. Say a child becomes fascinated by climate change after watching a few documentaries. Instead of stopping there, they might design an infographic for their school bulletin board or start a campaign to reduce plastic at home. Suddenly, the digital realm isn't just a source of information—it's a launchpad for real-world impact.

And what fuels all of this? Curiosity. That restless impulse to understand more, to ask why, to chase after new questions. It's the heart of critical thinking—and yet, curiously, much of today's digital design suppresses it. Algorithms reward what's familiar. Instant gratification discourages deeper inquiry. To nurture curiosity, we must give children permission to linger in uncertainty, to follow tangents, to wonder aloud.

Modelling this curiosity is more powerful than any lecture. A parent might remark, "I read something odd today and I'm still thinking about it," or ask, "What did you see online that made you stop and think?" These seemingly small moments tell children that digital life isn't about certainty—it's about discovery.

But all of this rests on a particular kind of relationship between adult and child—one based on trust and ongoing dialogue, not surveillance. Children are more likely to reflect critically when they feel their thoughts are welcome, even when those thoughts are messy or half-formed. This requires patience on the adult's part: listening without immediately correcting, resisting the urge to "fix" their thinking too quickly. It's guidance, not governance, that sets the tone.

Schools, too, must shoulder part of the responsibility. Media literacy shouldn't be siloed into special lessons; it belongs across the curriculum. Analysing adverts in English, deconstructing political rhetoric in history, comparing news coverage in geography—all of these activities teach students to think clearly and ethically about the media they consume. And when students are invited to produce media themselves—be it a short film, a blog, a podcast—they begin to appreciate the principles of accuracy, clarity, and responsibility from the inside out.

In the end, raising critical thinkers in a digital world isn't about wrapping children in metaphorical bubble wrap or limiting their exposure. It's about giving them the intellectual tools to move through complexity with confidence. To recognise that not all information is created equal. To understand that what they believe is shaped—sometimes subtly, sometimes blatantly—by the media they encounter. And to feel empowered not only to question, but to choose and contribute with integrity.

When we encourage curiosity, teach discernment, and model honest dialogue, we're not just helping children survive online. We're helping them grow into thoughtful, resilient citizens. The future will, inevitably, be digital—but it will belong to those who can think deeply, question wisely, and act with conviction. That future begins with the questions we're willing to ask today.

Teaching Kids to Question What They See Online

In a digital landscape saturated with images, videos, headlines, opinions, and persuasive content, helping children develop the ability to question what they encounter online is no longer optional—it is essential. The internet has become the primary gateway through which many young people access information, form their opinions, and engage with the world. Yet within this seemingly boundless resource lies a spectrum of content that ranges from credible and informative to manipulative and outright false. Teaching children how to navigate this terrain with discernment requires more than simply instructing them to be careful. It demands a systematic nurturing of digital literacy and media scepticism from an early age.

Digital literacy goes far beyond the ability to operate devices or navigate apps. It encompasses the capacity to find, evaluate, and use digital information critically and responsibly. At its heart lies an inquisitive mindset—one that does not take digital content at face value but probes its source, intention, and reliability. Media scepticism, similarly, is not about mistrust for its own sake, but about fostering a healthy questioning attitude. When children learn to ask "Who made this?", "Why was it made?", and "What is missing from this picture?", they begin to reclaim agency in a media environment designed to steer their attention and beliefs.

The challenge is that the online world does not naturally reward scepticism. In fact, many platforms are designed to encourage rapid consumption, emotional reactions, and automatic sharing. Algorithms feed users content that aligns with their previous behaviour, creating an illusion of consistency and truth. Headlines are written to provoke, not to inform. Videos autoplay before one has time to reflect. The internet favours immediacy, not deliberation. In this context, helping children to slow down and ask thoughtful questions becomes an act of empowerment.

One of the most effective ways to introduce these skills is through guided exposure. Rather than shielding children from questionable content, parents and educators can use real-world examples to teach critical evaluation. A viral post making a dubious claim about health, a trending video with misleading edits, or a sensational news story that lacks cited sources can all serve as teachable moments. Sitting with a child and examining such content together—discussing how to trace the original source, how to assess the credibility of the author, and how to spot emotional manipulation—provides practical skills that abstract instruction cannot match.

For example, a parent might come across a headline shared on social media claiming that a new study has found chocolate improves academic performance. Rather than immediately accepting or dismissing the claim, they can ask their child to help investigate: "Where is this study published? Who funded it? Is the headline consistent with the actual findings?" Such a conversation transforms a passive reading experience into a mini-investigation, one that teaches the child to move from surface impression to deeper inquiry.

Children should also be introduced to the concept of bias—not only in media producers but in themselves. Every viewer brings assumptions and emotional responses that colour their interpretation of content. Helping children recognise their own biases is an advanced but important part of digital literacy. This might begin with questions like, "Why do you think you agreed with that post?" or "How would someone with a different background see this?" These questions foster empathy as well as critical thinking, and they prepare children to engage constructively in diverse information environments.

Media scepticism also involves understanding the techniques used in digital persuasion. Children need to learn how visuals, music, language, and pacing are employed to create particular effects. An emotionally charged video, for instance, might use slow motion, music, and selective edits to evoke outrage or pity, regardless of factual accuracy. Teaching children to notice these techniques—not to be immune to emotion, but to recognise when it is being used strategically—gives them greater control over how they respond.

Schools have a significant role to play in this educational process. Integrating media analysis into literacy, history, or science lessons can deepen students' understanding of how information is constructed. For instance, comparing news reports from different outlets about the same event helps students see how language and framing shape public perception. Analysing advertising techniques in a media studies class can reveal how products are sold not through rational arguments but through association, fear of missing out, or idealised imagery. These exercises build analytical muscles that extend far beyond the classroom.

Equally important is creating a home environment that values questioning. When children are encouraged to ask why, to challenge assumptions respectfully, and to express doubt without fear of dismissal, they learn that uncertainty is not a weakness but a sign of thoughtful engagement. Parents who model this attitude themselves—who openly wonder, correct their own mistakes, and demonstrate a willingness to change their minds—convey that truth-seeking is a dynamic and lifelong process.

Yet fostering digital literacy is not just about evaluating individual pieces of content. It is also about understanding the broader ecosystem in which information circulates. Children should be taught how information spreads online, how algorithms work, and how virality is often a function of emotion rather than truth. A popular story is not necessarily a reliable one, and a shared post is not the same as a verified fact. When children grasp the mechanics behind what appears on their screens, they are better equipped to resist manipulation.

The social dimensions of digital information also matter. Children often encounter content through peer networks, where group dynamics can influence belief and behaviour. If everyone in a friend group is sharing a particular meme or following a certain influencer, there may be pressure to conform or accept without question. Teaching children to distinguish between popularity and reliability helps them navigate these social pressures with greater confidence. It also prepares them to be digital leaders—individuals who set standards of thoughtfulness and responsibility in their online communities.

The goal is not to create digital cynics, but digital citizens—curious, discerning, and engaged. This means striking a balance between scepticism and open-mindedness. Children should be able to interrogate a claim without reflexively rejecting it, to hold space for complexity rather than retreating into certainty. It means teaching them that it's okay to say, "I don't know," and to seek out more information before forming an opinion.

Technology can aid this process when used strategically. Many educational platforms now offer media literacy modules, fact-checking exercises, and interactive simulations that expose the mechanics of misinformation. When integrated into a broader framework of discussion and reflection, these tools can reinforce the skills and attitudes necessary for critical digital engagement.

Ultimately, teaching children to question what they see online is about equipping them to think for themselves in a world that is constantly trying to think for them. It is about preparing them not just to survive the digital age, but to contribute to it meaningfully—

by asking better questions, seeking deeper answers, and sharing information responsibly. This is not a one-off lesson but an ongoing conversation, one that evolves alongside technology and deepens as children grow.

The role of adults in this process is not to have all the answers, but to model the inquiry. It is to walk alongside children as they learn how to read between the lines, evaluate what is real, and remain grounded in truth while navigating the noise. In doing so, we raise not just digital natives, but digital thinkers—capable of engaging with the world not only with intelligence, but with integrity.

Spotting Misinformation and Fake News

In a world where information travels faster than it can be verified, the ability to distinguish fact from fiction is a foundational skill for any digitally literate individual. For children growing up in this media-saturated environment, the challenge is particularly acute. They are not just passive recipients of content; they are active participants—watching, sharing, liking, and commenting—often before they've had the chance to fully process what they're engaging with. The risks of misinformation are far from abstract: falsehoods about health, history, science, and current events can influence beliefs, fuel fear or prejudice, and skew a child's understanding of how the world actually works. Teaching children how to spot misinformation is not merely a safety measure; it is a vital aspect of preparing them to think clearly, act responsibly, and participate ethically in a digital society.

The internet is not designed to prioritise truth. It is structured to prioritise engagement. Whether it's a shocking claim, a viral meme, or a sensational headline, digital content succeeds when it captures attention and provokes a reaction. Misinformation thrives in this climate because it often exploits the very elements that drive online interaction: emotion, immediacy, and shareability. A fabricated news story about a celebrity's death, for instance, can spread across platforms within minutes, fuelled by alarm and curiosity. By the time a correction is issued, the damage is already done—the falsehood has taken root in the public consciousness.

Children are especially vulnerable to such content because they are still developing the cognitive tools necessary for critical evaluation. Their understanding of authority, evidence, and plausibility is in formation. Moreover, they often access content through social channels, where the source is not a news organisation or educator but a friend, influencer, or algorithmically curated feed. The familiarity of the messenger can lend undue credibility to the message, even when that message is demonstrably false.

Helping children navigate this complexity starts with cultivating a healthy scepticism—not a blanket distrust of everything they see, but a habit of inquiry. When a child encounters an extraordinary claim online, the instinct should not be immediate belief or dismissal, but investigation. Encouraging them to ask, "Where did this come from?", "What do I know about the source?", and "Can this be verified by a credible authority?" lays the foundation for discernment.

One practical technique is to teach children how to "read laterally." Unlike traditional reading, which progresses top to bottom, lateral reading involves opening multiple tabs, checking other websites, and comparing sources in real time. When presented with an unfamiliar claim, children can be taught to step outside the original page and look at what other reputable outlets or fact-checkers have said. This method, widely used by journalists and digital researchers, exposes children to a broader context and helps them see whether a claim is isolated or widely accepted.

Fact-checking tools can support this process. Websites like Snopes, Full Fact, and PolitiFact maintain extensive databases of debunked stories and claims. Encouraging children to use these resources—perhaps by making it a shared activity—can demystify the verification process. For instance, if a child sees a post claiming that drinking hot water cures COVID-19, a quick search on a fact-checking site can reveal that this is a persistent myth with no scientific basis. Going through that process together not only corrects misinformation but reinforces the idea that truth is something we pursue actively, not something handed to us passively.

Another powerful tool is the CRAP test—a framework used to assess the reliability of sources by looking at Currency, Reliability, Authority, and Purpose. Though the acronym may amuse younger children, its application can be quite serious. Is the information up to date? Are the sources cited and verifiable? Who is the author, and what are their qualifications? What is the motive behind the content—to inform, entertain, persuade, or provoke? Teaching children to apply these questions helps them move beyond surface impressions and into deeper evaluation.

Visual literacy is equally important. Misinformation is not limited to text; it often appears in manipulated images, memes, or videos. A digitally altered photo can appear convincing at first glance, especially when paired with emotive captions. Children should be encouraged to question not just what a picture shows, but what it *means*. Who created this image? Has it been altered? Does it align with known facts? Tools like reverse image search can help verify whether an image has appeared in other contexts or has been used misleadingly.

Case studies can be particularly effective in bringing these concepts to life. Take, for example, the infamous case of a doctored image circulated during a natural disaster, showing sharks supposedly swimming through flooded streets. Many viewers accepted it as real because it was dramatic and shared by peers. Exploring such examples with children—showing them how to trace the image, examine metadata, and identify inconsistencies—can be both instructive and empowering. It also helps them understand that not everything that "goes viral" is trustworthy.

Children also benefit from understanding the psychology of misinformation—why people create it, why others believe it, and why it spreads. Misinformation is often designed to provoke strong emotions—anger, fear, outrage, or awe—because these emotions increase the likelihood of sharing. Discussing this dynamic with children helps them see how they, too, can be influenced. Asking, "How does this post make you feel, and why?" opens a reflective space that connects emotional awareness with critical thinking.

Equipping children to spot misinformation also involves talking about the broader digital ecosystem. Algorithms do not simply show content randomly; they curate feeds based on previous engagement. If a child clicks on conspiracy theory videos, their feed may begin to offer more of the same, reinforcing skewed perspectives. Teaching children about algorithmic bias—not as a technical abstraction but as a real influence on what they see—helps them contextualise their information exposure and seek out diversity of thought.

Equally important is discussing the consequences of misinformation. Children may not realise the ripple effects of sharing false information. A rumour about a classmate, a viral hoax about a vaccine, or a misleading post about a global event can contribute to real harm. When children understand that their digital actions have offline consequences, they are more likely to pause before sharing. Framing this not as a rule to obey, but as a responsibility to others, taps into their emerging sense of ethics and community.

Parents can reinforce these lessons by modelling critical behaviour themselves. Narrating thought processes aloud—"This looks suspicious. Let me check another source," or "This headline is really dramatic. I wonder what the full article says"—shows children that critical evaluation is part of everyday media use. It also normalises doubt as a healthy, intelligent response to an overabundance of information.

Schools, too, can embed misinformation education across subjects. In science, students can evaluate the credibility of health claims. In history, they can compare primary and secondary sources. In media studies, they can analyse how narratives are shaped by perspective. These exercises build a culture of inquiry that transcends disciplines and prepares students for real-world engagement.

What underpins all these efforts is a respect for the intelligence of the child. Rather than shielding them from misinformation or dictating what to believe, we trust in their capacity to learn how to evaluate. This trust is not naïve; it is strategic. It recognises that children, like adults, are capable of critical thought when given the right tools, guidance, and opportunities to practise.

Ultimately, teaching children to spot misinformation is about more than protecting them from falsehoods. It is about nurturing intellectual independence, emotional awareness, and civic responsibility. It is about helping them become not just smart consumers of information, but thoughtful participants in a shared reality. As they grow, they will encounter increasingly complex and subtle forms of digital influence. The skills they build now—of questioning, verifying, and thinking beyond the headline—will serve them not only online, but in every facet of their personal, academic, and professional lives. And as these young thinkers mature, they will contribute to a culture where truth is not assumed or imposed, but pursued with care, rigour, and a commitment to the common good.

Understanding Algorithms and Echo Chambers

One of the most invisible yet powerful forces shaping our children's understanding of the world today is the algorithm. Every time a child watches a video, clicks on a post, searches for a topic, or lingers over an image, algorithms are quietly at work—learning, predicting, and curating what will appear next on their screen. These lines of code are not merely technical tools; they are the architects of digital experience, selecting which content is seen and which remains hidden. For children, who are still learning how to think critically and develop independent viewpoints, this unseen influence can significantly affect how they form opinions, perceive truth, and relate to others.

Algorithms, at their most basic level, are sets of instructions designed to solve problems or automate decision-making. On social media platforms, search engines, and streaming services, they determine what content is shown to each user. While the intention behind algorithmic design is often benign—enhancing user experience, improving relevance, and keeping people engaged—the consequences of this curation are far-reaching. Children are not interacting with a neutral, comprehensive view of the internet. Instead, they are engaging with a highly personalised feed shaped by what they've clicked on before, who they follow, what they watch, and how long they engage with certain types of content.

This content personalisation can create what is known as an echo chamber—a digital environment where a user predominantly encounters information that aligns with their existing beliefs, interests, or preferences. Over time, this reinforces a particular worldview and limits exposure to alternative perspectives. For adults, echo chambers can entrench political opinions, cultural biases, or ideological positions. For children, the effects are even more subtle and potentially formative. A child who consistently watches videos promoting a particular lifestyle, social narrative, or opinion may begin to believe that this is the universal norm, not realising that their digital experience is being shaped behind the scenes.

Understanding how algorithms work—and what they don't do—is the first step in helping children engage more thoughtfully with digital content. Algorithms are not inherently intelligent or moral. They do not distinguish between truth and falsehood, quality and clickbait, education and manipulation. They are designed to optimise for engagement, which means they show more of what keeps users on a platform. This may include uplifting stories, but it can also include sensational headlines, emotionally charged content, or controversial opinions—anything that prompts a reaction. For children who are emotionally impressionable, the result can be a skewed sense of reality, fuelled by repetition and intensity rather than balance and accuracy.

Take, for instance, a twelve-year-old interested in fitness. They start watching workout videos, which the platform's algorithm then interprets as a preference. Soon, the child's feed is saturated not just with fitness advice, but potentially with content promoting unrealistic body standards, extreme dieting, or toxic comparisons—particularly if those videos are gaining traction with other users in similar demographics. What began as a healthy interest can be subtly distorted by an algorithm that favours popularity over nuance. Without awareness or guidance, the child may absorb messages that are not only misleading but potentially damaging to their mental and physical well-being.

Similarly, consider the case of a teenager exploring political topics online. They search for information on a current event and click on a video that aligns with one ideological perspective. The algorithm then amplifies similar content, and over time, the teen is less likely to encounter opposing views. This repetition creates the illusion of consensus—everyone I see agrees with this, so it must be true. What's more, exposure to more extreme content often happens gradually, as algorithms push users toward increasingly provocative material in order to maintain interest. This phenomenon, sometimes referred to as "radicalisation by algorithm," is not reserved for fringe topics; it can occur in mainstream discourse as well, affecting how young people understand social, cultural, and political realities.

Helping children recognise the role of algorithms in shaping their online experience is an act of digital empowerment. Rather than treating algorithms as mystical or opaque, adults can explain them in accessible, age-appropriate ways. One approach is to draw analogies to everyday experiences. For example, just as a shopkeeper might recommend products based on what you bought last time, a digital platform recommends content based on your past interactions. The difference is that in the digital space, this "shopkeeper" is tracking every scroll, click, pause, and reaction—and using that data to make increasingly precise predictions about what will keep you watching.

This understanding invites children to reflect on their own patterns. What do they see most often on their feed? How does that make them feel? What have they *not* seen recently that they used to enjoy or learn from? Encouraging this kind of meta-awareness can help children step outside the stream of content and examine the structure that delivers it. This doesn't mean they'll stop using digital platforms, but it does mean they can begin to use them more consciously.

It also highlights the importance of actively seeking diversity in digital experiences. Children should be encouraged to follow a range of voices, explore new perspectives, and question the homogeneity of their feeds. Parents and educators can model this by sharing a variety of articles, videos, and viewpoints, demonstrating how to engage respectfully with ideas that differ from one's own. When children are exposed to a broad spectrum of content, they are less likely to develop polarised thinking and more likely to appreciate the complexity of real-world issues.

Another practical strategy is teaching children to pause before sharing content, especially if it evokes a strong emotional reaction. Algorithms are designed to reward content that triggers fast engagement, but critical thinking requires slow reflection. Asking questions like, "Is this from a trustworthy source?", "Could there be another side to this story?", or "Why might someone want me to believe this?" helps disrupt the automatic impulse to like, share, or repost. These questions are simple but powerful tools for building digital resilience.

Understanding algorithms also opens the door to important conversations about autonomy and agency. If a child realises that their online experience is being shaped by forces beyond their control, they may initially feel powerless. But reframing this as an opportunity—"Now that you understand how this works, you can make better choices"—transforms that powerlessness into ownership. Children can learn to reset their algorithms by engaging with different types of content, clearing their watch history, or using platforms that offer more transparent recommendation systems.

Schools can reinforce this education by integrating algorithmic literacy into digital citizenship curricula. Lessons might include simulated environments that show how different user behaviours produce different content streams, or projects where students analyse how their own search histories influence their digital suggestions. These activities make the abstract concrete, helping students see the cause-and-effect relationship between their actions and their online environment.

It's also vital to address the emotional dimension of echo chambers. Part of the appeal of personalised content is that it feels affirming. When children see videos, posts, or articles that align with their values, tastes, or humour, it creates a sense of belonging and validation. This is not inherently negative, but it can become problematic when it shields them from discomfort or alternative views. Teaching children to tolerate, even welcome, cognitive dissonance—the feeling of holding multiple ideas in tension—helps them grow intellectually and emotionally. It also prepares them for real-life interactions, which are rarely as neatly curated as their digital feeds.

Ultimately, the aim is not to turn children into digital sceptics who distrust every post or video, but to help them become thoughtful navigators of a complex media environment. Understanding algorithms and echo chambers equips them with the insight to question, the confidence to explore, and the wisdom to recognise when their perspectives may be narrowing. It encourages a balance between familiarity and novelty, affirmation and challenge, personal interest and public responsibility.

As adults, we cannot dismantle the algorithmic architecture of the internet overnight, but we can help children see it clearly. We can teach them that what they see online is not a complete picture, but a curated selection tailored to their past behaviour. We can show them how to disrupt that cycle by making deliberate choices, seeking out difference, and thinking critically about what they consume. In doing so, we prepare them not just to survive in a digital world, but to shape it—one thoughtful click, question, and conversation at a time.

Encouraging Meaningful Digital Engagement

In a world increasingly defined by digital interaction, the way children engage with technology is shaping not only how they learn but how they think, communicate, and relate to the world around them. As screens become embedded in nearly every facet of modern life, the distinction between passive consumption and active learning becomes critical. It is no longer sufficient to manage screen time through limits alone. What truly matters is how that time is spent—whether children are passively scrolling through endless streams of algorithmically curated content or actively engaging with technology in ways that stimulate curiosity, creativity, and critical thought.

Passive digital consumption typically involves repetitive, unstructured engagement with media designed to capture attention rather than inspire insight. This includes activities such as mindlessly watching video compilations, endlessly swiping through social feeds, or clicking from one distraction to another without a clear purpose. While such activities can offer moments of leisure and mental rest, they often fail to provide the deeper engagement required for intellectual development or personal growth. Over time, excessive passive use can even dull attention spans, reduce motivation, and diminish the capacity for sustained focus—a concerning pattern, particularly during the formative years of cognitive and emotional development.

By contrast, meaningful digital engagement is characterised by intentionality, interaction, and reflection. It transforms screens from sources of distraction into tools for discovery. Children who use technology to create, explore, collaborate, or solve problems are not merely using digital tools—they are engaging with them actively, building skills and insights that extend well beyond the screen itself. Whether composing music with a digital synthesiser, constructing a virtual world in a sandbox game, or participating in an online course about space exploration, the emphasis is on doing, not just watching.

The key to fostering this kind of engagement lies in shifting both mindset and environment. Children must be guided to see technology not simply as entertainment, but as a platform for learning and self-expression. This does not mean stripping screens of all fun or spontaneity. Rather, it means expanding their digital repertoire to include content and activities that encourage thought, spark curiosity, and build competence.

One effective strategy is to integrate digital tools with personal interests. A child fascinated by animals might use a tablet to film and edit a documentary about local wildlife. Another drawn to storytelling might explore interactive fiction or design a choose-your-own-adventure game. When technology aligns with intrinsic motivation, it becomes a conduit for deeper engagement. The child is not just using a device—they are directing it towards a goal, investing in a process, and reflecting on an outcome. This agency is crucial. It cultivates a sense of ownership that passive consumption simply cannot provide.

Real-world examples illustrate the power of this approach. Consider a nine-year-old who becomes engrossed in an online platform for learning to code. Initially drawn in by the promise of creating simple animations, she begins experimenting with increasingly complex scripts, seeking out tutorials, and eventually building an interactive quiz for her classmates. What started as screen time evolves into an interdisciplinary project involving logic, design, literacy, and peer feedback. Importantly, the screen here is not the end in itself—it is the medium through which learning, connection, and creativity unfold.

Parents and educators play a vital role in facilitating these shifts. Conversations about digital use should centre not only on limits but on purpose. Asking children what they are doing online, what they've learned, or what they're proud of creates an atmosphere of interest and accountability. It signals that their digital activities matter and that thoughtful engagement is both expected and valued. Instead of imposing top-down rules, adults can collaborate with children to identify goals, evaluate outcomes, and adjust habits as needed. This co-constructive approach fosters independence while ensuring support.

Another useful intervention is to cultivate digital curiosity through modelling. When adults use technology to research a question, build a project, or explore a new skill, and do so openly, they demonstrate that screens are tools for lifelong learning. A parent experimenting with a language-learning app, a teacher using a mapping tool to design a virtual field trip, or a carer creating a digital photo album with a child all provide templates for what active, enriching screen use can look like. These examples offer both inspiration and permission for children to use technology in similarly constructive ways.

Schools, too, have a pivotal role in promoting meaningful digital engagement. Educational settings should go beyond simply digitising textbooks or gamifying worksheets. Instead, they should harness technology's capacity to personalise learning, support inquiry, and connect students with authentic audiences. For instance, students might use digital platforms to collaborate on a climate research project with peers in another country, blending science, communication, and cultural awareness in one initiative. The emphasis is not on the screen as a novelty, but as a bridge to real-world application.

Critical to this effort is ensuring that digital engagement is not overly structured or adult-directed. Children need space to experiment, take creative risks, and follow their own questions. A healthy digital environment allows for both guided learning and open-ended exploration. For instance, a child might start with a task—like learning to create a stop-motion video—and then branch out into composing their own sound effects, scripting narratives, or exploring animation techniques. This kind of emergent engagement fosters deeper investment and a more sustained connection to learning.

Balancing structured and unstructured engagement also supports the development of self-regulation. Children who are given opportunities to pursue their interests within thoughtful boundaries learn to manage their own time, evaluate their progress, and reflect on their choices. This capacity is far more protective against digital overuse than external enforcement alone. When children are empowered to set their own goals and measure their own success, they are more likely to use technology with intention rather than habit.

Of course, fostering meaningful digital engagement also requires access to quality resources. Not all apps, games, or platforms are created equal. Adults must be discerning curators, seeking out content that is age-appropriate, challenging, and designed with pedagogical integrity. Resources that invite open-ended exploration, support mastery through feedback, and encourage collaboration tend to be more beneficial than those that rely on extrinsic rewards or rote tasks. Evaluating digital tools through the lens of what they ask the child to *do*—not just what they deliver—can help filter out superficial experiences.

It is also important to pay attention to the emotional tone of digital engagement. Meaningful use does not always mean academic use. It can include activities that bring joy, foster connection, or provide comfort. A child video-calling a friend to co-create a digital art piece, or using a meditation app to practise mindfulness, is engaging with technology in ways that nurture emotional well-being. These experiences matter. They remind us that digital learning is not limited to facts and skills—it also encompasses relationships, identity, and resilience.

Encouraging children to reflect on their digital habits is another key dimension of this work. When children are invited to assess how their screen time makes them feel—energised or drained, connected or isolated—they begin to develop metacognitive awareness. Keeping a simple screen journal, discussing digital highs and lows at dinner, or setting weekly intentions for digital use are small but powerful practices. They move screen time from something that "just happens" to something that is actively shaped.

As the digital landscape continues to evolve, so too must our expectations. The goal is not to eliminate screens or to fear their presence, but to ensure that their use enriches rather than diminishes children's lives. This requires a shift in perspective—from managing technology to mentoring its use; from enforcing control to cultivating curiosity. It involves recognising that meaningful engagement is not a luxury, but a necessity for digital flourishing.

Ultimately, when we support children in shifting from passive consumption to active learning, we are doing more than enhancing their screen time. We are strengthening their sense of agency, deepening their capacity for focus and reflection, and equipping them with the tools to navigate a complex world with intelligence and care. Screens are neither heroes nor villains. They are mirrors, amplifiers, and gateways. And when used with purpose, they become instruments of growth—not just for what children know, but for who they are becoming.

The Role of Curiosity in Digital Awareness

In an age where technology permeates nearly every dimension of a child's life—from learning and play to communication and self-expression—the way adults introduce, discuss, and model digital engagement has lasting consequences. Much of the prevailing narrative around children and screens has been shaped by fear: fear of addiction, misinformation, online predators, and lost innocence. While these concerns are not unfounded, an overemphasis on danger can paradoxically leave children more vulnerable, not less. When the discourse around technology is framed primarily by anxiety, children may retreat into secrecy, develop shame around their digital interests, or disengage from opportunities to explore the digital world critically and reflectively. What they need instead is a foundation of curiosity—one that encourages questions, invites exploration, and treats digital awareness as a shared, evolving process rather than a set of fixed warnings.

Curiosity is the seedbed of critical thinking. It propels children to ask how things work, why people behave as they do online, what lies behind the headlines, and what they can create rather than merely consume. It also serves as a powerful antidote to both naïveté and cynicism. A curious child is less likely to accept digital content at face value and more likely to examine, compare, and reflect. At the same time, curiosity tempers the impulse to reject technology outright, recognising that digital tools—like all tools—can be shaped toward different ends. In this way, curiosity does not just foster digital competence; it nurtures a confident, open-minded posture toward a rapidly changing world.

Parents have a vital role to play in cultivating this disposition. Their responses to digital questions, habits, and mistakes often determine whether a child will feel safe to explore and inquire, or compelled to hide and disengage. When a child shares something they've seen online, the adult's reaction can either open the door to dialogue or shut it down. A response grounded in curiosity—"That's interesting. What made you click on that?"—signals to the child that their digital life is not off-limits or shameful, but a legitimate topic for discussion. It invites the child to think more deeply about their choices, while also affirming that the parent is a safe and interested partner in that exploration.

This contrasts starkly with approaches rooted in fear or control, which often provoke defensiveness or secrecy. If a child is met with immediate judgement or panic when disclosing a digital experience—especially one that was confusing, upsetting, or boundary-testing—they are less likely to bring similar issues forward in the future. Over time, this erodes trust and hampers the child's ability to learn from their experiences. Curiosity, by contrast, creates a culture of reflection. It models the idea that mistakes are learning opportunities, and that questions—even uncomfortable ones—are welcome.

Real-world examples help illustrate the power of this approach. A parent notices that their eleven-year-old is watching a series of conspiracy-themed videos on a video-sharing platform. The fearful reaction might be to forbid further viewing, remove access to the platform, or label the content as dangerous and ridiculous. The curious response, however, begins with a question: "What do you find interesting about these videos?" From there, the parent might explore what claims are being made, how the presenter tries to build credibility, and what evidence—if any—is provided. This doesn't mean endorsing the content; it means using it as a springboard for inquiry. In doing so, the parent not only addresses the specific issue but equips the child with skills to question similar content in the future.

Fostering curiosity also means modelling it. Children are remarkably attuned to the digital habits and attitudes of the adults around them. If a parent treats technology as either a necessary evil or a source of mindless escape, children may internalise that ambivalence. If, however, they see adults using technology to solve problems, research unfamiliar topics, experiment with creative tools, or engage in thoughtful conversation, they are more likely to adopt similar habits. Curiosity is contagious. A parent who pauses a video to ask,

"What do you think the creator was trying to say here?" or who explores how an app was designed, demonstrates that digital environments can be sites of inquiry as well as entertainment.

This modelling extends to how adults handle their own uncertainties. When parents admit they don't know how an app works, or express genuine interest in a game their child enjoys, they humanise the learning process and show that curiosity has no age limit. These moments build relational bridges. They also reposition adults as co-learners rather than gatekeepers, which encourages children to take more initiative in reflecting on their digital experiences.

Schools, too, can support this curiosity-driven approach. When educators move beyond rote digital literacy lessons and instead encourage students to bring their digital questions, confusions, and discoveries into the classroom, they transform learning into a collaborative endeavour. Projects that ask students to investigate how algorithms shape their feeds, explore the economic models behind popular platforms, or analyse online discourse patterns make digital awareness a living subject. This not only increases engagement but also validates students' lived experiences in digital spaces.

One important aspect of fostering curiosity is helping children develop a comfort with ambiguity. The digital world is full of contradictions, incomplete information, and evolving norms. Teaching children that it's okay not to have immediate answers—and that part of curiosity involves sitting with uncertainty—can relieve the pressure to adopt definitive positions before fully understanding an issue. A curious mindset resists oversimplification. It encourages children to ask, "What else might be going on here?" or "Who might see this differently?" These questions expand perspective and cultivate intellectual humility.

Equally, curiosity needs scaffolding. Left entirely unguided, children may pursue digital content that is too advanced, disturbing, or manipulative. The goal is not unbounded exploration but supported autonomy. Parents can help children set intentions for their digital time—asking what they hope to learn, make, or understand—and then reflect afterward on what they found valuable. This process doesn't require formal assessments. Informal check-ins—"What did you find most interesting today online?"—can reveal much about the child's evolving interests and comprehension. These conversations also help children build a reflective muscle, which is critical for both self-regulation and lifelong learning.

Digital curiosity can also be nourished through creative expression. Encouraging children to make rather than just consume—whether through writing blogs, designing games, creating videos, or composing digital art—allows them to explore the inner workings of digital tools while expressing their own voice. This not only strengthens technical skills but deepens understanding. A child who edits a video learns about narrative flow, audio synchronisation, and platform conventions. A child who builds a website gains insight into design logic, coding structure, and user experience. In each case, the screen becomes a site of experimentation rather than passive input.

It is also essential to recognise the emotional dimension of digital curiosity. For some children, especially those who are anxious, perfectionistic, or have experienced shame around their digital habits, curiosity may feel risky. They may fear making mistakes, disappointing adults, or being judged for what they find interesting. In these cases, the adult's tone and timing are crucial. Rather than interrogating or correcting, the adult should express genuine interest and encouragement. The message must be: "I'm glad you're asking questions. Let's explore this together." Creating emotionally safe spaces for curiosity is a prerequisite for genuine digital awareness.

As the digital environment continues to evolve—introducing new platforms, trends, and threats—curiosity remains one of the most resilient tools a child can possess. It allows them to keep learning even when adults are not present. It gives them the confidence to explore without succumbing to every new trend or narrative. And it grounds their digital awareness in an attitude of engagement rather than avoidance.

Ultimately, cultivating curiosity in digital contexts is not simply about avoiding harm or improving media literacy metrics. It is about shaping the kind of thinkers and citizens children will become. A curious child is more likely to resist propaganda, value evidence, appreciate nuance, and act with empathy. These qualities are foundational not only to digital awareness but to democratic participation, intellectual development, and emotional maturity.

Parents who foster this kind of curiosity are not just managing screen time—they are mentoring minds. They are creating conditions in which questions flourish, reflection deepens, and growth becomes a shared enterprise. In doing so, they shift the narrative around technology from one of fear to one of discovery, and they prepare their children not only to navigate the digital world but to shape it with thoughtfulness, creativity, and courage.

Chapter 5
Social Media and Emotional Resilience

Social media has woven itself into the very fabric of how young people see the world—and indeed, how they come to understand themselves within it. For today's children and teenagers, platforms like TikTok, Instagram, Snapchat, and whatever new app emerges next are not simply time-fillers or escapist diversions. They are arenas where identity is explored, social standing negotiated, and emotional needs either met or magnified. With every post, like, or scroll, young people are enacting a digital performance of self. Sometimes this performance brings connection, even joy. Other times, it leaves them exposed, judged, or adrift.

At the heart of this chapter lies a rather thorny paradox: social media can provide space for genuine self-expression and community, and yet—almost in the same breath—it can chip away at well-being, warp self-image, and erode emotional resilience. Managing this contradiction requires more than tracking screen time or enforcing blanket rules. It calls for a much deeper grasp of how these platforms shape emotional development, and a sustained effort to help children engage with them critically, compassionately, and—crucially—with an anchored sense of who they are.

One of the most pervasive emotional undercurrents of social media is the push-pull between connection and comparison. On the surface, these platforms extend the promise of closeness: maintaining friendships, finding like-minded communities, following role models. But behind that inviting façade is a constant, often invisible, ranking of social worth—measured in likes, followers, views, and comments. A simple photo becomes a public spectacle, its value determined not by the memory it captures but by the reactions it garners. For children and adolescents still forming their sense of self, this can be deeply destabilising. The mirror they hold up to themselves is a fickle one, and often, brutally honest.

Psychologists have termed this dynamic the "like-driven self-worth trap," and it's not hard to see why. When social approval becomes the yardstick for self-esteem, a child's confidence is no longer something they carry from within—it's outsourced, subject to the shifting tides of online validation. A well-received selfie may buoy them up; a post met with silence might plunge them into self-doubt. And so begins a feedback loop: self-expression is no longer authentic, but strategic, filtered through an invisible audience's presumed expectations.

Breaking this loop isn't easy. It requires a subtle reframing—moving away from the idea that online attention equals worth, and towards a view of digital spaces as just one of many venues for expression, not the judge and jury of one's identity. This shift can't happen through stern lectures or vague affirmations. It needs lived example, real dialogue, and above all, the slow strengthening of emotional resilience. That is, the ability to feel disappointment, embarrassment, or rejection—and still remain rooted in one's own value.

Another facet of digital life that deserves close attention is the way it complicates social conflict. Cyberbullying, while sadly not new, has taken on more insidious forms. It doesn't end with the school bell. It follows children into their bedrooms, creeping in through their phones at all hours. The anonymity of burner accounts, the cruelty of group chat exclusions, the sting of viral mockery—these are not rare occurrences. They can cause real, lasting harm, especially when children feel they have nowhere to turn.

Spotting the signs is vital. A child becoming withdrawn, showing anxiety around their phone, or suddenly dreading school may be sending up distress flares. But identifying the problem is only the beginning. Children must also be given the tools to respond—technical ones like blocking or reporting, yes, but also emotional ones: self-advocacy, empathy, and the confidence to seek support without fear of being shamed or dismissed. These lessons are best taught before the crisis, as part of a wider emotional education that treats online life not as an exception but as a continuation of the offline world.

Privacy, often discussed as a technical setting or legal issue, is actually deeply personal—especially for children. In sharing snippets of their lives online, young people may reveal more than they intend: their moods, their friendships, even their emerging identities. The pressure to be visible, to "keep up," can lead to oversharing, or to posting things that later feel painfully out of step with who they're becoming.

A teenager venting about a friendship breakdown may not consider how their words could be screenshotted and circulated beyond their intended circle. A child mimicking influencers might not grasp what it means to be visible to strangers. Instead of handing down rigid rules, parents can create moments of reflection. Asking, "Would you feel okay if this popped up in your memories a year from now?" or "Who are you posting this for, really?" opens space for thoughtful engagement. It's not about scolding—it's about fostering self-awareness.

Lurking beneath all this is a larger cultural problem: the way digital platforms reward spectacle over sincerity, reaction over reflection. Outrage travels fast. So does sarcasm. In such an environment, how do we nurture empathy? How do we teach children that behind every comment is a person, often feeling just as unsure, hopeful, or wounded as they are?

The answer doesn't lie in control, but in character. Empathy isn't something children automatically carry into digital spaces—it must be cultivated. It begins with perspective-taking: helping them imagine the emotional impact of their words, consider the context behind a post, or simply ask, "What might this person be going through?" Encouraging children to pause before responding, to think about how they themselves would feel on the receiving end, builds the habits of mind that lead to kinder, more considered online interactions.

And here's something that may seem obvious, but is easily forgotten: emotional security offline is one of the best buffers against the volatility of social media. When children feel known, accepted, and capable away from the screen—through hobbies, physical activity, strong family connections—they are less likely to unravel when digital life gets messy. A child who is comfortable in their own skin is far more likely to treat social media as a tool, not a measure of their worth.

Teachers have a critical part to play in this, too. Digital citizenship shouldn't be an isolated topic, tacked on at the end of term. It should be woven into lessons, discussions, and creative projects. Analysing online rhetoric, crafting thoughtful media, exploring the ethics of influence—these aren't extras. They are essentials. And when students themselves lead the way, through peer initiatives or digital storytelling, the impact can be transformative.

In the end, helping children thrive emotionally in a social media world isn't about removing all risk. Life, online or off, will never be free of bumps and bruises. It's about helping them meet those bumps with steadiness—with the emotional strength to navigate criticism, the clarity to question what they see, and the compassion to treat others well.

This chapter delves into all of these themes—drawing from research, lived experience, and practical wisdom. It offers tools not for shutting down digital life, but for guiding children through it with heart and integrity. Because while social media will continue to evolve, one thing remains constant: the need for young people to feel seen, valued, and strong in who they are—regardless of who's watching.

The Social Media Dilemma

Social media, in its short lifespan, has transformed how we connect, communicate, and construct identity—especially for children and adolescents. Once a peripheral form of communication, it is now central to the social lives of many young people. Platforms such as Instagram, Snapchat, TikTok, and newer variants of interactive spaces provide real-time access to friendships, trends, and expressions of self. For many children, these platforms are their social playgrounds, their diaries, their stages, and their mirrors. Yet embedded within these digital forums is a tension that can be difficult to navigate: the simultaneous promise of connection and the peril of comparison.

The social media dilemma is not a question of whether these platforms are inherently good or bad; it is a recognition that their effects are multifaceted and context-dependent. On the one hand, they offer young people opportunities to maintain friendships across distances, discover communities of shared interest, express creativity, and engage with ideas and issues they might never otherwise encounter. On the other, these same platforms intensify pressures related to appearance, popularity, and performance—magnifying insecurities and, in many cases, feeding a quiet but persistent sense of inadequacy.

This dual nature is perhaps most evident in the way social media shapes children's self-perception. Whereas previous generations grew up comparing themselves primarily to their immediate peers, today's young people are exposed to a vast, curated feed of peers, influencers, and celebrities—each carefully constructing an image that highlights success, beauty, humour, or glamour. Children scrolling through their devices are not only catching up with friends; they are being silently measured against images of "better" lives. It is this subtle shift—from social connection to social comparison—that lies at the heart of the dilemma.

Comparison itself is not inherently harmful. Developmentally, children and adolescents are wired to look to others as reference points. They model behaviours, absorb cues, and benchmark themselves as part of learning how to belong. The issue arises when the standards of comparison become distorted by the unique structure of social media. When children consistently compare their full, imperfect lives to the highly filtered highlight reels of others, they are at risk of internalising unrealistic expectations about what life, success, or even happiness should look like. The effect is cumulative and often invisible, eroding self-worth with every swipe.

Research into this phenomenon has shown that heavy social media use is associated with increased anxiety, depression, and feelings of loneliness in young people—not necessarily because of the time spent online, but because of the nature of the engagement. Passive consumption, especially of content that invites comparison, correlates with more negative emotional outcomes than active, communicative use. A child who spends time interacting with close friends online is more likely to feel connected. A child who spends the same time scrolling through influencer content or watching others' interactions from the sidelines may feel isolated despite being digitally 'plugged in.'

Real-world examples bring this dynamic to life. A thirteen-year-old girl may enjoy following fashion influencers on Instagram. Initially, she finds inspiration and creative ideas. But over time, she begins to feel that her own clothes are inadequate, her body not quite right, her experiences too plain. Her own posts become more performative—posed, filtered, edited—not out of vanity, but from a deepening desire to belong to the aesthetic she sees repeatedly celebrated. With each like, she experiences a fleeting sense of affirmation. With each post that gains little traction, she questions her worth. This is not narcissism. It is the psychological architecture of social media doing precisely what it was designed to do: capture attention and generate engagement by appealing to the most emotionally vulnerable parts of the user.

Parents and caregivers, often unfamiliar with the emotional mechanics of these platforms, may overlook the quiet toll they can take. They may notice mood swings, preoccupation with online activity, or self-critical comments but misinterpret these signs as typical adolescence. While developmental turbulence is to be expected, the digital environment often amplifies what might otherwise be passing insecurities. The problem is not just what children see, but what they infer—about themselves, their value, and their place in their peer group.

Helping children navigate this line between connection and comparison requires thoughtful engagement. It is not enough to demonise social media or issue blanket restrictions. Such approaches can inadvertently increase secrecy and shame. Instead, children need guided conversations that help them reflect critically on what they see and feel online. Asking questions like, "How does your feed make you feel?" or "What do you think that person is trying to communicate with that post?" opens up space for analysis and emotional literacy.

Equally important is encouraging children to reflect on their own motivations for posting. Are they sharing to express themselves, to connect with others, or to seek approval? None of these reasons are inherently wrong, but self-awareness is key. When children can articulate why they are posting and how they feel about the responses they receive, they are less likely to become caught in the trap of seeking digital validation.

Educators and mental health professionals can support this process by introducing frameworks for understanding social media dynamics. Media literacy programmes that unpack the construction of online identities, explore the use of filters and editing, and discuss the economics of attention can demystify what children often take at face value. When they learn that influencers are often paid to promote products, that engagement is driven by algorithms, and that 'likes' are designed to trigger dopamine responses, children are better positioned to reclaim agency in how they interpret and participate in online spaces.

Another promising strategy is encouraging intentional digital use. When children are supported in choosing what platforms to use, what content to follow, and when to disengage, they begin to experience social media as a tool rather than a trap. For example, a child interested in photography might use a platform to share their work, connect with other young photographers, and receive constructive feedback. In this context, social media fosters growth, not comparison. The focus shifts from external validation to intrinsic development.

Of course, this kind of engagement requires a supportive environment. Children need to feel secure in their offline relationships in order to approach online experiences with confidence. Families that prioritise connection—through conversation, shared activities, and emotional availability—create a buffer against the social anxieties that digital comparison can provoke. When a child knows they are valued and accepted unconditionally, they are less likely to tie their self-worth to digital metrics.

Part of fostering this security involves helping children develop a broader sense of self. When identity is tied solely to appearance, popularity, or performance, it becomes fragile—especially under the gaze of a global audience. But when children cultivate multiple dimensions of self—artist, reader, friend, thinker, helper—they are more resilient to the pressures of comparison. Encouraging offline pursuits, celebrating effort over outcome, and highlighting strengths beyond the digital sphere all contribute to this sense of groundedness.

Social media is unlikely to become less influential in children's lives; if anything, its presence will deepen and diversify. What we can do is equip children with the emotional tools to navigate its effects. We can teach them that connection is not the same as comparison. That visibility is not the same as worth. And that behind every polished post is a real person—uncertain, complex, and just as human as they are.

By reframing social media not as a threat but as a context—one that can both nurture and challenge emotional resilience—we invite children into a more thoughtful relationship with the digital world. They will still feel the pull of comparison, but they will also have the language to name it, the perspective to contextualise it, and the confidence to step back when needed.

Ultimately, the social media dilemma is not one to be solved, but to be understood and engaged with deliberately. Connection and comparison will always coexist in some measure. Our role is to help children strengthen the former while softening the latter—guiding them not away from digital spaces, but toward wiser, kinder, and more authentic participation within them.

The Like-Driven Self-Worth Trap

For many young people today, the line between online performance and personal identity has become increasingly blurred. At a time in their lives when self-image is being formed and social belonging is paramount, the digital metrics of approval—likes, shares, views, and comments—have evolved into powerful indicators of self-worth. Social media platforms, designed to reward attention with validation, create an environment where visibility is equated with value, and approval is measured in numbers. This dynamic has produced what might be termed the *like-driven self-worth trap*, a psychological loop in which children and adolescents begin to define themselves by their online reception rather than their intrinsic qualities, values, or efforts.

To understand how young people fall into this trap, it is essential to consider the mechanisms at play. Social media platforms are not neutral tools for connection; they are engineered systems that capitalise on the brain's reward pathways. When a post receives a high number of likes, the user's brain releases dopamine—a neurotransmitter associated with pleasure and reinforcement. This experience, though fleeting, is powerful, and it encourages repetition of the behaviour that produced it. In this way, the young person is conditioned to seek digital approval, often unconsciously, as a form of emotional sustenance.

Over time, the need for validation can become compulsive. Children start to post not for expression, but for applause. They may delete images that fail to gain traction, tailor their appearance or activities to please their perceived audience, or obsessively check their notifications in the hope of reassurance. This creates a fragile foundation for self-esteem—one that rises and falls with public approval and is easily shaken by criticism, indifference, or invisibility.

The psychological cost of this dynamic is profound. Children who tether their self-worth to digital metrics often experience heightened anxiety, mood instability, and a distorted sense of self. They may become hyper-attuned to how they are perceived, constantly comparing themselves to peers or influencers who seem more popular, attractive, or successful. These comparisons, driven by algorithmic exposure to curated and idealised content, can erode confidence and fuel self-doubt. Even high-achieving or socially connected children are not immune. Indeed, those who are most invested in their digital personas may be the most vulnerable to emotional fluctuations triggered by online engagement.

Real-world examples illuminate the subtle but pervasive nature of this phenomenon. A fifteen-year-old boy might feel proud of a video he made showcasing his artwork. He posts it, hoping to share his passion. When it receives only a handful of likes, compared to a peer's comedic skit that goes viral, he begins to question whether his interests are valid or worth pursuing. Or a twelve-year-old girl, initially confident in her appearance, begins to notice that her selfies receive fewer reactions than those of her classmates who conform more closely to prevailing beauty standards. She starts using filters to reshape her features, not as a form of creative expression, but in an attempt to meet an invisible and ever-shifting threshold of approval.

These are not isolated incidents; they reflect a broader cultural trend that equates public affirmation with personal value. And while this dynamic is not exclusive to children—adults, too, fall prey to the allure of digital popularity—its impact on developing minds is uniquely significant. Children are still learning to internalise values, regulate emotions, and form stable identities. When external validation becomes the dominant source of esteem, it crowds out the slower, deeper work of building self-respect from within.

Helping children detach their self-esteem from digital validation requires a multi-layered approach—one that combines emotional support, reflective dialogue, and practical strategies. The first step is to name the dynamic. When adults openly discuss the seductive nature of likes and the pressures of online performance, they normalise the experience and create space for reflection. A parent might say, "It's easy to feel good when people like your post—but have you noticed how quickly that feeling fades?" or "Do you ever feel nervous about what to share because of how people might react?" These questions invite children into a conversation, not a lecture. They also signal that the adult is not dismissive of their digital world, but genuinely interested in understanding it.

Equally important is helping children identify alternative sources of self-worth. These may include effort, creativity, kindness, resilience, humour, or critical thinking. By celebrating these qualities consistently—both online and offline—adults reinforce the message that value is not dependent on audience response. For example, if a child writes a thoughtful post that doesn't receive many likes, the adult might acknowledge the quality of the content rather than the reaction it received. "I loved how clearly you explained your idea. It made me think." This kind of feedback strengthens internal motivation and detaches validation from popularity metrics.

Schools can play a significant role by fostering environments that promote self-awareness and media literacy. Lessons that explore how social platforms manipulate engagement, how filters and edits create illusions, and how attention can be monetised provide children with critical tools for understanding their digital experiences. More importantly, these lessons should be linked to discussions about identity, emotion, and community. When children are encouraged to ask, "What does this post say about who I am and what I value?" or "How do I feel before and after spending time on this app?" they begin to reclaim agency over their digital lives.

At home, modelling is equally powerful. Children observe how adults interact with technology and internalise those habits. When adults constantly check their phones for likes or interrupt conversations to engage with digital feedback, they signal that approval is paramount. But when adults use technology to learn, to connect meaningfully, or to create without expectation of applause, they offer a different model—one grounded in intrinsic interest and purposeful action. Parents who share their own struggles with validation—"Sometimes I catch myself checking how many people liked my post, and I have to remind myself why I shared it"—also provide valuable context, showing that these feelings are common and manageable.

Another key strategy is encouraging intentional posting. Children can be supported in asking themselves, "Why do I want to share this?" and "What will I feel if it doesn't get much attention?" These questions help separate genuine expression from the need for affirmation. If the desire to post is rooted in wanting to share an achievement, spark a conversation, or document a memory, the act becomes more meaningful and less dependent on response. Conversely, if the primary motivation is to gain approval, the child may choose to pause or reflect further.

Boundaries around digital use can also help reduce dependence on online feedback. Designated tech-free times, such as during meals, study periods, or before bed, provide emotional breathing space and allow children to connect with other aspects of their identity. Encouraging screen-free hobbies—sports, music, crafts, reading, nature—reaffirms that joy and fulfilment exist beyond the digital world. These activities also serve as sources of mastery and pleasure that are not contingent on audience approval.

Of course, none of these strategies work in isolation. Children must feel safe, supported, and understood in order to examine and reshape their relationship with digital validation. This requires patience. A child who has internalised the message that likes equal worth will not shift their mindset overnight. But with consistent encouragement, open dialogue, and positive modelling, they can begin to build a self-image that is stable, nuanced, and resilient.

Ultimately, the challenge of the like-driven self-worth trap is not about removing children from social media, but about preparing them to engage with it from a position of strength. It is about teaching them that self-worth is not something to be earned through applause, but something to be discovered through effort, reflection, and connection. It is about helping them understand that their value is not measured in likes, but in the integrity of who they are—online and offline.

When children internalise this message, they are no longer at the mercy of algorithms or fleeting trends. They can participate in digital culture without being defined by it. They can share, express, and connect without performing for approval. And most importantly, they can grow into young people whose confidence is anchored not in how they are perceived, but in the quiet, enduring knowledge of their own worth.

Cyberbullying and Online Safety

The digital world, for all its promise and potential, has also introduced new forms of harm that many parents and educators are still learning to understand. Among the most pressing of these is cyberbullying—a term that encompasses a wide range of online behaviours designed to intimidate, shame, humiliate, or harass others. Unlike traditional bullying, which is typically confined to specific times and spaces such as the playground or the classroom, cyberbullying is omnipresent. It can follow a child from school to home, from day into night, and from one device to the next. Its permanence, reach, and capacity for anonymity make it uniquely damaging, particularly to the developing emotional and social resilience of children and adolescents.

Understanding how to recognise, prevent, and respond to cyberbullying begins with acknowledging that digital harassment is not just a technological issue—it is a relational and psychological one. It arises in the social dynamics of peer groups, in the shifting norms of online behaviour, and in the emotional vulnerabilities of young people seeking connection and belonging. To address it effectively, we must move beyond fear-based narratives and towards empathetic, informed strategies that empower both children and the adults who care for them.

Recognition is the first step. Cyberbullying can take many forms, some obvious, others more insidious. Direct forms include threatening messages, public shaming, exclusion from digital groups, and the sharing of private information or images without consent. Indirect forms, which can be just as damaging, include passive-aggressive comments, the spreading of rumours, the use of memes to ridicule, or the systematic ignoring of someone's posts in group conversations. These actions may be subtle, but their psychological impact is significant. Children experiencing cyberbullying often exhibit changes in mood, behaviour, and routine. They may become withdrawn, anxious, or irritable. Sleep disturbances, reluctance to attend school, loss of interest in previously enjoyed activities, and secrecy about online behaviour are also common indicators.

It is crucial that adults recognise these signs not simply as typical adolescent moodiness, but as potential signals of distress. However, recognising the issue is only part of the solution. Children must also be supported in naming and articulating their experiences. This requires trust. Many victims of cyberbullying hesitate to come forward, fearing shame, disbelief, or the loss of access to their devices—an action that, from their perspective, may seem like further punishment. Creating an open, non-judgemental space where children feel safe discussing their online lives is fundamental. Adults should make it clear that they are allies, not enforcers—that their goal is to support, not to control.

Preventative education is a powerful tool in reducing the incidence and impact of cyberbullying. Children need to understand not only what constitutes digital harassment, but why it happens and how it affects people. Teaching empathy—helping children see the person behind the profile—is perhaps the most effective form of prevention. When children are taught to pause and consider how their words or actions might feel from the other side, they are less likely to engage in harmful behaviour. This can be reinforced through stories, role-play, and critical discussions about online interactions. For example, examining a real or hypothetical post that seems funny on the surface but humiliates someone in the subtext can prompt valuable insights into the emotional costs of digital 'banter.'

Digital citizenship education should also include practical strategies. Children should learn how to manage privacy settings, block or report users, and preserve evidence through screenshots. Understanding these tools equips children not only to protect themselves but also to assist peers who may be struggling. Empowering children with this knowledge fosters a sense of agency, transforming them from passive recipients of digital culture into active, responsible participants.

The role of bystanders in cyberbullying dynamics must not be overlooked. In many cases, online harassment is perpetuated not only by the aggressor, but by the silence or complicity of others. Encouraging children to speak up, show support, or report abusive content when they witness it helps to shift the social norms around what is acceptable online behaviour. Creating a culture of digital solidarity—where kindness is visible and valued—is essential in building safer online communities.

When cyberbullying does occur, response matters immensely. The immediate goal is to stop the harm, but the longer-term goal is to help the child process and recover from the experience. This involves listening without interruption, validating the child's emotions, and refraining from overreaction. For example, instead of saying, "Why didn't you just block them?" or "You need to toughen up," an adult might say, "That sounds incredibly hurtful—thank you for telling me. Let's think together about what we can do next." Such responses communicate respect, empathy, and partnership.

In some cases, it may be appropriate to involve the school, especially when the cyberbullying overlaps with offline relationships or impacts the child's learning. Many schools now have designated safeguarding leads or pastoral staff trained to handle digital issues. However, involving the school should be done with the child's consent and involvement, unless there are immediate safety concerns. This ensures that the child remains central in the process and feels a sense of control over the response.

More serious incidents may warrant engagement with legal authorities, particularly when threats of violence, hate speech, or non-consensual sharing of explicit material are involved. Children and parents alike should be made aware that certain forms of cyberbullying are not just inappropriate—they are unlawful. However, invoking legal pathways should be done thoughtfully and sensitively, with consideration for the child's emotional wellbeing and the broader context of the harassment.

An equally important aspect of addressing cyberbullying is supporting the child in rebuilding their confidence and online identity. Victims often feel a loss of control over their digital presence and may become wary of all online interaction. Helping them re-establish a sense of agency is critical. This might involve setting new boundaries, joining supportive online communities, or gradually re-engaging with platforms in ways that feel safe and affirming. Therapeutic support can also be beneficial, particularly when the bullying has led to significant emotional distress or trauma.

Preventing future incidents means creating ongoing opportunities for dialogue. Cyberbullying is not a one-time issue; it evolves with technology, trends, and group dynamics. Regular check-ins, both informal and structured, keep lines of communication open. Asking children, "How are things going online this week?" or "Have you seen anything lately that made you uncomfortable?" normalises digital life as a topic of family discussion. It also helps adults stay informed about emerging platforms, behaviours, and risks.

Equipping children to handle online conflict with maturity is part of a broader commitment to developing their emotional intelligence. They need to learn how to disagree respectfully, how to cope with criticism, and how to distinguish between malice and misunderstanding. These are not just digital skills—they are life skills. When children feel emotionally supported and intellectually prepared, they are less likely to feel helpless in the face of digital cruelty.

Cyberbullying is a complex issue that touches on technology, psychology, peer relationships, and family dynamics. There is no single solution, but there is a clear direction: one that values empathy over punishment, education over restriction, and collaboration over control. When adults approach the issue with clarity, compassion, and consistency, they create the conditions in which children can learn not just to protect themselves, but to thrive online.

By cultivating awareness, fostering emotional resilience, and building cultures of digital kindness, we can transform social media from a source of stress into a space where young people are seen, heard, and valued for who they are—not targeted for who others think they should be. In doing so, we help them step into the digital world not with fear, but with confidence, compassion, and the wisdom to use their voices wisely.

Privacy in a Public Digital World

For today's children and adolescents, the distinction between public and private life is increasingly opaque. From the moment a young person opens a social media account, uses a learning app, or plays an online game, they begin weaving a digital footprint—often without understanding its permanence or potential implications. The instinct to share, to connect, and to be seen is natural, particularly during developmental stages when identity is actively forming. Yet in a digital world where personal information is not just observable but trackable, storable, and exploitable, teaching children how to protect their privacy is both a moral imperative and a practical necessity.

The concept of privacy itself has evolved dramatically. Whereas older generations understood privacy in spatial terms—what is said behind closed doors or kept within the family—digital privacy is more complex. It is not only about what one chooses to share, but also about what is passively collected, inferred, and repurposed. Children may assume that because they are not posting their home address or phone number, they are being cautious. However, digital surveillance operates on subtler levels. A photograph tagged with a location, a quiz answered on a social app, a browsing pattern on a game site—all these fragments contribute to a profile that can be used for marketing, manipulation, or more nefarious purposes.

This reality can feel abstract to children, who often approach technology with trust and immediacy. Their focus is on interaction—sharing a joke, posting a picture, joining a group—rather than on the long-term consequences of those interactions. Therefore, the first step in teaching children about privacy is to demystify how information flows in digital spaces. Rather than framing privacy as a rule to be obeyed, it should be introduced as a skill to be developed: a combination of awareness, discernment, and digital etiquette.

To do this effectively, the conversation must start early and evolve over time. Young children can begin by understanding the difference between personal and public information: names, birthdays, schools, addresses, and photographs are not just casual facts, but data points. They should learn to ask, "Who is this for?" and "Who might see this?" before posting or sharing. These questions, simple as they seem, encourage a pause—a moment of reflection that interrupts impulsivity and builds the foundation of responsible digital behaviour.

As children grow, their engagement with technology becomes more complex, and so must their understanding of privacy. Adolescents, in particular, may resist adult guidance if it feels intrusive or moralistic. Therefore, the tone of these conversations must be collaborative rather than controlling. Discussing real-world examples—such as influencers who've had private content leaked, or news stories about companies misusing user data—can anchor abstract concepts in relatable narratives. For instance, a teenager who admires a social media celebrity may be more receptive to discussing privacy when shown how even public figures struggle to maintain boundaries between their public and private selves.

Real-life situations often serve as powerful teaching moments. Take, for example, the case of a thirteen-year-old boy who enthusiastically joins a gaming platform and begins streaming his gameplay. At first, he shares only his game screen and username. But over time, in response to friendly chat messages, he reveals his first name, his town, and what school he attends. He doesn't see this as risky—after all, he's just chatting. Yet in this interaction, he has unknowingly made himself traceable. A parent, noticing this, has an opportunity not to shame but to explore: "What made you feel comfortable sharing that? What might someone do with that information?" These questions not only raise awareness but also respect the child's agency, framing the discussion as a shared inquiry rather than a lecture.

The rapid pace of technological change means that children are often using platforms that parents or teachers know little about. From anonymous sharing apps to location-based games, the tools themselves constantly evolve. What remains constant, however, is the principle of context. Children must learn that privacy is not about secrecy, but about control—about choosing what to share, with whom, and for what purpose. They must understand that different contexts call for different behaviours: what is appropriate in a private chat with a close friend is not appropriate in a group forum or public profile.

This is especially important when it comes to images. The sharing of photos and videos is now a central feature of digital communication, but many children lack a clear understanding of what it means to lose control over an image once it's uploaded. They may delete a post, assuming it disappears, without realising that screenshots or backups may exist elsewhere. Teaching children to think about digital permanence—not with fear, but with foresight—helps them navigate these decisions more wisely. Questions like, "Would I be okay with a teacher or future employer seeing this?" or "Does this image represent who I really am?" prompt reflection and self-regulation.

Privacy education must also address the commercial side of digital interaction. Many platforms are 'free' only in the monetary sense; users pay with their attention and personal data. Children should understand how companies track their activity, personalise content, and use algorithms to shape their experience. Explaining this is not about creating paranoia, but about fostering critical engagement. When a child realises that the ads they see are not random, but based on their behaviour, they begin to see themselves not just as users but as participants in a system. This awareness is the starting point for ethical decision-making about what they click on, what permissions they grant, and what data they offer.

Building habits of digital privacy can be supported through practical actions. Encouraging children to keep their profiles private, to use aliases where appropriate, and to avoid geotagging their posts helps them exercise control over their digital presence. Showing them how to use privacy settings, how to review app permissions, and how to manage their digital footprint reinforces the message that privacy is an ongoing practice, not a one-time precaution.

However, no amount of technical knowledge can substitute for emotional maturity. Children must also be equipped to handle the social dynamics that test their boundaries. Peer pressure to overshare, the desire to impress, or the fear of exclusion can all lead to lapses in judgement. Creating space for children to talk about these pressures without fear of reprisal enables them to reflect and recalibrate. Rather than punishing mistakes, adults should treat them as learning opportunities, reinforcing the idea that digital privacy is not about perfection, but about progress.

At the heart of digital privacy is the concept of respect—respect for oneself and respect for others. Children who are taught to value their own privacy are more likely to respect the boundaries of their peers. They learn not to share images or stories without consent, not to forward private messages, and not to use others' information as a source of gossip or leverage. This mutual respect is the cornerstone of digital citizenship, and it must be modelled by the adults in their lives.

Parents and educators can further support this development by sharing their own strategies and reflections. When a parent explains why they limit their own social media exposure or how they manage online privacy, it reinforces the idea that these are lifelong skills, not just childhood rules. When a teacher discusses how they navigate professional boundaries online, it helps students see that privacy is relevant beyond adolescence. These conversations position privacy not as a constraint, but as a form of dignity and self-determination.

Ultimately, teaching children how to protect their personal information in a public digital world is about more than safety. It is about cultivating discernment, strengthening identity, and promoting autonomy. It is about helping them understand that while the digital world may invite them to share everything, they have the right—and the responsibility—to decide what remains theirs. By guiding children to develop a thoughtful, principled approach to digital privacy, we prepare them not only to survive the public nature of modern life, but to thrive within it—confident in their boundaries, conscious of their choices, and empowered to be fully themselves, both online and off.

Teaching Empathy and Digital Kindness

The online world, despite being driven by innovation and connectivity, often struggles to reflect the civility we aspire to in our physical communities. While digital platforms have made it easier than ever to interact across distances and differences, they have also created an environment where detachment and anonymity can distort human interaction. For children growing up in this digital context, learning to communicate with empathy and kindness online is not just about good manners—it is about cultivating the moral and emotional skills necessary for healthy relationships, ethical engagement, and responsible citizenship in an increasingly digital society.

Empathy, at its essence, is the ability to understand and share the feelings of others. It is the foundation of social harmony, allowing individuals to anticipate the emotional impact of their words and actions. In offline settings, empathy is often reinforced through visual and verbal cues—tone of voice, facial expressions, body language—all of which provide immediate feedback. In digital interactions, these cues are frequently absent or diminished, which can make it harder for young users to assess how their words might affect someone else. This disconnect often results in comments being more abrupt, jokes more cutting, and disagreements more polarised than they might be face-to-face.

Teaching empathy in digital contexts, therefore, requires a deliberate effort to bridge this gap. Children must be guided to recognise that behind every username, avatar, or screen name is a real person with feelings, struggles, and vulnerabilities. This is not always obvious, particularly on platforms that reward provocation or popularity. In some online environments, harshness is normalised, and children may mimic behaviours that are perceived as clever or assertive, not realising they are participating in a culture of exclusion or harm.

To counter this, adults must first acknowledge that digital empathy is not automatic. It must be taught, reinforced, and modelled consistently. One effective approach is to use digital scenarios as teaching tools. For example, when a child encounters a harsh comment on a YouTube video or a classmate's Instagram post that receives mocking replies, a parent or teacher might ask, "How do you think that person felt reading those comments?" or "What do you think was going through the mind of the person who posted that?" These kinds of questions prompt children to consider emotional consequences and begin to internalise the perspectives of others.

Incorporating digital kindness into these conversations helps translate empathy into action. Digital kindness is not about being overly polite or avoiding conflict at all costs—it is about communicating with integrity, fairness, and compassion, even in disagreement. It means using online platforms not just to express opinions, but to uplift, include, and build others up. This can take many forms: offering encouragement, defending someone being targeted, acknowledging others' contributions, or simply using language that conveys respect. Such behaviours may seem small, but in an environment where cruelty can spread rapidly, kindness is radical.

Real-world examples help reinforce this message. Take the story of a secondary school student who noticed a peer being excluded in a group chat. Rather than ignoring the situation, she messaged the classmate privately to express support and then raised the issue with a trusted adult. Her intervention disrupted the cycle of exclusion and demonstrated that digital spaces can be used to build bridges rather than walls. Highlighting stories like these shows children that they have power in online spaces—not just to protect themselves, but to shape the culture around them.

Another crucial dimension is ethical literacy. Many children understand right from wrong in traditional contexts, but may not immediately apply those principles online. They might know that teasing is hurtful, but not realise that forwarding a private meme or screenshot can cause lasting harm. They might value honesty but see no harm in exaggerating online to fit in. Ethical digital behaviour requires reflection: what are the motives behind my actions? Who might be affected by this? Would I do or say the same thing if we were in the same room?

To foster this kind of ethical reflection, children need opportunities to engage in dialogue, not simply follow rules. Rather than saying, "Don't post mean comments," we can ask, "What kind of online environment do you want to be part of?" This approach encourages ownership and agency. When children are involved in setting expectations for their own digital conduct, they are more likely to uphold those standards and help others do the same. Classrooms and families that co-create digital charters or community agreements often report higher levels of respect and cooperation, because the values are shared rather than imposed.

Model behaviour from adults is also instrumental. Children watch how we interact online—how we respond to criticism, how we talk about others on social media, how we engage in public discourse. If we respond to disagreement with mockery or sarcasm, they may do the same. If we publicly shame others for mistakes, they may mimic that strategy in peer conflicts. By contrast, when adults model thoughtful engagement, compassionate language, and restraint, they show that digital spaces can reflect the same values we champion offline.

Schools can enhance these efforts by embedding empathy and kindness into digital citizenship curricula. This goes beyond technical safety to include collaborative projects, peer mediation training, and cross-cultural exchanges that deepen understanding and reduce prejudice. Encouraging students to create positive content—such as gratitude campaigns, inclusive profiles, or kindness challenges—shifts the focus from avoiding harm to actively doing good. These initiatives demonstrate that empathy is not merely reactive; it can be a proactive force that transforms online culture.

At home, cultivating empathy begins with everyday conversations. When children talk about online conflicts or friendships, adults can listen with curiosity rather than judgement. Questions like, "What did you think they meant by that?" or "Have you felt that way before?" invite exploration and build emotional vocabulary. Even seemingly trivial interactions can become opportunities for growth. A discussion about a silly comment thread or an awkward emoji exchange can reveal deeper insights into how children interpret and navigate digital communication.

It is also important to recognise the emotional toll that digital interactions can take. Even positive feedback, when tied to popularity metrics, can create pressure. A child who posts a heartfelt message and receives limited engagement may feel invisible. One who is used to frequent praise may feel compelled to perform or present a curated version of themselves. Empathy must extend inward as well—helping children recognise and respond to their own feelings with kindness and understanding. Teaching self-compassion is foundational to fostering compassion for others.

Developing empathy and digital kindness is not about perfection. Children will make mistakes, sometimes act impulsively, and occasionally participate in online interactions they later regret. The goal is not to eliminate all missteps, but to build the capacity to learn from them. When adults respond to these moments not with punishment but with perspective, they create a learning environment that encourages growth. A child who says something hurtful online can be guided to reflect, apologise, and make amends—thus learning that mistakes, when addressed with integrity, can lead to deeper maturity.

Over time, these lessons shape how children show up in digital spaces—not just as users, but as citizens, friends, and ethical communicators. They learn that their words matter, that silence can either condone or resist harm, and that kindness is not weakness but strength. They also begin to see the online world not as separate from the "real" world, but as part of it—one in which their actions carry weight and their empathy can ripple outward in ways they may never fully see.

By teaching empathy and promoting digital kindness, we are not just improving online behaviour. We are raising thoughtful, compassionate individuals who know how to engage with difference, who understand the emotional impact of their choices, and who use their voices not to dominate, but to connect. This is not only a digital skill—it is a human one, and its relevance will endure regardless of how the technologies change. Through every click, comment, and conversation, our children can learn that kindness is not just possible online—it is essential.

Chapter 6
Tech as a Tool for Growth, Not a Distraction

It's all too easy—especially in an age of escalating concern over digital dependency, fractured attention spans, and relentless screen exposure—to cast technology in the role of villain when it comes to childhood development. The dominant narrative tends to frame screens as the chief culprit behind a host of social and cognitive ailments, sapping creativity, derailing meaningful connection, and stalling healthy growth. But that lens, while not without merit, often misses the fuller picture. Technology, after all, isn't inherently harmful or helpful; the real question lies in how we choose to wield it. What we prioritise, what we model, what we enable—all these choices shape whether screens become tools for enrichment or engines of distraction.

Digital media, when thoughtfully engaged with, can be so much more than a vehicle for passive consumption. It can, in the right hands, become an open stage for exploration, creativity, and intellectual play. A child sketching imaginative characters on a tablet, a teenager editing a short film on their mobile, or a curious learner building a simple game using a coding interface—these aren't trivial pastimes. They're expressions of ingenuity and discipline, often cloaked in the language of leisure but grounded in very real educational value. Behind such projects lie planning, experimentation, iterative learning—skills as applicable in the classroom as in broader life.

Still, a pervasive myth lingers: that all screen time is equal, flat, and void of meaningful substance. It's a convenient simplification, but a false one. The difference between hours lost to mindless scrolling and time spent storyboarding an original comic on a digital design app is profound. The former dulls the senses; the latter sharpens them. The key lies in exposure to the right kind of digital experiences—ones that invite active participation, spark curiosity, and emphasise the creative process rather than the end product.

In recent years, educational technology has matured in notable ways. Admittedly, the digital learning terrain is uneven, and not all platforms are created equal. But tools like Khan Academy, Duolingo, Scratch, or Tinkercad have emerged as genuinely engaging environments. They're not merely digitised worksheets—they offer adaptive learning, exploratory thinking, and, on occasion, a touch of wonder. Crucially, these platforms don't displace human teachers; rather, they extend the reach of learning, allowing children to practise, reflect, and revisit concepts on their own terms.

This kind of engagement also cultivates autonomy—a subtle but vital shift in mindset. A student who completes a self-paced coding challenge or builds a 3D model on their own isn't just learning facts or techniques; they're learning that they can steer their own progress. That sense of agency—of being the architect of one's own learning experience—can be deeply empowering. It teaches young people that technology is not simply something that happens to them, but something they can shape and direct.

Outside formal education, digital tools are also opening doors to an entrepreneurial spirit once reserved for adults with capital and connections. The web has flattened many of the traditional barriers to entry. A teenager with a smartphone can launch a podcast, write and publish a blog, design merch, or crowdsource support for a community initiative. These ventures aren't just experiments—they're formative experiences, often involving budgeting, branding, communication, and perseverance.

Picture a twelve-year-old crafting and selling handmade jewellery online—not just perfecting a skill, but learning to price, present, and promote her creations. Or a teen who sets up a YouTube channel explaining algebra tricks, gradually honing his public speaking and technical editing abilities in the process. These aren't idle pursuits. They represent a shift in the digital dynamic—from consumption to contribution, from distraction to direction.

Parents have an important role in encouraging this shift. Too often, screen use becomes a site of friction—a flashpoint for rules, arguments, and control. But if reframed, it can also be a place of shared exploration. Watching a documentary together, playing a collaborative game, co-creating digital stories or music—these are small but meaningful ways to turn screen time into family time, into moments of mutual learning.

And in those moments, parents can do more than supervise—they can engage. Asking a child why they chose a particular colour palette for a digital drawing, or how they learned a specific game mechanic, does more than show interest; it signals respect. It communicates that the child's digital world is valid, worthy of conversation, and, by extension, that the child's choices within it carry weight.

That said, none of this negates the need for balance. Children still require unplugged time—space for daydreaming, for fresh air, for messy physical play. The point isn't to maximise digital engagement but to ensure that, when it happens, it feeds rather than stifles growth. It's about seeing digital play as a new strand in the broader fabric of play itself, not as its replacement. Passive entertainment has its place—but it shouldn't eclipse the opportunities for creation, connection, or discovery that tech can offer.

Looking further ahead, it becomes clear that the digital skills children are acquiring now are not merely useful—they are foundational. The world they will inherit is not just online—it is algorithmic, automated, and deeply interwoven with machine intelligence. In this reality, knowing how to code is important. But knowing how to adapt, how to question, how to empathise across virtual divides—that will matter just as much, if not more.

The conversation about AI and emerging tech must, therefore, begin at home. Children are already encountering intelligent systems—recommendation engines, voice assistants, predictive text. These tools are powerful, yes, but also opaque. Parents can help demystify them by inviting questions: How does this algorithm decide what to show you? Who built it? What assumptions might be baked into it? These are not technical queries alone—they are ethical ones, and they are critical to the development of a thoughtful, questioning digital citizenry.

For parents, this role requires humility as well as curiosity. It means acknowledging the limits of one's own knowledge, learning alongside one's child, and cultivating a household culture where digital exploration is both safe and celebrated. The same enthusiasm we show for a child's painting or sporting effort should be extended to a clever bit of code or a well-edited video. The effort is no less real, the learning no less rich.

Technology is not a neutral presence in our lives. It shapes us—our habits, our thinking, our relationships. But that shaping is not inevitable. It can be directed, guided, even resisted, where needed. Children can be taught to approach technology not just as consumers, but as conscious participants—individuals who understand the structures they inhabit and who feel empowered to shape them with intelligence and care.

This chapter offers a map for that kind of engagement. It draws on concrete examples, practical insights, and a belief in the creative potential of children when given the right tools and encouragement. By shifting our focus from fear to possibility, from limitation to cultivation, we begin to see technology not as a threat to childhood, but as a means of enriching it. The challenge is not to eliminate screens, but to illuminate their potential—to help children become not just fluent in the digital language, but wise in its use.

The Creative Potential of Digital Tools

When we think about children and technology, the dominant narratives often focus on consumption—hours spent scrolling, gaming, or watching videos. But this perspective overlooks one of the most dynamic and promising dimensions of digital engagement: the opportunity for young people to use technology as a springboard for creative expression and intellectual development. Far from being a distraction or a passive activity, digital tools—when thoughtfully introduced and appropriately used—can unlock new forms of artistry, problem-solving, and idea generation that were previously inaccessible to most.

Creativity today is no longer confined to paper, canvas, or stage. It exists just as vividly on touchscreens and digital interfaces. A child composing music through GarageBand on a tablet, a teenager animating a short film using Blender, or a young learner building an interactive story through a coding platform like Scratch is engaging in profoundly creative acts. These tools do not replace traditional forms of expression; rather, they expand the vocabulary through which children can make sense of the world and their place in it. They lower barriers to entry, invite experimentation, and offer immediate feedback—key ingredients in the creative process.

The democratisation of creative tools is one of the most transformative aspects of the digital age. Previously, producing a short film required expensive equipment, technical expertise, and often adult supervision. Today, a smartphone and a basic editing app are enough to craft a compelling narrative. The same applies to publishing, music composition, digital illustration, and even game design. Platforms like Canva, Procreate, Tinkercad, and BandLab make it possible for children to create sophisticated works across mediums, often without formal instruction. This accessibility matters. It tells children that creativity is not reserved for the gifted or the professionally trained—it is something they can claim, explore, and develop at their own pace.

Real-world examples demonstrate how children are harnessing these tools with remarkable ingenuity. Consider the case of a ten-year-old who begins creating stop-motion videos using household objects and a mobile phone. Initially, the videos are simple and spontaneous, but over time, they become more complex—incorporating scripted dialogue, set design, and character development. Through this process, the child is not only learning technical skills but engaging in storytelling, pacing, and visual composition. Similarly, a thirteen-year-old might use a blogging platform to publish reflective essays or fan fiction, discovering a love for writing and building a sense of audience that fuels further exploration.

These digital platforms do more than provide new formats for expression—they cultivate habits of mind. The iterative nature of digital creation encourages resilience. A child who records and re-

records a podcast segment, or edits a photo multiple times to achieve the desired effect, is practising persistence and refining their attention to detail. The collaborative features of many digital tools also promote interpersonal learning. Children working together on a Google Slides presentation or contributing to a shared digital comic learn how to give and receive feedback, negotiate ideas, and combine their strengths.

Crucially, technology allows for multi-modal creativity. Children are not forced to choose between writing and drawing, between sound and visuals. They can mix media, blend genres, and move seamlessly between modes of expression. This integrated approach suits the natural inclinations of many young learners, especially those who may not flourish in traditional academic settings. A child who struggles with written essays might thrive when asked to produce a video essay, voiceover project, or interactive infographic. By allowing multiple points of entry, digital creativity can reveal strengths that standard assessments miss.

Parents and educators often wonder how to encourage this kind of digital engagement without letting screens dominate or dilute attention. The answer lies in framing technology as a tool, not a pastime. When children are encouraged to use devices to create rather than consume, the relationship to the screen shifts. A parent might ask, "What are you making today?" rather than "How long have you been on your device?" This subtle reframing reinforces agency and intention. Likewise, teachers can design assignments that allow for creative digital outputs—inviting students to submit a podcast instead of a written report, or a digital zine in place of a conventional poster.

Support from adults does not require technical expertise. What matters most is the willingness to be curious, to ask questions, and to celebrate effort. When a child shares a piece of digital artwork or a short video, the adult response should mirror how we react to other forms of creativity. Asking about the process, the choices made, and what the child learned along the way helps them deepen their understanding and take pride in their work. It also opens the door to conversations about aesthetics, intention, and audience—critical components of creative development.

There are also rich opportunities to connect digital creativity to real-world contexts. A child creating a poster about environmental issues on an online design platform can be encouraged to print and distribute it at school. A digital recipe book created as a family project can be shared with relatives or uploaded to a community website. When digital creations move beyond the screen and into social contexts, children see that their ideas matter and can make an impact. This reinforces the value of what they are doing and inspires further exploration.

In addition, creative use of technology helps children develop a sense of digital identity—not in terms of personal branding, but in terms of their voice, interests, and values. The act of choosing what to create, how to present it, and where to share it invites self-reflection. It encourages children to consider how they want to be seen and what they want to contribute. This process is foundational to developing a healthy relationship with technology—one in which the screen is a mirror of thought, not a mask of conformity.

Yet the creative potential of digital tools is not without its tensions. The risk of comparison, performance anxiety, or fixation on feedback metrics such as likes and views can undermine intrinsic motivation. This is where adult guidance is most needed—not to eliminate these risks, but to help children navigate them. Supporting a child in reflecting on why they create, how they define success, and what they enjoy about the process reinforces a focus on growth and learning rather than approval or competition.

Educators and caregivers should also be aware of the disparities in access to high-quality digital tools. While many platforms are freely available or low-cost, devices, connectivity, and supportive learning environments are not equitably distributed. Ensuring that all children have the opportunity to explore their creative potential with technology is a broader social responsibility. It requires investment not only in hardware but in digital pedagogy, teacher training, and culturally relevant content.

The creative potential of digital tools is vast, but it is not automatic. It must be cultivated through opportunity, encouragement, and intentional use. When children are given the space, support, and resources to explore, they can turn screens from distractions into studios—from sources of noise into instruments of voice. They can draw, write, design, compose, film, code, and invent. In doing so, they develop not only technical competence but also the deeper capacities that creativity fosters: imagination, resilience, empathy, and innovation.

As technology continues to evolve, so too will the ways children create with it. The tools will change, but the impulse to express, to connect, and to shape ideas into form will remain. By embracing this impulse and guiding its digital expressions, we help children see themselves not merely as users of technology, but as its shapers—thoughtful, inspired, and empowered to contribute meaningfully to the world around them.

Educational Apps and Platforms That Work

The exponential rise of educational technology has revolutionised the landscape of learning for children, making it more accessible, engaging, and personalised than ever before. Yet amid the sheer volume of apps, games, and platforms claiming to enhance cognitive development or academic achievement, many parents and educators are left wondering which tools genuinely support meaningful learning—and which simply masquerade as educational while delivering little more than distraction. To navigate this digital terrain with discernment, we must look beyond flashy interfaces and marketing slogans to consider the actual educational value offered by technology. The goal is not merely to keep children occupied, but to facilitate learning that is active, purposeful, and developmentally enriching.

Constructive tech use begins with identifying tools that align with sound pedagogical principles. The most effective educational apps and platforms are those that foster deep thinking, support mastery through feedback and repetition, and adapt to the individual learner's pace and needs. These tools do not treat learning as entertainment or gamification alone but as a process that involves curiosity, challenge, and reflection. They are structured to engage children not just cognitively, but emotionally—by offering content that is relevant, stimulating, and responsive to their efforts.

Take, for instance, the widespread success of Khan Academy. What began as a library of simple maths tutorials has grown into a comprehensive platform covering subjects such as science, economics, computing, and the humanities. Its strength lies in the clarity of its explanations, the scaffolded nature of its content, and its mastery-based approach. Learners are not pushed forward until they demonstrate understanding, a model that reduces anxiety and builds confidence. Moreover, its real-time feedback helps students correct misconceptions as they occur. Teachers and parents can track progress through detailed dashboards, which enhances transparency and provides a basis for tailored support.

Another standout is Duolingo, a language-learning app that blends playful design with rigorous content. Although often perceived as a game, Duolingo's structure is pedagogically sound. It uses spaced repetition to enhance memory retention and offers contextualised vocabulary to promote application rather than rote recall. What distinguishes Duolingo is its ability to turn practice into a habit, making language learning a daily exercise that is both enjoyable and effective. For children, particularly those who might find language learning intimidating in formal settings, this kind of low-pressure, incremental exposure can be transformative.

For younger learners, apps like Endless Alphabet and Montessori Crosswords focus on phonics, vocabulary, and early literacy through interactive storytelling and puzzle-solving. Their visual and auditory design is rooted in child development research, promoting multisensory engagement. Unlike many flashy alternatives, these apps avoid overstimulation and encourage children to slow down, think, and explore. This design philosophy respects the child's cognitive process and supports more sustained attention.

When it comes to numeracy, Prodigy has gained popularity for blending role-playing game mechanics with maths challenges. The platform adapts questions to the learner's level and rewards effort with progress in an interactive fantasy world. While some educators have raised concerns about the gamified incentives overshadowing the content itself, when used thoughtfully, Prodigy can act as a motivational supplement to classroom instruction. It is particularly effective for children who benefit from visual and kinesthetic learning styles.

Older children and adolescents are increasingly turning to platforms like Quizlet and Brainscape, which use digital flashcards to support revision and self-testing. These tools promote metacognitive awareness by helping students identify what they know and what they need to revisit. Unlike traditional flashcards, these platforms use algorithms to adjust the frequency of questions based on confidence ratings, enhancing efficiency and reinforcing long-term retention. Importantly, they also allow students to create their own content, thereby reinforcing agency and personal engagement with the material.

Coding platforms such as Scratch and Tynker deserve special attention for their ability to teach computational thinking and logic in an accessible and creative way. Scratch, developed by the MIT Media Lab, allows children to build animations, games, and interactive stories by sequencing blocks of code. This visual approach demystifies programming and nurtures problem-solving in a playful, non-threatening format. Tynker, while similar, offers more structured courses aligned with school curricula and is ideal for learners ready to delve into more advanced coding languages.

The educational value of these platforms lies not only in the subjects they teach but in how they teach them. They reinforce core executive functions—such as working memory, cognitive flexibility, and inhibitory control—by requiring planning, persistence, and adaptive reasoning. They also support intrinsic motivation when learners see the tangible outcomes of their efforts, whether in the form of a functioning app, a completed level, or a personalised achievement badge. These forms of feedback, while simple, are psychologically meaningful and help anchor learning in positive reinforcement.

One must also consider the social dimension of educational platforms. Collaborative tools like Google Classroom, Padlet, and Flipgrid allow students to share ideas, provide peer feedback, and co-create content in real time. These platforms blur the boundaries between learning and dialogue, encouraging children to see themselves not just as recipients of information, but as active participants in a learning community. When used in a school or family setting, such tools can foster communication skills and collaborative problem-solving—key competencies in both academic and future workplace environments.

Practical implementation, however, requires intentional adult involvement. Even the most effective educational apps can become unproductive if used without context, reflection, or guidance. Adults need not be experts in the apps themselves but should be willing to engage with children about their use. Asking questions such as "What did you find challenging today?", "How did you solve that problem?", or "What would you like to learn next?" helps make learning visible and reinforces metacognition.

It is also essential to strike a balance between structured and exploratory use. While some platforms offer guided pathways with clear objectives, others are open-ended, encouraging children to direct their own learning. Both have value. A child who uses a design app like Canva to create an infographic on a topic of interest is engaging in research, synthesis, and visual communication—all under their own steam. Similarly, a student using Google Earth to explore global geography at their own pace is likely to retain far more than through passive instruction alone. These moments of curiosity-driven learning are not supplemental—they are central to building lifelong learners.

Equity must also be at the forefront of any discussion about educational technology. Not all children have equal access to devices, broadband, or adult support. While many of the best platforms are free or low-cost, their effectiveness is contingent on broader infrastructural conditions. Schools, libraries, and community centres play a vital role in bridging this divide, as do policies that prioritise digital inclusion and parental education. Without these supports, the promise of educational technology risks becoming yet another vector of inequality.

That said, when access and support are in place, educational apps and platforms can significantly enhance the learning experience. They allow for differentiation, offer immediate feedback, and support a variety of learning styles. They can help a child who struggles with traditional methods find their stride, or challenge an advanced learner to stretch their thinking. More than anything, they can make learning feel personal—anchored not in obligation but in discovery.

As parents and educators consider the role of digital tools in children's lives, the key is not to reject or uncritically embrace technology, but to engage with it mindfully. This means evaluating platforms not by their popularity or polish, but by their capacity to support real learning. It means being curious about what children are doing on their screens, and willing to guide them towards tools that feed rather than flatten their intellect. And it means recognising that in a world increasingly shaped by technology, knowing how to use it constructively is not just a digital skill—it is a foundational one for the modern learner.

Encouraging Digital Entrepreneurship

Children today are growing up in a world where the boundaries between consumer and creator are increasingly blurred. With access to sophisticated digital tools, global audiences, and decentralised platforms, the opportunity for young people to engage in entrepreneurial activity has never been more within reach. And yet, much of their interaction with technology remains rooted in passive consumption—watching videos, scrolling social feeds, or playing games designed by others. Encouraging digital entrepreneurship means shifting this paradigm: guiding children to see themselves not merely as users of content, but as capable builders, problem-solvers, and innovators within the digital landscape.

Digital entrepreneurship is not simply about starting a business or monetising skills. It is a mindset—one that values initiative, creativity, experimentation, and resilience. It teaches children that they can create value using the tools at their fingertips and that their ideas, however nascent, can be developed into something tangible. This mindset aligns closely with the foundational principles of twenty-first-century learning: critical thinking, collaboration, self-direction, and adaptability. By cultivating these qualities through entrepreneurial practice, we prepare children not just to participate in the digital world, but to shape it.

The first step is helping children recognise that building something online is within their capability. Many already engage in creative pursuits—designing avatars, editing videos, writing fan fiction, or creating digital art. These hobbies, when nurtured with the right scaffolding, can evolve into entrepreneurial ventures. A child who enjoys drawing may begin creating digital stickers or character designs, which can be sold on platforms like Redbubble. A teenager who plays with music production apps might develop a portfolio of tracks and distribute them via Bandcamp or SoundCloud. What matters is not the scale of the endeavour, but the realisation that digital creativity can extend beyond personal satisfaction to shared value.

Real-world examples illustrate how young people are already making this shift. Consider the case of a fourteen-year-old who learned to code using free online resources and built a simple productivity app to help classmates track homework. After sharing it on social media and refining it based on peer feedback, the app gained traction in their school and eventually reached a wider student network. What began as a modest tool became a meaningful project with users, a brand identity, and potential for further development. In this scenario, the child did not wait for formal instruction or external validation; they identified a problem, devised a solution, and took action—hallmarks of entrepreneurial thinking.

Teaching children to adopt this approach begins with encouraging them to ask questions about the digital tools and content they encounter. Instead of accepting apps or games as finished products, they can be guided to explore how they were made, who made them, and what decisions went into their design. This kind of critical inquiry fosters technical curiosity and empowers children to move from passive users to active creators. Once they begin to understand the mechanics behind their favourite digital experiences, the idea of making their own becomes far less intimidating.

Another essential element is fostering a tolerance for failure. Entrepreneurship, by nature, involves trial and error. Whether a child is starting a blog, launching a YouTube channel, or creating an online shop for handmade crafts, setbacks are inevitable. Videos may not get views, products may not sell, and technical glitches may abound. The adult role here is to frame these experiences not as defeats, but as data—valuable insights that inform future attempts. When a child is taught to analyse what didn't work, to pivot, and to try again, they are developing the very resilience that distinguishes successful creators from discouraged dabblers.

This mindset extends beyond digital skills into broader life lessons. When children run a small online project—whether it's managing a community around shared interests, tracking their own publishing schedule, or coordinating orders and feedback—they develop time management, communication, and accountability. They learn how to prioritise tasks, meet deadlines, and adapt based on user feedback. These are not hypothetical learning outcomes—they are the daily realities of digital entrepreneurs, and they prepare children for both academic success and professional adaptability.

Schools and parents can support this development by creating spaces where entrepreneurial thinking is not only allowed but encouraged. In the classroom, this might mean project-based learning that integrates technology and real-world problem-solving. Rather than assigning abstract reports, educators might challenge students to develop digital solutions to school-wide issues—such as improving communication, enhancing environmental awareness, or building peer mentoring platforms. These projects can be interdisciplinary, combining language, computing, design, and ethical reasoning. When students see that their ideas can have a tangible impact, they develop a sense of agency that transcends the classroom.

At home, parents can encourage entrepreneurial thinking by showing interest in their children's digital passions and supporting their exploratory projects. A child interested in gaming might be invited to design their own game mechanics or character scripts. A young writer might be encouraged to compile their stories into an e-book and learn about self-publishing. Parents do not need to be experts in the tools themselves. What matters more is their willingness to ask questions, provide encouragement, and help children frame their efforts within broader contexts of value and impact.

Importantly, digital entrepreneurship also offers a platform for children to explore social responsibility. Many young entrepreneurs use their projects to raise awareness about causes they care about or to contribute to their communities. A child might sell eco-themed stickers to support environmental charities or create content about mental health awareness for peers. These ventures teach children that entrepreneurship is not solely about profit—it can also be a vehicle for advocacy, inclusion, and positive change. When children understand that they can use digital tools to serve others as well as themselves, they begin to see their role in the digital world as one of contribution, not just consumption.

However, with opportunity comes responsibility. As children step into online entrepreneurship, they must also be taught about digital ethics, privacy, and intellectual property. They need to understand the importance of consent, attribution, and transparency. Just as we teach traditional ethics in business education, so too must we instil a sense of digital integrity. This includes respecting the work of others, protecting their own ideas, and communicating honestly with their audience or users. These conversations are not peripheral—they are central to ensuring that the digital creators of tomorrow are not only innovative but principled.

Digital entrepreneurship also presents an opportunity to address equity. While the tools for creation are more accessible than ever, disparities in access to devices, stable internet, and mentoring still persist. Schools and communities must actively work to provide all children with the resources needed to explore and develop their entrepreneurial ideas. Programmes that offer shared devices, workshops, mentorship, and exposure to real-world role models can help level the playing field. Without such support, the most creative and driven children may still find themselves locked out of the opportunities that digital entrepreneurship affords.

What we ultimately want is to raise a generation of children who do not simply wait to be entertained, instructed, or employed—but who understand their capacity to shape the digital world with intelligence, creativity, and heart. Encouraging digital entrepreneurship does not mean pressuring children to build a business or chase profit. It means cultivating a mindset of initiative and ownership. It means showing them that their ideas matter and that they have the tools to bring those ideas to life. It means teaching them that success is not about overnight fame, but about persistence, impact, and growth.

When children learn to build rather than merely consume, they begin to see themselves not as passengers in the digital age, but as pilots. They discover that they have a voice, a skillset, and a platform—and that, with the right guidance and support, they can use these to create something meaningful. In doing so, they are not just learning about entrepreneurship—they are learning about who they are and what they are capable of achieving. That, ultimately, is the promise of digital entrepreneurship: not simply the creation of products, but the cultivation of purpose, curiosity, and agency in a connected world.

Using Technology for Family Bonding

Technology is often viewed as a wedge in family life—a source of isolation, distraction, and disconnection. The archetypal image of each family member staring at their own screen, lost in separate digital worlds, feeds the narrative that technology is inherently corrosive to relationships. Yet this perspective is, at best, one-sided. While it is true that unmoderated screen use can create emotional and physical distance within households, it is equally true that technology, when used mindfully and collaboratively, can become a powerful tool for bringing families closer together. It is not the presence of screens that determines their impact on family life, but the nature of the interactions they facilitate.

The concept of turning screen time into shared time is not about simply occupying the same room while using separate devices. It is about intentional engagement—using technology as a conduit for conversation, cooperation, and mutual discovery. When parents and children experience media together, they move from passive consumption to active co-creation of meaning. Watching a documentary side by side, playing a cooperative game, or co-editing a digital photo album all represent moments where technology ceases to be isolating and instead becomes relational. These shared experiences can spark dialogue, generate laughter, and even cultivate empathy, particularly when adults model curiosity and emotional responsiveness.

One of the most accessible ways to use technology for family bonding is through co-viewing. This involves not just watching television or online content together, but engaging with it critically and emotionally. Parents might choose a film that raises moral questions, introduces new cultures, or addresses issues relevant to their child's life. Rather than simply watching and moving on, they can initiate discussions that deepen understanding and invite multiple perspectives. Asking questions such as "What do you think that character was feeling?" or "Would you have made the same choice?" transforms entertainment into a platform for ethical thinking and shared reflection. These conversations help children feel heard and understood, while also exposing them to the values and reasoning styles of their parents.

Gaming, too, has emerged as a surprisingly rich context for intergenerational connection. While often maligned for its addictive potential, gaming can also offer opportunities for collaboration, problem-solving, and even storytelling. Cooperative games that require players to work together toward a common goal—such as "Minecraft," "Overcooked," or puzzle-based adventures—foster communication and strategy. When parents join in, not as overseers but as teammates, they gain insight into their child's interests and thinking patterns. For the child, having a parent take their digital world seriously is a form of validation that strengthens trust and emotional closeness. Even competitive games, when framed with a spirit of fun and sportsmanship, can become sites of healthy rivalry and humour.

Technology also opens doors for families to create together. Digital tools for photo editing, video production, music composition, and graphic design are increasingly accessible and user-friendly. A family might start a private YouTube channel to document holidays and milestones, create a digital scrapbook of shared memories, or collaborate on a music mix that reflects their tastes and history. These projects are not just fun—they are acts of storytelling, memory-making, and identity formation. They provide children with the sense that their experiences matter and that their voice has a place in the family narrative.

Educational platforms offer another path to shared screen time. Parents can join their children in exploring topics of mutual interest, whether it be learning a new language through Duolingo, exploring science concepts via interactive simulations, or visiting virtual museum exhibits together. These shared intellectual pursuits create a dynamic where parents and children are co-learners. This flattens the traditional authority gradient and encourages children to see learning as a lifelong, joyful endeavour rather than a school-bound task. It also demonstrates that technology can be a source of wonder, not just entertainment.

Communication technologies can be particularly valuable for families separated by distance. Video calls with grandparents, shared online calendars, family group chats, and collaborative playlists all allow dispersed family members to remain present in one another's lives. These digital touchpoints, though small, weave continuity and closeness across geographical boundaries. When children see these tools used to nurture real relationships, they learn that technology can be an expression of love, not merely a device for distraction.

However, using technology to foster connection does not happen automatically. It requires intentionality, boundaries, and adaptability. Adults must be willing to engage on their child's terms, within the digital spaces that the child finds meaningful. This means resisting the impulse to dismiss a game, video, or app simply because it seems trivial. It also means being attuned to the emotional tone of shared experiences. If screen time together becomes laced with judgement, correction, or frustration, its bonding potential is lost. The aim is not to monitor or critique but to participate, to observe, and to ask open-ended questions that invite the child to articulate their thoughts and feelings.

Equally important is the ability to recognise when screens are detracting from family life rather than enhancing it. Not all digital interaction is bonding, and there are times when a screen-free meal, walk, or board game offers a richer form of connection. The goal is not to elevate technology above other forms of family engagement, but to integrate it meaningfully and selectively. Families should reflect on how they use technology together and ask whether their current habits support their relational goals. If not, small adjustments—such as scheduling a weekly family game night, co-watching a series with planned discussion, or collaborating on a digital project—can redirect the course.

Shared screen time also provides a natural context for modelling digital citizenship. As children observe their parents' online behaviour, they learn how to engage respectfully, evaluate content critically, and balance online and offline life. When a parent pauses a film to discuss a stereotype, declines to post an unflattering photo of someone without consent, or admits to needing a break from social media, they are teaching by example. These small acts communicate volumes about how to use technology ethically and reflectively. They also reinforce that digital engagement is not a solitary pursuit but a social act with implications for self and others.

Technology can also become a tool for rituals and celebration. Families might use a shared calendar app to plan weekly meals, record voice notes for birthdays, or host virtual talent shows with extended relatives. These traditions, while mediated by screens, are rich with emotional significance. They create a sense of continuity and collective identity. They show that bonding is not about physical proximity alone—it is about shared attention, mutual investment, and the willingness to be present with one another, even through a screen.

It is also worth noting that using technology for family bonding requires a shift in how we talk about screens in the household. If the dominant narrative is one of limitation and guilt—"You've had enough screen time," "You're always on that thing"—children may come to view their digital world as a point of tension rather than potential. By reframing the conversation to focus on content, context, and connection, adults can foster a more nuanced and constructive dialogue. Asking, "What have you learned today?" or "What can we explore together?" signals curiosity rather than control, and opens the door to richer interaction.

As technology continues to evolve, so too will the ways in which families engage with it. Augmented reality, virtual experiences, and interactive storytelling will offer new formats for collaboration and shared exploration. The principles, however, remain constant: intentionality, empathy, presence, and the willingness to see screens not as obstacles but as opportunities. Technology does not have to pull families apart. With thoughtful use, it can draw them closer—helping them learn together, laugh together, and grow together in ways that enrich their relationships and deepen their sense of belonging.

When families reclaim screen time as shared time, they change the narrative. They move from passive coexistence to active connection. They demonstrate that the digital world, far from being a threat to intimacy, can be a canvas upon which meaningful relationships are written, frame by frame, click by click, moment by moment.

The Future of Technology and Parenting

As the digital landscape continues to transform at an astonishing pace, the task of parenting grows more complex. We are no longer preparing children for a world merely influenced by technology—

we are preparing them for one defined by it. Artificial intelligence, automation, immersive virtual environments, and adaptive digital platforms are not distant concepts on the horizon; they are already embedded in daily life. Whether it is a child asking questions to a virtual assistant, completing assignments in AI-enhanced educational apps, or observing their parents use machine learning-based tools at work, the influence of these technologies is pervasive. The critical challenge for parents today is not simply managing their children's screen time, but equipping them with the skills, ethics, and mindset required to thrive in a future shaped by intelligent systems and constant digital evolution.

This task begins with a fundamental shift in perspective. Parents must move beyond the dichotomy of 'tech as a threat' versus 'tech as a tool' and instead see it as an ecosystem—a living, shifting environment in which children will need to operate with discernment, creativity, and resilience. The tools themselves will change. What matters most is the child's ability to adapt, question, and contribute meaningfully within that environment. This means fostering digital literacy that extends far beyond how to navigate devices. It means teaching children to understand how technologies work, what values they embed, and how they influence behaviours, relationships, and opportunities.

Artificial intelligence is a particularly important focal point. Increasingly, AI is not only used to deliver content but to shape it—through personalised learning platforms, recommendation algorithms, automated feedback systems, and intelligent tutors. These systems can enhance learning efficiency and engagement, but they also raise critical questions about agency, bias, and data privacy. A child using an AI-based writing assistant might learn to refine their grammar and style, but they might also become overly reliant on suggestions that limit their original expression. A family using AI-curated content might benefit from convenience but remain unaware of how their preferences are being tracked, analysed, and monetised.

Helping children engage critically with AI begins with transparency. Parents can demystify these tools by discussing how they operate, where their data goes, and what their limitations are. Rather than banning or uncritically embracing AI, they can encourage reflection: "What do you think the app is trying to guess about you?" or "Why might it be showing you that result?" These questions cultivate a mindset of inquiry and self-awareness. They help children see themselves not just as users of AI but as participants in a feedback loop that can be observed, questioned, and influenced.

Automation, too, will play a major role in shaping children's futures—particularly in the workforce. Jobs that once required human input are now being handled by algorithms, robots, or remote-controlled systems. At the same time, new roles are emerging that require hybrid skills: the ability to work with intelligent machines, interpret complex data, and apply creative and emotional intelligence in tandem with technical know-how. Preparing children for this reality does not mean training them for specific careers that may no longer exist in two decades. Rather, it means nurturing a portfolio of cognitive and emotional skills that are transferrable, resilient, and adaptable.

Problem-solving, collaboration, ethical reasoning, and the capacity to learn independently are at the heart of future-readiness. Technology can support the development of these skills, but it cannot replace them. Parents can create environments where children are encouraged to ask big questions, experiment with solutions, and take intellectual risks. A child who builds a game using a coding platform, runs a simulation to explore climate change, or co-creates a digital project with peers is not just gaining technical proficiency—they are practising how to think, iterate, and collaborate in ways that mirror real-world demands.

Equally important is emotional resilience. The digital world can be disorienting and overwhelming, especially for young people who are bombarded with information, comparisons, and shifting social norms. As intelligent systems become more persuasive—anticipating needs, nudging behaviour, and shaping attention—children will need a strong internal compass. Parents can help by anchoring children's sense of self in values rather than metrics. Instead of praising popularity or perfection, they can affirm curiosity, kindness, and effort. Instead of focusing on achievement within a narrow frame, they can broaden the definition of success to include exploration, growth, and meaningful contribution.

The ethics of digital engagement will be an increasingly important area of parental guidance. As children begin to interact with AI agents, participate in virtual environments, or use platforms that simulate human conversation, they will encounter moral dilemmas that previous generations never faced. Is it acceptable to manipulate an algorithm to get a better score? Should a child believe everything a chatbot tells them? What does it mean to create a digital version of oneself, and who controls it? These are not abstract philosophical questions—they are becoming daily realities. Parents must be willing to explore them openly, modelling humility, critical thinking, and ethical reflection.

Emerging technologies such as augmented and virtual reality also present both exciting opportunities and new considerations. These tools can make learning more immersive and interaction more vivid, but they also blur the line between simulation and experience. A child who spends significant time in a virtual world may struggle to integrate those experiences with their offline identity. Helping children develop a healthy sense of digital presence—one that is grounded, conscious, and socially aware—will be essential. Parents can do this by fostering dialogue around how digital experiences make children feel, what they learn from them, and how they impact their relationships.

Equipping children for the future also involves modelling adaptability. When parents demonstrate curiosity about new technologies, ask for help when they are unsure, and reflect on their own digital habits, they signal that learning is lifelong and that flexibility is a strength. This counters the common narrative of technological generational divide and builds a culture of shared exploration. A parent who says, "I've never used this app before—want to figure it out together?" offers not only a learning opportunity but a relational one. It shifts the dynamic from control to collaboration and invites children to take pride in their knowledge while remaining open to others' insights.

Practical steps also matter. Families can create routines that balance digital engagement with offline experiences, ensuring that technology enhances rather than eclipses core developmental needs. They can use digital tools for co-learning, family storytelling, or creative collaboration, reinforcing that screens are not merely consumption devices but canvases for shared meaning. They can also stay informed about trends in educational technology, data policy, and youth culture, so they are better equipped to support children's navigation of complex environments.

Looking ahead, it is likely that children will not only use emerging technologies but shape them. Many will become designers, programmers, policymakers, and thought leaders whose decisions influence how technology is deployed and whom it serves. Cultivating a sense of responsibility alongside competence is therefore crucial. Children should be encouraged to think not only about what technology can do but what it should do—and for whom. They should be taught to ask who is included in digital narratives and who is left out, whose values are embedded in design choices, and how digital tools can be used to solve real problems rather than reinforce inequalities.

Parents are uniquely positioned to guide this development, not because they know more about technology, but because they know more about their children. They understand their personalities, their fears, their motivations, and their dreams. This insight is invaluable when helping a child find their footing in a world where identities, economies, and relationships are increasingly mediated by digital systems. By combining emotional attunement with a willingness to engage with technological change, parents can offer children something no device can replicate: a sense of meaning, belonging, and direction.

The future of technology and parenting is not about control—it is about cultivation. It is about preparing children to meet complexity with clarity, to engage innovation with integrity, and to step into the unknown not with fear, but with confidence. As intelligent machines grow more capable, it is human intelligence—ethical, emotional, and relational—that will become more essential than ever. In this context, the role of the parent is not to resist the future, but to raise children who are ready to shape it wisely.

Chapter 7
Setting Digital Boundaries Without Power Struggles

For many households today, screens have become the flashpoint in an ongoing tug-of-war between generations. Managing when, how long, and for what purpose children engage with digital devices often turns into a daily negotiation—one that leaves parents feeling like reluctant referees and children cast as persistent challengers. It's remarkable, really, how a simple piece of glass and circuitry can become so emotionally loaded. Screens are no longer neutral tools; they're vessels of expectation, sites of anxiety, and symbols of deeper cultural friction. And yet—this tension needn't be inevitable. When digital boundaries are shaped with empathy, a clear sense of purpose, and a spirit of collaboration, they can foster mutual respect rather than resentment. This chapter explores how families might move away from policing screen time toward something more sustainable: guiding it with resolve and responsiveness, without losing the thread of connection in the process.

At the root of many digital conflicts lies a straightforward dynamic: children often resist rules that feel arbitrary, especially those imposed without explanation or inclusion. When a parent abruptly bans screens after 8 p.m. to encourage better sleep or family bonding, the intention may be noble—but if the rule arrives without context, it's likely to be met with confusion or defiance. To the child, it can feel punitive, as though a favourite pastime is being punished rather than redirected. Predictably, this can lead to a cat-and-mouse game: covert usage, heightened emotional reactions, and ultimately, a growing disconnect between parent and child. Harsh restrictions might buy temporary obedience, but they rarely instil the kind of internal discipline that lasts.

Shifting from control to connection requires a change in tone, not just in tactics. Children—particularly those approaching adolescence—are more likely to engage with boundaries that feel just and participatory. This doesn't mean putting every house rule to a vote or relinquishing authority; rather, it means treating children as active participants in shaping the norms that affect their daily lives. When parents invite them into the conversation around digital use, it creates a space for dialogue—and, more importantly, for buy-in.

One particularly effective approach is to draft a family digital agreement—not as a list of prohibitions delivered from on high, but as a co-authored document that reflects shared values and rhythms. It should lay out expectations not only for children but for adults too, reinforcing that everyone in the household is subject to the same principles of respect, balance, and presence. A younger child might propose no screens at dinner, while an older sibling may request uninterrupted online time after finishing homework. These negotiations, when carried out in good faith, are less about compromise and more about collective ownership.

For such agreements to work, they must be rooted in clarity and upheld consistently. Rules should be straightforward enough to be remembered, and consequences should follow logically from the behaviour in question. If a child uses a device during a screen-free hour, the response might be a gentle reminder or a calm conversation—not a dramatic confiscation. When enforcement is predictable and explanations are transparent, children are far more inclined to respect the structure.

Physical and temporal boundaries serve to anchor these agreements in everyday life. Declaring certain spaces—bedrooms, the dining table, or bathrooms—as screen-free zones reclaims those areas for rest, connection, or solitude. Similarly, establishing screen-free windows of time—perhaps the first half-hour after school or the wind-down before bedtime—helps preserve mental clarity and emotional presence. These boundaries aren't about deprivation. They're about carving out room for rhythms that nurture, rather than distract.

Yet all of this hinges on a simple truth: what parents model carries more weight than what they say. Children are always watching. If a parent insists on device-free meals but spends dinner glancing at text messages, the double standard quickly erodes credibility. On the other hand, when a parent puts the phone down mid-scroll to make eye contact, or chooses not to answer a work email during family time, those actions speak volumes. Modelling mindful technology use—however imperfectly—is perhaps the most powerful form of teaching available.

That said, no one expects parents to be digital monks. Authenticity, more than perfection, is what matters. Admitting your own struggles with screens—the urge to check social media first thing in the morning, or the temptation to reply to emails late at night—makes you human, not hypocritical. It also opens the door to mutual understanding. A parent might say, "I've noticed I'm on my phone too much in the evenings. I'm going to start charging it in the hallway—want to try it with me?" In that moment, you're not just setting a rule; you're inviting a shared experiment in better habits.

Of course, not every boundary will be met with enthusiasm. Screens serve many functions in children's lives: entertainment, connection, identity, even sanctuary. When a parent enforces limits, it can trigger resistance—sometimes loudly so. But friction isn't always a sign that something's wrong. Often, it means the limit touches something important. The goal here is not to avoid conflict altogether, but to handle it with steadiness and compassion.

Meeting resistance with empathy can defuse defensiveness. Acknowledging the moment—"I get that it's frustrating to stop mid-game"—goes a long way toward preserving trust. Offering gentle transitions—"You've got ten more minutes before we switch off"—gives children time to adjust. And when emotions flare, as they will, a parent's calm response provides an anchor. Shouting back or doubling down on punishment often escalates the situation; consistency, patience, and a measured tone tend to do far more over time.

Importantly, boundaries should not be carved in stone. Children grow. Technologies evolve. Family needs shift. What works now may not hold next month—or even next week. Perhaps a period of increased screen time during illness or a school holiday is perfectly reasonable. Or perhaps a teenager's growing independence calls for a recalibration of rules. The point is not rigidity, but responsiveness. Families that treat digital agreements as living documents—subject to review, refinement, and feedback—are better equipped to maintain a sense of shared direction.

That flexibility should include space for children's voices. They won't always express concerns gracefully, but even poorly timed complaints can contain useful insight. Checking in occasionally—"Are the screen rules still working for you?" or "Is there anything that feels unfair?"—sends a clear message: your input matters. Not every suggestion needs to be implemented, but the invitation itself affirms respect and openness.

Ultimately, setting digital boundaries is not a logistical exercise. It's a relational one. When those boundaries emerge from shared understanding, are held with empathy, and evolve with time, they create more than structure—they create a culture. Children raised in such an environment don't just learn what's expected of them; they begin to understand why the expectations exist. They internalise the idea that limits are not there to restrict them, but to support their flourishing.

In a world where screens beckon from every corner—offering stimulation, distraction, and escape—the real task isn't to eliminate them. It's to integrate them wisely, so that technology becomes part of a life rooted in purpose, connection, and care. This chapter offers a path toward that integration, one not paved with ultimatums or endless negotiation, but with clarity, intention, and a deep respect for the developmental journey of both child and parent.

Why Harsh Restrictions Backfire

When it comes to managing screen time, many parents are motivated by a deep desire to protect their children—from addictive behaviours, from inappropriate content, from losing themselves in a world of digital distraction. These concerns are well-founded, and they reflect a genuine commitment to nurturing healthy development in an age where screens are omnipresent. Yet too often, this well-meaning impulse leads to approaches that inadvertently make the problem worse. Harsh restrictions—rigid limits, sudden bans, or zero-tolerance policies—may offer temporary relief or a fleeting sense of control, but over time, they can damage trust, fuel resentment, and drive unhealthy patterns of behaviour underground.

Understanding why harsh restrictions backfire requires us to look not just at what rules are being enforced, but how and why they are being set in the first place. Children, particularly as they enter middle childhood and adolescence, are hardwired to seek autonomy. Their brains are developing rapidly, especially in areas related to identity, independence, and emotional regulation. When adults impose limits without dialogue, explanation, or flexibility, they often provoke resistance—not because the limits are unreasonable, but because the child experiences them as a threat to their growing sense of agency.

The dynamic here is not unlike a power struggle over bedtimes or food preferences. A seven-year-old who feels controlled may respond with tantrums; a teenager may withdraw, rebel, or find ways to subvert the rules altogether. What distinguishes screen-related power struggles, however, is that digital technology holds a unique emotional and cognitive appeal. It offers instant gratification, social belonging, creative expression, and escapism. When access to these experiences is suddenly cut off or heavily policed, the deprivation is not only logistical but deeply psychological. Children may not have the vocabulary to articulate this, but they feel it—intensely.

A common example is the overnight device ban. A parent, alarmed by their child's late-night gaming or texting habits, decides that all screens must be handed in by 7pm. There is no prior conversation, no gradual adjustment, no accommodation for homework or downtime. The child, blindsided and frustrated, perceives the new rule as arbitrary and unfair. They may argue, plead, or lash out. If the rule is enforced with threats or punishments, the conflict escalates. If the child acquiesces outwardly but continues to use devices in secret, the parent feels undermined. Trust erodes, and what was intended as a protective measure becomes a source of tension, secrecy, and emotional distance.

Such patterns are not inevitable. They arise when screen rules are implemented reactively, without attention to context, communication, or relational dynamics. Children resist not because they are inherently defiant, but because they are trying—however clumsily—to assert control over their environment. When adults respond by doubling down—by increasing the rigidity of rules or intensifying punishments—they often trigger more of the very behaviour they are trying to prevent. The result is a cycle of conflict and concealment that is emotionally exhausting for both parties.

Avoiding this cycle requires a fundamental rethinking of how digital boundaries are approached. First and foremost, rules must be anchored in dialogue. Children are far more likely to accept limits when they understand the rationale behind them and when they feel that their needs and perspectives have been considered. This does not mean giving in to every demand or negotiating endlessly. It means creating a culture of mutual respect, where rules are explained in developmental terms—"We're setting a screen curfew because your brain needs rest to function well," or "We're limiting social media because constant notifications can affect your concentration and mood."

These kinds of explanations matter. They shift the focus from control to care. They help children see that rules are not punitive but protective, designed to support their well-being rather than diminish their freedom. When children feel that adults are working with them rather than against them, they are more likely to cooperate—even if they don't always agree.

Another important strategy is predictability. Harsh restrictions often feel arbitrary because they are introduced without warning, often in response to parental frustration. A child who has been allowed unlimited gaming for months suddenly finds their device taken away for a week after a poor grade or a forgotten chore. From the child's perspective, this feels less like a consequence and more like a punishment rooted in emotion. Over time, such inconsistencies undermine a child's trust and can provoke ongoing defiance.

By contrast, when expectations are clearly established and consistently reinforced, children know where they stand. If a child knows that screen time ends at 8pm every night, or that privileges are earned by meeting responsibilities, they are less likely to argue—and more likely to take ownership of their choices. This predictability fosters emotional safety. It also teaches children about boundaries in a way that prepares them for future self-regulation.

Modelling is also key. Children are exquisitely attuned to hypocrisy. A parent who demands that phones be put away at the dinner table but checks their own messages under the napkin sends a confusing message. When adults preach balance but exhibit compulsive tech behaviours themselves, their credibility erodes. Conversely, when parents model healthy digital habits—pausing notifications during family time, resisting the urge to multitask, taking digital detoxes—they send a powerful, implicit message: screens are tools, not masters.

Perhaps most critically, families must create alternatives. Harsh restrictions often fail because they focus solely on what children can't do, rather than what they can. Taking away a device without offering meaningful, age-appropriate alternatives leaves a vacuum. Children are left bored, disconnected, or excluded, which increases the allure of the prohibited activity. If a child loses gaming time but gains no other outlet for fun, autonomy, or social connection, their resentment grows. Offering alternatives doesn't mean bribing or distracting. It means enriching the offline environment so that screens become one option among many—not the only source of stimulation or pleasure.

This might include encouraging outdoor play, creative projects, shared hobbies, or downtime that isn't always hyper-productive. It also means acknowledging that digital experiences are not inherently inferior. A child who plays an online game with friends is engaging socially and cognitively. A teenager editing videos for fun may be developing real creative and technical skills. The goal is not to demonise technology, but to help children find balance and develop a thoughtful relationship with it.

Finally, parents should recognise that screen-related behaviour often signals deeper needs. A child who disappears into YouTube for hours after school may be coping with anxiety, boredom, or social rejection. A teenager who insists on texting late into the night may be navigating fragile friendships or seeking emotional support. When parents respond only with restriction, they risk missing the underlying message. Instead of asking, "How do I stop this behaviour?" it may be more fruitful to ask, "What is this behaviour trying to tell me?" This mindset shift opens space for empathy, connection, and problem-solving.

To be clear, boundaries are essential. Children need structure to thrive, and they benefit from clear, consistent expectations about screen use. But harsh, reactive restrictions are rarely effective in isolation. They may win the battle, but they lose the war—eroding trust, fuelling secrecy, and turning screens into a source of rebellion rather than responsibility.

The alternative is harder, but far more sustainable. It involves listening, explaining, collaborating, and modelling. It requires patience, flexibility, and a willingness to learn alongside one's child. But the reward is a home environment where digital boundaries support not only behavioural management but emotional growth, self-regulation, and mutual respect. In a world where screens are likely to play a lifelong role in our children's personal and professional lives, this approach is not just preferable—it is essential.

Creating a Family Digital Agreement

In many households, conversations around technology often erupt into conflict, frustration, or silence. Parents worry about excessive screen time, content exposure, and social media pressures. Children, in turn, may perceive rules as arbitrary, unfair, or rooted in adult misunderstandings of their digital world. As the divide between generations' digital fluency widens, so too does the gap in communication. Yet amid these tensions lies a powerful, underused strategy that can realign families around shared values and expectations: the creation of a family digital agreement. Done thoughtfully, this collaborative approach fosters clarity, accountability, and mutual respect—helping to transform technology from a source of friction into a point of connection.

A family digital agreement is not a list of dos and don'ts hastily written on a fridge note after an argument. Nor is it a static document meant to police behaviour through fear of punishment. At its best, a digital agreement is a living, evolving expression of a family's intentions—how its members want to use technology in ways that protect wellbeing, support learning, and nurture relationships. It is built through dialogue, reflection, and compromise, with every voice in the family—adults and children alike—given space to contribute.

The act of co-creating such an agreement serves multiple functions. First, it demystifies rules by making the rationale behind them explicit. Rather than simply being told, "No screens after 8pm," a child understands that screen-free evenings allow for better sleep and uninterrupted family time. This contextualisation transforms rules from rigid limitations into shared commitments grounded in logic and care. When children know *why* a boundary exists, they are more likely to respect it—and more willing to remind others of its importance.

Second, a collaborative agreement helps surface differing assumptions and priorities. A parent might assume that gaming is purely recreational, while their child sees it as a space for social bonding and creative expression. Talking through these perspectives allows each party to see the other more clearly and moves the conversation from opposition to understanding. It also helps parents realise that not all screen use is equal. Scrolling aimlessly through social media differs substantially from video-calling a friend, attending an online class, or building a digital art portfolio.

The process of crafting a digital agreement begins with observation and conversation. Families benefit from first spending a few days noticing their current tech habits without judgement. How much time is spent on devices? When is screen use most helpful or most disruptive? What emotions or behaviours tend to follow prolonged screen time? These observations provide a baseline for discussing what is working and what might need adjustment. Rather than declaring immediate change, families can begin from a place of shared curiosity: "What do we notice about how we're using technology? What might we want to change or keep?"

From there, the agreement can take shape as a set of core principles—flexible, age-appropriate, and adapted to the specific rhythms of the household. Some families may prioritise device-free meals; others may focus on setting boundaries around homework, bedtime, or weekends. The important thing is that the rules feel relevant and realistic. If an agreement feels too strict or abstract, it will not last. If it is too vague, it will be ignored. Striking the right balance requires honest input from everyone, including the youngest members of the family.

Consider the example of a twelve-year-old who proposes that Friday evenings be set aside for a family film night—with everyone agreeing to put phones away except for emergencies. This rule, initiated by a child, becomes more meaningful because it reflects their desire for connection and shared experience. At the same time, the rule applies to all family members equally, which reinforces fairness. Such shared accountability fosters a sense of unity: the digital agreement is not something done *to* the children but *with* them and *for* everyone.

What makes the agreement effective over time is its adaptability. Children grow, technologies evolve, and family needs change. An agreement made with a ten-year-old will not suffice when that child becomes a teenager navigating social media or managing online coursework. Regular check-ins—perhaps once a term or every six months—allow families to revisit their digital norms and adjust as needed. These sessions do not need to be formal; they might involve a casual weekend conversation, a shared Google Doc with suggestions, or even a walk-and-talk that invites reflection. The goal is not to achieve perfect adherence but to cultivate awareness and responsiveness.

These revisions also allow families to reflect on what's going well. Too often, digital agreements are treated solely as disciplinary measures. But they can also be a place to celebrate growth: a child who is managing their screen time independently, a parent who has modelled putting work emails aside on weekends, a sibling who reminds others of the agreed screen-free hour after dinner. Acknowledging these small successes reinforces the agreement's positive spirit and encourages continued effort.

Another powerful feature of a family digital agreement is its potential to cultivate empathy. When children are invited to help create rules that apply to the whole family, they begin to see technology from multiple vantage points. A child may learn that their younger sibling's screen time is more limited not as punishment, but because younger children are more vulnerable to over-stimulation. A parent may realise that their teen's resistance to screen curfews is driven not by defiance, but by a fear of missing out on late-night group chats. These insights can reduce friction and support more nuanced compromises.

Digital agreements can also serve as an entry point into broader ethical and safety conversations. As children mature and engage with more complex digital environments, the agreement can include discussions about online privacy, respectful communication, cyberbullying, and media literacy. For instance, families may agree not to share photos of each other online without consent, or to talk openly about any distressing content encountered. These rules do more than manage screen time; they establish a family culture of integrity, responsibility, and mutual protection in the digital world.

Importantly, the agreement must include consequences—but these, too, should be co-developed and transparent. Rather than reactive punishments, consequences can be framed as logical outcomes that support reflection and repair. If a rule is broken—say, devices are used during screen-free hours—the family might discuss why it happened, what could be done differently next time, and whether any adjustments are needed. This process avoids shame and encourages children to take responsibility without fear.

Incorporating humour, rituals, or visual aids can also make agreements more engaging. Younger children may enjoy drawing pictures of screen-free zones or helping design a poster of their favourite offline activities. Older children might prefer a shared digital calendar that includes agreed-upon screen breaks, or a family chat where tech-free plans are proposed and celebrated. These playful elements remind everyone that digital agreements are not about restriction, but about intentional living—and that screen time, when managed thoughtfully, can coexist with deep connection, creativity, and wellbeing.

Ultimately, a family digital agreement is not a quick fix or a disciplinary tool. It is a living practice—an ongoing conversation that reflects a family's values, priorities, and evolving realities. It requires patience, compromise, and above all, a willingness to listen. But its rewards are profound. Families who approach screen use collaboratively tend to experience less conflict, deeper understanding, and more meaningful engagement both online and offline.

In a culture often polarised between extremes—total control or total freedom—a family digital agreement offers a middle path. It acknowledges the importance of boundaries without denying the complexity of modern digital life. It respects children's voices while upholding parental guidance. And it models the very qualities—

empathy, accountability, flexibility—that children will need to thrive in a digital world. By creating such an agreement together, families are not just managing technology—they are building a foundation for communication, resilience, and mutual respect that will serve them long after the screen is switched off.

Screen-Free Zones and Time Blocks

In homes across the world, the subtle hum of screens has become the background noise of everyday life. Whether it's televisions flickering in the living room, phones buzzing at the dinner table, or tablets in bedrooms late into the night, technology now permeates nearly every corner of the domestic landscape. While these devices offer entertainment, education, and connectivity, their constant presence also fragments attention, shortens conversations, and diminishes opportunities for presence and reflection. It's no surprise, then, that families seeking greater balance often turn to the concept of screen-free zones and designated time blocks as practical strategies to reclaim attention, restore boundaries, and foster more meaningful interaction.

Creating screen-free zones and time blocks is not about demonising technology or enforcing rigid austerity. Rather, it's about designing intentional pauses in the digital flow—spaces and moments where human connection, physical activity, and emotional attunement take precedence. The aim is not to impose discipline for its own sake but to cultivate a home environment that supports wellbeing, cognitive development, and relational closeness. When implemented thoughtfully, these boundaries become less about restriction and more about ritual—predictable rhythms that support healthier, more harmonious living.

Establishing screen-free zones begins with identifying parts of the home that should prioritise interpersonal connection, rest, or focus. For many families, the dining table is the most intuitive place to start. Shared meals represent a rare opportunity in the day where members of the household can come together, exchange stories, and check in with one another. When devices are present—whether in use or simply within reach—they introduce a low-level distraction that can derail even the most well-intentioned conversation. By making the dinner table a device-free space, families create a buffer around a vital social ritual, allowing attention to be directed inward rather than outward.

Bedrooms are another critical area to consider. The presence of screens in sleeping areas has been shown to disrupt sleep hygiene in both children and adults. The blue light emitted from devices can interfere with the body's production of melatonin, making it harder to fall and stay asleep. Moreover, late-night scrolling, gaming, or texting fragments mental rest and may lead to emotional overstimulation just when the brain should be winding down. By keeping bedrooms screen-free—particularly in the hour before bedtime—families not only protect sleep quality but also reinforce the notion that rest and restoration are sacred aspects of life, deserving of their own undisturbed spaces.

Some families also choose to designate screen-free zones in areas meant for play, reading, or creative work. A corner of the living room transformed into a reading nook, an art station in the kitchen, or a play area in the garden can serve as powerful invitations for offline engagement. These spaces, adorned with books, puzzles, craft materials, or musical instruments, provide tactile alternatives to digital entertainment. While children will still gravitate toward screens out of habit or boredom, the existence of inviting, screen-free spaces helps rewire the impulse to reach for a device as the default.

Equally important to physical space are temporal boundaries—predictable, manageable time blocks where screens are deliberately set aside. These might include the first hour after school, when children can decompress through unstructured play or conversation; the final hour before bed, when screens are swapped for quieter activities; or designated family time on weekends. These intervals don't need to be lengthy or austere to be effective. What matters is their consistency and the quality of interaction they protect.

The structure of these time blocks can vary according to age, personality, and daily routines. A younger child might benefit from multiple short breaks, while a teenager may prefer longer stretches of device access punctuated by clearly defined downtime. Flexibility is key. Families who approach time blocks as adaptable guidelines rather than strict edicts are more likely to gain buy-in from children and teens. The goal is not perfection but participation—a shared agreement to step away from screens at moments that matter, in order to create space for other aspects of life to flourish.

One of the greatest benefits of establishing screen-free zones and time blocks is the way they reinforce self-regulation. Instead of relying on parental enforcement alone, children begin to internalise a rhythm where screens are one part of the day—not the organising principle of it. They learn to anticipate screen-free intervals, to plan their use more thoughtfully, and to develop a broader repertoire of ways to pass time and cope with boredom. These are critical life skills, particularly as they move into adolescence and eventually adulthood, where self-discipline around digital engagement becomes essential for emotional and mental health.

Families can enhance the effectiveness of these boundaries by involving children in their design and maintenance. A family discussion about where and when screens are most disruptive can yield surprisingly thoughtful input from children, who may already recognise that tech sometimes intrudes on family connection or rest. When a child suggests that phones stay off during movie nights so everyone can focus, or that homework time be screen-free unless required for study, their ownership of the idea makes it more likely to stick. These moments also validate the child's capacity for insight and self-governance, rather than casting them as passive recipients of adult control.

Of course, screen-free zones and time blocks will occasionally be tested. A family dinner may be interrupted by a work call, or a child may sneak a device into their room. These lapses are opportunities, not failures. Rather than reacting with punishment or shame, parents can respond with reflection: "What made it hard to follow the plan today? What can we do differently tomorrow?" This keeps the focus on growth, not guilt, and helps children see boundaries not as rigid rules, but as habits worth returning to—even after a misstep.

Technology can also be used to support these boundaries. Some families use device settings or parental controls to create automatic downtimes, where apps are locked during screen-free periods. Others establish charging stations in public areas, which not only keep bedrooms device-free but also encourage a more communal relationship with technology. Timers, visual schedules, or daily planners can help younger children conceptualise when screen time begins and ends. These tools should never replace conversation, but they can reinforce it—turning abstract ideas into tangible routines.

Importantly, screen-free zones and time blocks should not be framed as sacrifices. They are, in essence, acts of protection—safeguarding time for rest, connection, creativity, and attention in a world that constantly seeks to fragment them. When children experience these boundaries as positive, nourishing, and chosen, they are more likely to see them not as punishments, but as a form of care.

One family, for instance, introduced a "Tech Sabbath" on Sunday afternoons, where all devices were powered down from noon until dinner. Initially met with resistance, the time gradually became a cherished interval for board games, bike rides, storytelling, and impromptu baking sessions. What started as an experiment in discipline became a family tradition rooted in presence and pleasure. Such examples demonstrate that screen-free time is not an absence—it is a possibility, a space in which deeper forms of life can unfold.

In a culture that prizes productivity, availability, and constant stimulation, the act of stepping away from screens is quietly radical. It signals that our attention is finite, that our relationships deserve focus, and that silence, rest, and daydreaming are not indulgences, but necessities. For children, growing up in this ethos fosters resilience, creativity, and a clearer sense of self. For families, it reclaims the texture of daily life—the subtle, often fleeting moments where connection deepens and memories take shape.

Establishing screen-free zones and time blocks, then, is not a battle to be won but a rhythm to be cultivated. It is an invitation to redesign the contours of time and space with greater intention. And in doing so, families find that amidst the noise of the digital world, they can still carve out spaces of calm, of meaning, and of shared presence—spaces where everyone, regardless of age, can simply be together.

The Role of Parents as Digital Role Models

In the discourse surrounding children's screen use, much attention is paid to the rules—how much time is appropriate, what content should be allowed, and when devices should be put away. Yet often overlooked is the most powerful form of digital guidance a child receives: the behaviour they observe in their parents. In households where boundaries are clearly articulated but inconsistently practised, where children are told to "get off their devices" while adults compulsively check emails or scroll social media during meals, a silent contradiction takes root. It is not the verbal instruction that lingers, but the daily habits that children witness. In this way, parents serve not only as caregivers or enforcers of rules, but as living models of how technology is integrated into daily life—for better or worse.

The psychological basis for this influence is well-established. From early childhood, children learn through imitation. They observe not only what adults do but how they do it—what excites them, frustrates them, distracts them, and engages them. This observational learning is particularly potent in emotionally charged contexts, such as the use of devices during family interactions. A child who sees their parent routinely interrupting conversations to check notifications absorbs an implicit lesson: attention is negotiable, and presence is conditional. Similarly, when a parent models digital mindfulness—pausing to put their phone away before engaging, or intentionally stepping back from screens to prioritise eye contact and shared experience—the child begins to internalise these behaviours as part of what it means to communicate respectfully and live attentively.

In modern households, the visibility of technology is almost constant. Children see adults using devices to work, relax, stay informed, navigate logistics, and maintain social ties. These behaviours are not inherently problematic. What matters is the context, the tone, and the degree to which parents are conscious of their example. A parent who uses a tablet to read the news each morning and then discusses an article over breakfast is demonstrating that technology can be a tool for engagement and intellectual curiosity. A parent who retreats into their phone immediately after work and grunts one-word replies when spoken to is modelling withdrawal and disconnection. The difference lies not in the device, but in the relational message being conveyed.

This is particularly significant because many of the behaviours parents seek to limit in their children—excessive screen time, constant checking, difficulty unplugging—are ones they themselves struggle with. A parent might express concern about their teenager's attachment to social media while themselves reaching for their phone within minutes of waking. This inconsistency does not go unnoticed. Adolescents, in particular, are highly attuned to hypocrisy and deeply resistant to rules that feel arbitrary or unreciprocated. If adults demand restraint but display none, their authority erodes. If, on the other hand, they demonstrate effort, awareness, and self-regulation—even imperfectly—they gain credibility. Children are not looking for perfection, but for authenticity. They respond not to declarations, but to example.

The implications of parental modelling extend to how technology is used in moments of stress or boredom. If children observe adults reflexively turning to screens when overwhelmed, distracted, or disengaged, they learn to do the same. Digital devices then become coping mechanisms—tools for avoidance rather than engagement. This can be especially harmful in emotionally charged environments. A child who witnesses a parent scrolling during conflict, disengaging during play, or checking messages during moments of vulnerability may interpret these behaviours as emotional unavailability. Over time, this can shape their own attachment patterns and their expectations for interpersonal connection.

By contrast, when parents use technology in ways that reflect thoughtfulness and balance, they demonstrate that digital life can coexist with emotional presence. This might involve narrating one's choices—"I'm setting a timer so I don't get stuck scrolling," or "I'm turning off notifications so we can focus on our time together"—to make invisible habits visible. These small verbal cues demystify self-regulation and reinforce that boundaries are not punitive, but protective. They show that technology is something to be managed, not something that manages us.

There are also opportunities for modelling through joint engagement. Parents who co-watch programmes with their children, play games alongside them, or explore digital tools together create space for shared learning and relational intimacy. In these moments, screens become bridges rather than barriers. Children learn how to evaluate content critically, how to express preferences respectfully, and how to use digital media as a platform for collaboration. They also witness how adults react to content—what they find funny, upsetting, inspiring—which opens the door to richer conversations about values, representation, and emotional response.

Equally important is the way parents model digital boundaries in the context of work. In an age where professional life often bleeds into the home via emails, alerts, and virtual meetings, children may struggle to distinguish between presence and availability. A parent may be physically in the room but mentally occupied with work messages. If this becomes the norm, children internalise a version of adulthood where constant responsiveness is equated with productivity, and personal boundaries are routinely sacrificed. This is not only unsustainable—it sets the stage for burnout, anxiety, and disconnection across generations.

To counter this, parents can be intentional about marking transitions—physically closing the laptop, setting an out-of-office message, or announcing, "I'm done with work for the day." These gestures, though simple, communicate a powerful message: that family life deserves undivided attention, and that boundaries around digital engagement are not only possible but necessary. In doing so, parents give children permission to protect their own time and attention in future academic, professional, and relational contexts.

Modelling also plays a vital role in digital citizenship—the norms and ethics of online behaviour. Children who see adults engaging respectfully online, crediting sources, maintaining privacy, and thinking critically about content are far more likely to adopt these behaviours themselves. When parents talk openly about misinformation, advertising, digital footprints, and cyber etiquette, they cultivate not only knowledge but discernment. These lessons are best absorbed not through lectures, but through lived experience—watching a parent fact-check an article, pause before commenting, or report problematic content with explanation. Such practices teach children that digital life is not detached from moral life—it is embedded within it.

Of course, no parent can model perfectly. There will be moments of distraction, inconsistency, and overuse. The key is not to avoid these entirely, but to use them as opportunities for repair and reflection. When a parent catches themselves prioritising a device over a conversation and says, "I'm sorry—I wasn't listening. Let me put this away," they model accountability and attentiveness. This teaches children that awareness is an ongoing process and that even adults must course-correct. It also reinforces the idea that self-regulation is not a state of mastery but a set of habits cultivated over time.

Children do not need parents who are flawless. They need parents who are present, self-aware, and willing to engage with technology consciously. By modelling digital habits that reflect values such as respect, curiosity, responsibility, and balance, adults shape a home environment where screens serve rather than dominate. They equip children with a blueprint not only for how to use technology, but how to live well within a digital world.

In a culture where screens often compete with relationships, parents must become not just rule-setters but role models—living examples of what it looks like to integrate technology into life with purpose, ethics, and care. The lessons children draw from these examples will outlast any app or platform. They will carry them into their own homes, their friendships, and their futures. And perhaps most importantly, they will carry with them the memory of being seen, heard, and valued by adults who chose, again and again, to be fully present.

Handling Resistance and Pushback

No matter how thoughtfully digital rules are established, some degree of resistance is inevitable. Screens are not just tools in the lives of children and teenagers; they are portals to friendship, creativity, validation, and escape. Consequently, any limit imposed on their use, however reasonable it may appear to an adult, is likely to provoke some form of emotional or behavioural pushback. Parents might encounter everything from eye-rolls and passive defiance to outright refusal or negotiation tactics. Understanding how to respond to this resistance without falling into cycles of conflict is key to maintaining both the boundary and the relationship.

One of the first principles to acknowledge is that pushback is a developmentally appropriate response. Children test limits not only to assert independence but to make sense of the rules imposed upon them. A ten-year-old might resist turning off the television not because they reject the boundary itself, but because the transition feels abrupt or the activity particularly engaging. A teenager might argue about screen curfews not to be difficult, but because they are navigating the complex social landscape of group chats, online gaming, or digital expression. In each case, resistance is not merely about the screen—it is about autonomy, connection, and perceived fairness.

Addressing this pushback effectively begins with preparation, not reaction. When rules are clearly communicated ahead of time, grounded in shared agreements, and revisited regularly, children are less likely to feel blindsided or powerless. For example, if a family has already discussed that all devices are turned off by 8:30pm on school nights, then a reminder at 8:15pm can reinforce predictability. Framing transitions with empathy—such as acknowledging that it's hard to pause a game mid-level—shows understanding without undermining the rule. The child may still protest, but they do so within a context of respect rather than rupture.

Tone is everything in these moments. If a parent responds to resistance with frustration or sarcasm, the conversation quickly shifts from content to emotion. The issue is no longer the screen rule but the tone of enforcement, which the child may experience as dismissive or authoritarian. A calm, consistent, and firm approach defuses this escalation. It sends the message that boundaries are not negotiable in the moment but also not imposed in anger. This kind of neutral authority—quiet confidence without aggression—can be profoundly stabilising for children, who often feel overwhelmed by their own emotional reactions.

Parents can also benefit from recognising that not all resistance requires immediate confrontation. A sulking teenager, a slammed door, or a brief argument may simply be part of the child processing disappointment or frustration. Allowing space for emotional expression, without interpreting it as disrespect or disobedience, can reduce unnecessary power struggles. The goal is not to suppress all resistance, but to distinguish between emotional protest and behavioural defiance. A child who mutters in frustration but still follows through with the rule is showing compliance, albeit reluctantly. This is a win, even if it doesn't feel like one in the moment.

That said, when resistance takes the form of consistent non-compliance—ignoring limits, sneaking devices, or refusing to participate in screen-free periods—parents need strategies that reinforce boundaries without eroding trust. One effective approach is to link privileges to responsibility in a transparent, non-punitive manner. For example, a child who consistently turns off devices on time might earn greater flexibility on weekends. Conversely, a child who breaks the agreement may be asked to reflect on the impact of their actions and to help problem-solve a solution. This process shifts the focus from punishment to accountability. It treats the child not as an adversary, but as a partner in finding workable solutions.

Real-world examples can illustrate how this plays out. Consider a parent who discovers that their child has been secretly using a tablet late at night. Instead of reacting with anger or confiscating the device indefinitely, the parent might sit down the next morning and ask, "What made it hard to stick to our screen rule last night?" The conversation might reveal that the child was struggling to sleep and turned to the device out of habit. Together, they might brainstorm alternatives—like keeping books by the bed or using a sleep timer. The device may still be removed temporarily, but the emphasis is on learning and repair, not retribution.

It is also crucial to address the emotional undertones of digital conflict. Sometimes, what appears as defiance is rooted in deeper feelings—anxiety about missing out, shame over being different from peers, or fear of social exclusion. A teenager asked to put their phone away during dinner might resist because they're expecting a reply to a vulnerable message sent to a friend. In these moments, parents should strive to see the child's perspective, even if they maintain the rule. Validating the feeling—"I get that it's hard to be cut off when you're in the middle of something important"—does not mean giving in. It means acknowledging the complexity of the experience. This approach preserves connection even amid disagreement.

Some families find it helpful to build in flexibility through limited exceptions. A special event, a late-night family film, or a conversation with a friend in a different time zone might warrant a temporary adjustment. These exceptions, when framed clearly, do not weaken the boundary—they reinforce its integrity by showing that it is responsive and thoughtful. However, it is essential that such flexibility is not driven by pleading or manipulation, but by mutual agreement. Children should understand that flexibility is a privilege earned through trust, not a loophole to be exploited.

Parents should also consider their own emotional triggers in screen-related conflicts. Often, adult frustration stems from a sense of losing control, feeling disrespected, or worrying about long-term outcomes. Recognising these triggers can help parents respond rather than react. A parent who is aware that their irritation is rooted in concern for their child's future can choose to express that concern constructively—by explaining, for example, how late-night screen use impacts sleep, mood, and learning. When children understand the emotional truth behind a boundary, they are more likely to respect it—even if they don't immediately agree with it.

Maintaining a long-term perspective is equally important. Resistance, by nature, is transient. What feels like a daily battle over devices today may become a non-issue next year, as the child matures or as household norms become more established. The key is to approach these conflicts with patience, consistency, and an eye toward growth. Each conversation, however imperfect, is an opportunity to teach values, reinforce habits, and build mutual understanding. Over time, these lessons accumulate. Children begin to internalise the expectations, not because they fear consequences, but because they recognise the logic, care, and consistency behind them.

Ultimately, handling resistance is not about eliminating opposition but about cultivating cooperation. It requires a balance of empathy and authority, structure and flexibility, firmness and grace. When parents approach digital boundaries with clarity and compassion, they lay the foundation for respectful relationships and responsible tech use. The resistance may still come—but so will the growth, the dialogue, and the slow but steady development of digital habits rooted in trust rather than coercion. And in a world where

technology is only becoming more central to daily life, that foundation may prove to be one of the most important gifts a parent can give.

Chapter 8
Raising Digitally Mindful Kids

In today's landscape, awash with glowing screens and ever-present pings, connectivity has become so ingrained in daily life it scarcely raises an eyebrow. Notifications punctuate every hour, entertainment lies a mere swipe away, and the line separating online from offline grows fainter by the day. For children born into this digital saturation, technology isn't an add-on or novelty—it's the canvas upon which much of their experience unfolds. And while the digital realm undeniably expands access to information, imagination, and interaction, it also carries the quieter, more insidious weight of distraction, compulsive engagement, and emotional detachment. Amidst all this, the notion of digital mindfulness stands out—not as a trend or parenting tactic, but as a necessary competency. It points toward a way of relating to technology with purpose, with attention, and, crucially, with a sense of self intact.

Cultivating digital mindfulness in children doesn't call for a rejection of screens, nor does it require constructing some artificial analogue utopia. Instead, it's about nurturing an approach to technology that is conscious, curious, and grounded. Mindful tech use means asking not just how much time is spent online, but what that time is for—what it brings, what it takes. It's about tuning into our motives and our moods. A child might begin to notice they're watching videos because they're interested, or perhaps simply because they're bored. A teenager may learn to spot the emotional hangover that lingers after scrolling through social media—and know when to step away.

Perhaps one of the most powerful shifts parents can encourage is helping children recognise that devices are tools, not default companions. Many young people reach for screens almost automatically—not from a place of joy or intention, but to fill a gap: boredom, anxiety, discomfort. The work begins with awareness. A simple observation—"I've noticed you often grab your tablet after school. What's going on for you around that time?"—can open a door. It doesn't accuse, doesn't presume. It invites reflection, a gentle nudge towards considering what's actually happening beneath the habit.

And that's the point, really: to foster reflection without resorting to shame. Just as children learn to identify hunger or fatigue, they can develop an awareness of their internal state as it relates to screen use. They can start to notice when they're becoming overstimulated or scattered, and begin to learn strategies for recalibrating—maybe it's taking a walk, diving into a different activity, or simply taking a moment to breathe. With time and support, this awareness becomes something stronger: a capacity for self-regulation, for choosing rather than reacting.

Adults, of course, play a central role here—not just in setting limits, but in modelling what intentional tech use looks like. Children pay more attention to what we do than what we say (as any parent who's ever barked "no phones at the table" while checking work emails mid-dinner knows all too well). When parents narrate their own choices—"I'm going to step away from my phone for a bit; my brain feels a bit foggy"—they demonstrate that managing one's digital environment is an ongoing, human process. It's not a performance. It's practice.

But there's a trap to avoid, too. If digital mindfulness becomes synonymous with denial—if the only message is "less screen, less screen"—then it begins to feel punitive. That's not the aim. Instead, stepping away from devices should be framed as an invitation—to discover richer, more varied experiences. Offline play offers something digital activities cannot fully replicate. It supports everything from emotional regulation and motor skills to imagination and empathy. Whether it's building something with their hands, running wild in the garden, getting lost in a story, or simply pottering about, children need these textures of experience to develop in full.

The good news is, creating opportunities for meaningful offline engagement doesn't require elaborate planning. It might be as simple as keeping a well-stocked art corner within arm's reach, going on impromptu walks to nowhere in particular, or establishing the occasional story night by candlelight, screens tucked away. These aren't anti-tech gestures. They're complements—reminders that pleasure and connection can be found elsewhere, not just in pixels.

In recent years, the idea of a "digital detox" has gained traction—often accompanied by images of dramatic retreats and total disconnection. But real life, especially family life, tends to resist such extremes. A more sustainable path might involve micro-detoxes: gentle pauses woven into the everyday. Maybe it's a nightly quiet time without devices. Or a Sunday morning walk before any screens are turned on. Or simply encouraging children to check in with themselves after long online sessions: How does your body feel? What's your mood like? These small, consistent pauses do more than reduce screen time—they reintroduce a rhythm that invites stillness, even boredom, as something generative.

And boredom, let's not forget, is not the enemy. In fact, helping children get comfortable with not being constantly entertained may be one of the greatest gifts we can offer. Over time, they learn that rest is not a void to be filled, but a fertile space where attention can settle and creativity can stretch its limbs. They begin to encounter themselves—not just as consumers of content, but as active minds capable of reflection, invention, even a bit of wonder.

What we're aiming for, ultimately, is not control, but capacity. The goal isn't to micromanage a child's screen use until they're 18 and out the door. It's to help them build a relationship with technology that is aware, flexible, and self-directed. And that takes time. Digital mindfulness doesn't sprout overnight. It grows slowly, seeded through repetition, through example, through conversations that may not land immediately but echo over time. It is shaped by the textures of home life, by the values we express (and embody), and by the space we leave for questions that don't have quick answers.

In that spirit, this chapter offers not a prescription, but a framework. It explores how families can nurture intentional screen habits without descending into rigid rules or reactive bans. It looks at ways to support emotional regulation, to enrich the offline world, and to model a kind of digital citizenship rooted in care rather than control. Drawing on both psychological insight and lived experience, it invites a deeper re-evaluation of what it means to be "connected"—and whether that connection extends inward, as well as outward.

At its heart, digital mindfulness is about reclaiming a sense of agency. For children, that means knowing they have options—choices in how, when, and why they engage with screens. For parents, it means leading not through fear or force, but through presence and practice. And together, within that shared space of intention, families can begin to write a new narrative—one not dominated by devices, but enriched by them, and by the connections that truly matter.

The Power of Intentional Tech Use

Modern childhood is unfolding in a world where screens are ever-present—woven into education, entertainment, communication, and even play. For many children, reaching for a device is no longer a deliberate act but an automatic response to boredom, transition, or emotional discomfort. This habitual engagement, though common, often comes at the expense of deeper focus, meaningful creativity, and real-world social interaction. It also shapes long-term habits of mind: how children learn to direct their attention, regulate their impulses, and engage with the world. Teaching children to use screens with intention—rather than defaulting to them mindlessly—is one of the most powerful and transformative interventions parents can make.

Intentional tech use begins with a simple yet profound question: *Why am I using this device right now?* It invites the user to pause, assess their internal state, and identify a purpose. Is the goal to learn something new? To connect with a friend? To relax after a challenging day? Or is it simply to fill a gap in time, avoid a feeling, or follow a habitual script? Helping children develop this reflective habit allows them to take ownership of their digital choices. They begin to move from passive consumers of content to active, discerning participants in their digital lives.

This shift is not about limiting screen time arbitrarily, nor about shaming children for their digital interests. It is about cultivating awareness and choice. When a child watches a science video because they are curious about black holes, the experience is fundamentally different—neurologically and emotionally—than when they click through random content for hours without noticing where the time went. One activity expands the mind; the other numbs it. One builds a sense of agency; the other fosters dependency. The key is not the screen itself, but the intention behind its use.

Cultivating this awareness starts early and grows through consistent modelling and conversation. Very young children can begin to articulate their motivations with prompts such as, "What are you hoping to do on the tablet today?" or "How do you think you'll feel after watching that show?" These questions are not meant to quiz or judge, but to nurture metacognition—the ability to think about one's own thinking. When children regularly reflect on their media choices, they build the mental muscles that support self-regulation, delayed gratification, and intentional engagement.

For older children and adolescents, the conversation can become more nuanced. Teenagers, especially, may use technology to navigate complex social dynamics, express identity, or manage stress. These are legitimate uses—but they are also vulnerable to distortion if left unexamined. A teenager who posts frequently on social media may benefit from questions like, "What do you enjoy most about posting?" or "How do you feel when you're waiting for people to respond?" These reflections can reveal patterns around validation, comparison, or avoidance, and offer a starting point for more balanced engagement.

Intentionality is also supported by structuring screen use around goals rather than time alone. Instead of saying, "You have 30 minutes on your device," a parent might say, "What do you want to do with your screen time today?" This shifts the focus from quantity to quality. The child begins to view their device as a tool to accomplish something—whether it's beating a level in a game, finishing an art project, or researching a topic for school—rather than a time-filler. Over time, they learn to plan their usage, monitor their progress, and evaluate their satisfaction, all of which reinforce executive functioning skills critical for academic and life success.

This approach also aligns with how digital fluency is evolving. In the future, the most successful digital citizens will not be those who consume the most content, but those who can curate, question, and create with intention. They will know when to log in and when to step back, how to manage digital distractions, and how to use technology as a lever for learning, collaboration, and innovation. These skills are not innate; they are cultivated through practice. Children need opportunities to use digital tools for meaningful purposes—and they need guidance in recognising when tech is enhancing their experience and when it is diluting it.

Real-world examples illuminate how this might look in practice. Consider a family where the child is passionate about nature. Rather than limiting screen use across the board, the parents help the child use a tablet to film and edit mini documentaries about local wildlife. This transforms the device from a passive outlet into an instrument of storytelling, observation, and technical skill. The child begins to associate technology with purposeful creation, not just consumption. At the same time, the parents remain attentive to the balance—encouraging outdoor exploration and real-time observation as the foundation for digital expression.

Another example might involve a child fascinated by mythology. Instead of defaulting to YouTube for entertainment, the parent suggests searching for animated retellings of world myths or interactive storytelling apps that allow the child to create their own versions. The screen becomes a bridge to literature, imagination, and even global cultural awareness. These engagements are still enjoyable, but they are rooted in curiosity and enriched by adult guidance.

It is important, too, to differentiate between different types of digital engagement. Passive scrolling, repetitive gaming, or endless video auto-play tend to produce a kind of mental sedation. Children emerge from these experiences dazed, dysregulated, or dissatisfied, often unsure how they spent their time. By contrast, active engagement—coding, writing, building, designing—tends to leave them energised, focused, and proud of their output. Teaching children to recognise this difference empowers them to choose experiences that genuinely serve their interests and wellbeing.

This does not mean that entertainment has no place. Watching a silly video, playing a casual game, or chatting with friends can all be valid and enjoyable uses of screen time. The issue is not entertainment per se, but unconscious defaulting. When every moment of silence, discomfort, or downtime is filled with digital noise, children lose the opportunity to learn from those spaces. Boredom, for instance, is a vital teacher. It invites creativity, introspection, and spontaneous play. Children who are constantly entertained miss the chance to discover what they can generate from within.

Parents play a central role in setting the tone for intentional use. This involves not only modelling but narrating their own choices. Saying things like, "I'm checking the weather before our walk," or "I'm going to read this article because I want to understand this topic better," makes the invisible visible. It shows that screens are not magic or mindless, but tools that require discernment. When children see adults make conscious choices, they internalise those patterns and begin to replicate them.

Schools, too, can support this mindset. Educators who integrate tech with purpose—using it to explore, collaborate, and solve problems—reinforce the idea that devices are instruments of engagement, not distraction. They can teach students how to evaluate sources, resist clickbait, and manage attention. These skills are part of a broader digital literacy that must be cultivated if we are to raise a generation that can think critically, feel deeply, and act responsibly in a digital age.

Finally, intentional tech use supports emotional intelligence. When children understand why they are using a device, they are better able to assess how it affects them. They can detect when it's helping or harming, when it's connecting or isolating. They become attuned to their internal signals—fatigue, frustration, satisfaction, curiosity—and they learn to trust those signals. This self-awareness lays the groundwork for emotional resilience and ethical behaviour online.

Helping children use technology with intention is not a single conversation—it is an evolving practice. It grows through everyday moments, subtle prompts, shared experiences, and honest dialogue. It requires patience, consistency, and a willingness to engage with discomfort. But the payoff is profound. Children who learn to pause before they swipe, to reflect before they post, and to act with purpose rather than compulsion are not only healthier digital users—they are more grounded, self-aware, and empowered individuals.

Intentional tech use is not about perfection. It is about presence. It is about raising children who don't simply inherit the digital world but shape it with integrity, curiosity, and care. And in doing so, they discover that the most powerful tool is not the screen itself—but their ability to choose how, when, and why they use it.

Mindfulness and Self-Regulation

Children today are growing up in an environment of perpetual stimulation. Screens are everywhere—on walls, in pockets, on wrists—offering an endless stream of content, conversation, and distraction. While digital access brings undeniable benefits, it also demands a level of internal control that developing brains are not naturally equipped to handle without support. One of the most important skills parents can nurture in this context is self-regulation—the ability to notice one's internal state, to pause before reacting, and to make choices aligned with one's needs and values. When combined with mindfulness, self-regulation becomes a powerful force that allows children to engage with technology thoughtfully and to know, from within, when it's time to step away.

Unlike rules imposed from the outside, self-regulation arises from within the child. It is not about obedience but about awareness. Helping children recognise when they have had enough screen time is not just a logistical matter—it is a developmental milestone. It means supporting them in learning to listen to their own minds and bodies, to identify the signs of digital fatigue, overstimulation, or emotional depletion, and to act on that awareness with confidence and autonomy.

This internal compass takes time to develop, especially in an age where external cues—likes, notifications, autoplay features—are designed to keep users hooked. Digital platforms are engineered to override natural stopping points. This makes the cultivation of internal signals all the more critical. Children must learn to detect their own thresholds, to differentiate between genuine enjoyment and compulsive use, and to distinguish between feeling relaxed and feeling numbed. These are subtle distinctions, but they form the foundation of digital wellbeing.

One practical way to begin this process is through body-based awareness. Even young children can learn to notice how their bodies feel during and after screen use. Are their eyes tired? Is their head buzzing? Are they irritable, sluggish, or restless? A parent might ask, after a television show or a gaming session, "How does your body feel right now?" or "What do you notice about your energy?" These questions are not meant to interrogate but to guide attention inward. Over time, children learn that their bodies hold valuable information about their needs and limits.

Emotional cues are equally important. Many children struggle to notice when screen time stops being fun and starts becoming draining. A child who begins a game excitedly may continue playing long past the point of enjoyment, driven by habit, challenge, or social expectation. When parents encourage reflection—"Did that feel good the whole time?" or "Were there moments you felt bored or frustrated?"—they help children build emotional literacy. They also disrupt the myth that more screen time is always better, inviting children to consider quality over quantity.

One effective method of nurturing this self-awareness is through the use of pause points—built-in moments where children are encouraged to check in with themselves. This could be as simple as a reminder every 30 minutes to stretch, drink water, or take a deep breath. These breaks create space between stimulus and response, allowing the child to assess whether they wish to continue or stop. Over time, the external prompt can become internalised, leading to spontaneous self-checks: "Am I still enjoying this?" "Do I need a break?" These micro-reflections build metacognition—the ability to think about one's own thinking—and support long-term habits of self-regulation.

Parents can reinforce these habits by modelling their own awareness. When an adult says, "I'm feeling a bit drained—I've been on my screen too long," or "I need to take a break from scrolling to clear my mind," they normalise self-monitoring and demonstrate that even grown-ups have limits. These expressions show that stepping away from technology is not a punishment but a form of self-care. They also teach that the decision to disconnect can come from within rather than from an external authority.

For adolescents, whose social lives are increasingly digital, the ability to self-regulate becomes even more nuanced. Teens may use screens not only for entertainment but for emotional regulation—escaping stress, managing anxiety, or seeking validation. While these uses are understandable, they can also become maladaptive if not tempered by mindfulness. Helping teens explore the emotional drivers behind their screen habits is essential. Questions such as "What do you usually feel before you pick up your phone?" or "How do you feel after scrolling through social media for an hour?" can open up space for reflection without judgement.

In some cases, digital overuse is a symptom of unmet needs—loneliness, boredom, academic stress, or lack of offline engagement.

Parents who respond only by limiting screen time, without addressing the underlying issue, may find their efforts met with resistance or secrecy. Instead, a more effective approach is to collaborate with the child in identifying what need the screen is fulfilling, and then to explore alternative strategies for meeting that need. For example, if a teenager spends hours online because they feel isolated, the focus might shift to building offline friendships or exploring group activities. The screen time is not simply restricted—it is replaced with something more nourishing.

This approach also applies to younger children. A child who becomes agitated when asked to stop using a device may not be addicted in a clinical sense, but they may be struggling with transitions. Parents can ease this process by offering advance notice, acknowledging the difficulty, and providing a clear next step. Saying, "I know it's hard to stop when you're having fun. Let's take a break now and then do something with our hands—maybe build or draw," validates the child's experience while guiding them toward self-regulation.

Another powerful tool is the use of reflective dialogue after screen time. Rather than ending the activity abruptly or with criticism, parents can invite a brief conversation: "What did you enjoy most about what you just did?" or "How did that activity affect your mood?" These questions create a natural feedback loop, helping children learn from their experiences and adjust future behaviour. Over time, they internalise these conversations and begin to conduct them on their own, silently assessing how different types of screen use make them feel.

Mindfulness exercises can also enhance self-regulation. Simple practices such as breath awareness, mindful movement, or body scans help children reconnect with the present moment and tune into their internal cues. These practices are especially useful when children feel overstimulated or dysregulated after screen use. A few minutes of quiet reflection, stretching, or deep breathing can restore balance and serve as a reset. Integrating mindfulness into daily life—whether at bedtime, during transitions, or after digital activity—teaches children that they have the tools to calm their minds and make conscious choices.

Parents must also be patient. Self-regulation is a skill that unfolds gradually. It is not linear, and setbacks are to be expected. Children may overuse screens one day and show great awareness the next. What matters is consistency and support. When children know that their parents are not monitoring them to punish but to empower, they are more likely to engage in honest reflection. The goal is not perfect behaviour, but growing insight.

Technology itself can support this process. Some families use screen time trackers, app usage summaries, or mindfulness reminders built into devices to help children visualise their habits. These tools, when used collaboratively, can spark meaningful conversations and reinforce the idea that screen use should be intentional, not automatic. The key is to ensure that the technology serves the user, not the other way around.

Ultimately, helping children recognise when they've had enough screen time is about more than managing behaviour—it is about developing character. It teaches responsibility, autonomy, and care for one's own wellbeing. It fosters a sense of agency in a world that constantly pulls at attention. And it lays the foundation for lifelong habits that support not only digital balance but emotional health, cognitive clarity, and relational depth.

Mindfulness and self-regulation are not luxuries in the digital age; they are necessities. By teaching children to listen to their internal signals, to pause and reflect, and to make choices rooted in awareness, we equip them not just to survive in a screen-filled world, but to thrive. They become not passive recipients of digital culture, but conscious participants—capable of deciding not just *what* to engage with, but *when* and *why*. And in a world that constantly demands their attention, that ability may be among the most valuable they ever acquire.

Encouraging Offline Play and Social Interaction

In a time when screens often feel like an extension of the self, many children are spending a growing portion of their lives in digital environments. They learn, play, communicate, and even rest with a device in hand. While technology offers children remarkable opportunities for exploration and connection, it can also crowd out essential aspects of development that occur only through real-world experiences—particularly offline play and in-person social interaction. The challenge for today's parents is not to eliminate technology but to create space alongside it, where imagination, movement, laughter, and face-to-face connection can flourish.

Offline play is not a nostalgic luxury—it is a developmental necessity. It fosters creativity, problem-solving, resilience, and emotional regulation in ways that digital engagement, however advanced, cannot fully replicate. When children play in the physical world, they interact with materials, environments, and bodies in dynamic ways. They test hypotheses, negotiate roles, take risks, and build narratives. These interactions shape neural pathways, refine motor skills, and cultivate a sense of agency. Play is the laboratory of childhood—where inner lives are made visible, where fears are worked through, and where a sense of self begins to form.

Equally important is the role of social interaction in this process. While digital platforms allow for constant connection, they often offer thin substitutes for the rich, multisensory experience of being with others in real time. In-person socialisation involves interpreting facial expressions, managing conflict, responding to tone and body language, and sharing unstructured moments of silence and spontaneity. These subtleties are the bedrock of empathy and emotional intelligence. Children who spend the majority of their social time online may miss critical opportunities to develop these skills, which can affect relationships throughout life.

Balancing digital life with offline experiences, then, is not simply about screen limits—it is about protecting and prioritising the kinds of play and interaction that allow children to thrive. This balance looks different for every family and every child. Some may need more guidance in stepping away from screens, while others might naturally gravitate toward outdoor exploration or hands-on activity. The key is to observe, listen, and create an environment that invites engagement with the world beyond the screen.

This begins with time. Children cannot engage meaningfully in play or socialisation if their schedules are packed with structured activities or dominated by passive entertainment. They need space—unhurried, unscheduled hours—to follow their curiosity, to become bored and find their way out of it, to build worlds with cardboard and mud, or to invent games that adults cannot decipher. These moments, though messy and unpredictable, are where creativity is born. Parents who defend this time—even in the face of cultural pressure toward productivity—are giving their children something profoundly valuable: the freedom to inhabit their own imaginations.

Space matters too, not just temporally but physically. Children are more likely to play and socialise offline when their environments support it. This does not require elaborate playrooms or curated toys. What matters is accessibility and openness. A backyard with uneven ground and scattered sticks can inspire more creative play than a screen-saturated living room. A table filled with art supplies, books, or building materials can beckon a child away from a tablet, if the environment itself invites tactile exploration.

Equally vital is the presence of social opportunities that are neither forced nor overly curated. Free play with peers—whether siblings, neighbours, or classmates—offers irreplaceable lessons in negotiation, cooperation, and emotional self-regulation. When children play together without adult direction, they encounter real dilemmas: Who gets to lead? What happens when someone quits? How do we make it fair? These experiences build resilience and empathy in ways that no app can simulate. They also teach that relationships are not transactional but dynamic and evolving.

Parents can facilitate this by creating space for social interaction without controlling it. This might involve inviting friends over for unstructured play, encouraging outdoor meetups, or simply turning a blind eye to the delightful chaos of a living room fort. It may also involve loosening the reins on mess, noise, and unpredictability—recognising that these are the natural by-products of engagement and growth.

The role of adult modelling is also significant. Children take their cues not just from what adults say, but from how they live. A parent who sets down their phone to be present, who invites their child for a walk or a board game, who values conversation over entertainment, is demonstrating that real-world connection matters. These gestures do not have to be grand. Sitting on the floor with a puzzle, asking thoughtful questions at dinner, or making time for shared chores can reinforce the message that life offline is rich, engaging, and worthwhile.

One of the most effective strategies for encouraging offline engagement is connecting it to a child's existing interests. A child who enjoys building games on a tablet might also enjoy constructing real-world structures with blocks or recycled materials. A teenager who curates photos online might be inspired by a photography class or a shared photo walk. The idea is not to separate digital and physical life, but to bridge them—to show that the passions nurtured online can take root and grow in the real world.

This bridging can also be useful in easing transitions away from screens. Rather than abrupt or punitive cut-offs, parents can create gentle transitions—using timers, visual cues, or shared activities that follow screen time. Saying, "When the show ends, let's go outside and check on the garden," frames disconnection not as a loss but as a shift. Children are more likely to move willingly when the alternative is framed as engaging rather than as a punishment.

At times, children may resist these transitions, particularly if screen use has become habitual or emotionally compensatory. In such cases, it is helpful to approach the issue with curiosity rather than confrontation. Asking, "What do you like most about playing that game?" or "What makes it hard to stop?" can yield insights into what the child is seeking—connection, mastery, escape—and guide parents in offering alternatives that meet those needs. This approach is not about replacing one stimulus with another, but about helping the child find richness in experiences that involve presence, agency, and real-world engagement.

There are also broader cultural forces to contend with. Many children feel that their offline lives are less relevant or meaningful than their digital ones. If their friends are online, if validation comes from likes, if memories are only counted when documented, then the real world may feel lacking by comparison. Countering this narrative requires a cultural shift within the family. Celebrating real-world experiences—without turning them into content—can help reclaim their value. A walk in the woods, a shared recipe, a heartfelt conversation—all of these moments matter deeply, even if they are not captured or shared.

Ultimately, encouraging offline play and social interaction is about rebalancing attention. It is about helping children see that the world outside their screen is not empty, but full—of texture, movement, story, and presence. It is about giving them the tools to engage with that world, and the confidence to find meaning in it. And it is about reminding them, gently and persistently, that while the digital world may be infinite in content, the real world offers something even more essential: the chance to be truly alive, in relationship with others, in the ever-unfolding moment of now.

Digital Detox Without Forcing It

In a world where screens have become ever-present companions, suggesting a digital detox to children can feel, at best, aspirational and, at worst, adversarial. For many families, the very mention of unplugging—even briefly—provokes resistance, anxiety, or outright rebellion. Yet, amidst growing evidence linking excessive screen use to diminished attention, disrupted sleep, reduced physical activity, and increased anxiety, the need for screen-free moments has never been more pressing. The challenge lies not in whether digital detoxing is beneficial, but in how to introduce it in a way that is gradual, respectful, and sustainable—without triggering conflict or making technology the enemy.

Contrary to popular imagery, a digital detox does not require sweeping interventions, dramatic declarations, or locking devices in a drawer for a week. In fact, such extreme measures often backfire, especially with children and teenagers who may already feel that their autonomy is under threat. When detoxing is imposed rather than invited, it tends to foster secretive behaviours, resentment, or overcompensation once restrictions are lifted. The more constructive—and enduring—approach is to slowly weave screen-free intervals into daily life until they feel natural, even welcomed. This requires patience, creativity, and above all, a shift in mindset from punishment to presence.

The starting point for any gradual detox is observation. Families benefit from pausing to notice when and how screens are being used. Are devices filling every transitional space—waking up, riding in the car, waiting for meals? Are they the default response to boredom or discomfort? Do children instinctively reach for a screen without considering alternatives? These patterns offer insight into where gentle shifts might be most effective. Rather than overhauling everything at once, parents can begin by selecting one moment in the day—perhaps breakfast, the walk home from school, or the last half-hour before bed—to consciously unplug. The key is to approach this not as a rule to enforce, but as a habit to explore.

Framing is critical. Children are more likely to accept screen-free moments when they are associated with something positive rather than with restriction. Rather than saying, "No screens after dinner," a parent might say, "Let's have a relaxed evening together and try playing a card game instead of watching something tonight." This subtle reframing shifts the focus from what is being taken away to what is being added: connection, interaction, novelty. Over time, the emphasis on presence rather than prohibition helps detox moments feel less like deprivation and more like enrichment.

In many families, screen use is woven into routines as a tool for transition, regulation, or reward. This is especially true for younger children, who may rely on screens to soothe, focus, or entertain. Removing the screen without offering an alternative is unlikely to succeed. The more effective method is to introduce substitutes that meet the same need while fostering real-world engagement. For example, if a child usually watches videos to unwind after school, they might be offered a chance to decompress through drawing, listening to music, or playing outside. The goal is not to replace one stimulus with another, but to help the child discover that their needs can be met in varied and enriching ways.

Gradual detoxing also benefits from rhythm. Children are more likely to accept screen-free time when it becomes predictable rather than arbitrary. A daily "quiet hour," a weekend morning without devices, or a family ritual such as reading aloud or going for a walk can serve as anchoring points in the week. These intervals become familiar over time and are less likely to provoke protest. They also provide moments of reset for attention and nervous system regulation, allowing both children and adults to re-engage with technology later in a more mindful state.

Importantly, these screen-free pockets do not need to be long to be effective. In fact, short, frequent pauses may have a greater impact on regulation and awareness than longer, more sporadic detoxes. Even five to ten minutes of tech-free transition between activities can help reset cognitive load, improve attention, and reconnect with one's body and environment. A child who learns to pause between watching a show and beginning homework is building a skill that will serve them far beyond the screen—namely, the ability to notice, reset, and choose with intention.

One particularly effective technique is co-participation. Rather than expecting children to unplug on their own, parents can model and share screen-free experiences. Reading together, playing a board game, cooking, gardening, or simply sitting and talking become ways of reclaiming attention and rebuilding relational intimacy. These shared moments matter, not only because they substitute for screen time, but because they affirm the child's importance. When adults put away their own devices to be present, they send a powerful message: "You are more interesting and more valuable than anything on this screen."

For adolescents, detoxing must be handled with even more sensitivity. Teens are often deeply embedded in digital networks that provide both social currency and emotional regulation. Cutting off access can feel like social exile or emotional withdrawal. Here, the conversation must shift toward partnership. Asking teens what kinds of screen-free time they find most restorative—or when they themselves feel "digitally full"—opens the door to mutual understanding. It might emerge that a teenager enjoys walking alone without their phone, drawing in a sketchpad, or working out without music. These preferences can be honoured and expanded. When detoxing becomes self-directed, rather than parent-imposed, it gains traction and respect.

Moreover, encouraging teens to reflect on the emotional aftermath of screen use—How did that scroll make you feel? Did that conversation energise or drain you?—helps them develop a more nuanced understanding of their own digital wellbeing. Over time, they may begin to pre-emptively take breaks not because they're told to, but because they recognise the need. This is the crux of mindful digital engagement: choosing to pause not because one must, but because one can.

Technology itself can be leveraged in this process. Ironically, digital tools can support detoxing when used with intention. Screen time apps, focus modes, or usage tracking can help children and adolescents visualise their habits and identify patterns. A child who sees that they've spent three hours watching short videos in one evening might be more open to experimenting with a new routine. Again, the emphasis must be on reflection, not guilt. The screen is not the enemy; the unconscious use of it is.

The language used around detoxing is just as important as the strategy. Words like "unplug," "reset," or "reconnect" are often more effective than "limit," "restrict," or "cut back." The goal is to reframe screen-free moments as forms of self-care and attention recovery, not as punishments for overuse. When children internalise this framing, they are more likely to protect these moments for themselves, seeing them not as obligations but as choices that support their wellbeing.

Ultimately, digital detoxing without force is about cultivating inner wisdom. It is about helping children and teenagers become aware of how screens affect their bodies, minds, and relationships—and then empowering them to make adjustments that serve their long-term growth. This is not a skill that develops overnight. It emerges slowly, through repeated exposure, honest dialogue, and the consistent modelling of mindful tech use by adults. It involves experimentation, reflection, and course correction. But over time, the rewards are significant.

Children who learn to pause before scrolling, to notice when their attention is waning, to value silence and real-world experience, are not just better screen users—they are more attuned human beings. They are more present in their relationships, more connected to their physical surroundings, and more capable of choosing their digital lives rather than being swept along by them. And perhaps most importantly, they are equipped with the inner compass necessary to navigate a world that will only grow more digitally saturated.

The digital world is not going away—nor should it. But the task before us is to ensure that our children are not consumed by it, that they do not lose themselves in the constant pull of algorithms and artificial urgency. By introducing screen-free moments gently, respectfully, and consistently, we allow them to rediscover the depth of their own attention, the pleasures of offline life, and the satisfaction of choosing presence over compulsion. And that, ultimately, is the true power of a digital detox—when it is chosen, not forced.

Helping Kids Develop a Healthy Relationship with Technology

At the heart of digital parenting lies a goal more nuanced than simply restricting screen time or policing online content. It is to help children develop a healthy, self-aware, and balanced relationship with technology—one that empowers them to engage meaningfully without being consumed. In an increasingly screen-saturated world, this objective demands more than control; it requires guidance, presence, and a deep understanding of how technology intersects with a child's emotional, cognitive, and social development.

A healthy relationship with technology is characterised by intentional use, emotional resilience, and internal regulation. It does not require that children avoid screens altogether, but that they engage with them thoughtfully—aware of their purpose, mindful of their effects, and able to step back when necessary. This capacity evolves over time and cannot be instilled through rules alone. It must be cultivated through lived experience, reflective dialogue, and consistent modelling from the adults in their lives.

One of the most important aspects of this relationship is agency. When children feel they are passive consumers—obliged to respond to every ping or compelled to watch one more video—they lose a sense of control over their digital environment. Conversely, when they learn to pause, assess, and choose their tech use with discernment, they gain mastery. This sense of ownership is critical. A child who understands why they are using a device and what they hope to get from the experience is far more likely to use it constructively.

The role of parents, then, is not to act as digital gatekeepers but as co-navigators—walking alongside their children, interpreting the digital landscape with them, and asking the questions that spark awareness. Instead of asking, "How long have you been on your phone?" it may be more effective to ask, "What drew you to it just now?" or "How are you feeling after being online?" These queries promote metacognition and invite the child to consider their emotional state, helping to establish a link between internal experience and digital behaviour.

This kind of reflective engagement is particularly powerful when paired with personal sharing. A parent who says, "I realised I was checking my emails all through dinner yesterday and felt disconnected from you," is not only modelling self-awareness but also showing that digital habits are something we all need to work on. This shared vulnerability dissolves the us-versus-them dynamic that so often characterises screen-time battles and opens up space for mutual growth.

Children also benefit from having opportunities to explore the full range of what technology can offer—not just entertainment, but creation, collaboration, and inquiry. A child who learns to use technology to code, design, research, or build gains a sense of empowerment that counters the passivity of endless consumption. Parents can support this by celebrating process over product: valuing effort, curiosity, and experimentation over polished output. This approach encourages children to use technology as a means of expression and problem-solving rather than merely as a way to pass the time.

Equally important is teaching children to notice and respect their own limits. This involves developing a vocabulary around the sensory, emotional, and cognitive effects of screen use. Does your head feel heavy after a long session? Do you get irritable when switching from a game to homework? Are you sleeping as well as you do on screen-light days? These questions are not meant to shame but to equip. They help children become fluent in reading their own internal cues and adjusting accordingly. In doing so, they begin to trust themselves to make wise decisions—an ability that will serve them well beyond childhood.

Technology should not become a battleground in family life, nor should it be treated as inherently harmful. The more effective approach is to treat it as a space for skill-building, self-discovery, and values alignment. For example, if a family values empathy and kindness, then discussions about online behaviour should connect to those values: "How do you think that comment would feel to someone reading it?" or "What do you want your online presence to say about who you are?" When technology use is framed within a moral and emotional context, it becomes a tool for character development, not just a habit to manage.

This framing is particularly crucial during adolescence, when identity formation and social belonging take centre stage. Teenagers may view their online lives as extensions of their social reality, and dismissive attitudes from adults can create distance. Rather than critiquing platforms wholesale, parents might ask what teens find meaningful or challenging about them. "What do you enjoy about being on TikTok?" or "What makes Instagram stressful sometimes?" These questions convey curiosity and respect, and they often lead to richer discussions about peer pressure, authenticity, and self-worth.

Trust plays a pivotal role in all of this. Children are more likely to develop a balanced relationship with technology when they feel trusted to make decisions, even if they sometimes falter. This does not mean abandoning oversight, but it does mean stepping back enough to let children experience natural consequences and learn from them. A missed homework deadline due to procrastination, a hurt feeling from a poorly worded message, or a sense of exhaustion after too much gaming can all be opportunities for reflection and recalibration—if handled with empathy rather than punishment.

Parents who approach these moments not with "I told you so," but with, "Let's talk about what happened," create a culture of learning rather than fear. They teach that digital mistakes are part of growth, not moral failures. This approach not only supports resilience but also reduces secrecy, making children more likely to come forward when something truly problematic occurs.

Developing a healthy relationship with technology also means learning when to disconnect—and discovering the richness of life without screens. This is not about forced deprivation but about balance. Offline experiences—play, nature, face-to-face conversation, creativity—provide grounding and contrast. They help children regulate, recharge, and reorient. When children are given the tools to enjoy offline life, they are less likely to rely on screens for emotional escape or constant stimulation.

Parents can facilitate this by making screen-free experiences accessible and appealing. This may involve creating tech-free rituals—reading aloud, evening walks, shared meals—or simply making room for unstructured play. These activities reinforce the message that real-world engagement is not only possible but deeply rewarding. And they give children the chance to be fully present, to connect with others, and to develop capacities that no screen can offer.

Ultimately, helping children build a healthy relationship with technology is not about fixing their habits, but about nurturing their humanity. It is about equipping them with the insight, flexibility, and inner strength to navigate an ever-changing digital landscape. It is about raising children who are not just literate in the mechanics of devices but fluent in the language of self-awareness, values, and choice.

This is the long game of digital parenting. It is not quick, and it is not perfect. But it is deeply worthwhile. Because when children learn to relate to technology as a tool—not a master—and when they are supported in making conscious, values-aligned decisions, they gain something far more important than screen balance. They gain the foundation for a grounded, empowered, and reflective life in a connected world.

Chapter 9
When Things Go Wrong: Navigating Digital Challenges

Even with the most carefully drawn boundaries, open lines of communication, and proactive parenting, there will inevitably be moments when a child's relationship with technology takes a challenging turn. Screens, by design, are captivating and immersive, tapping into psychological triggers that can easily overwhelm a child's still-maturing self-control. For some, what begins as innocent engagement gradually morphs into dependency, secrecy, or emotional unrest. When such situations arise, it's crucial that parents resist panic or harsh discipline, instead approaching matters with clear-headedness, empathy, and a well-informed strategy.

The digital era has brought with it behavioural and psychological complexities previous generations of parents simply did not face. Take screen addiction, for example: once a marginal concern, it is now widely acknowledged as a pattern where children struggle to disengage from digital content despite its adverse effects—be it disrupted sleep, falling grades, deteriorating mental health, or strained family ties. This can creep in quietly: irritability when devices are taken away, relentless urges to go online, or dishonesty about time spent glued to screens. On occasion, the consequences are far more visible—emotional meltdowns, social withdrawal, or obsessive preoccupation with games, social media, or videos.

Parents caught in this storm often find themselves overwhelmed, weighed down by guilt or uncertainty about the best course of action. Some respond with a clampdown—harsh restrictions or confiscation of devices without much explanation—while others recoil, hoping the problem will simply fade away. Neither path offers a sustainable solution. Instead, what is essential is an unflinching assessment of behaviour, an understanding of the child's underlying needs, and a steady commitment to rebuilding habits and trust through supportive, compassionate intervention.

It's important to remember that not all problematic screen behaviour springs from addiction. Sometimes screens serve as a coping mechanism—children might turn to them out of stress, boredom, or as a way to dodge uncomfortable feelings. Though these digital escapes might provide fleeting comfort, they often conceal deeper struggles: anxiety, academic frustrations, or social conflicts that demand attention. Parents who notice this pattern should resist jumping to reprimand. Rather, adopting a tone of curiosity—asking gently, "What's happening that makes this feel like your only option right now?" or "What else helps you feel calm besides your device?"—can open a crucial conversation, digging beneath the surface to unearth the root causes.

Then there is the pressing matter of online safety, particularly when children interact with strangers on digital platforms. From seemingly innocent game chats to social media, the internet abounds with potential dangers. Predators often masquerade as peers, exploiting a child's natural trust and curiosity. The fallout from such encounters can be devastating, spanning emotional manipulation, exposure to explicit material, or sharing of private information.

Parents must strike a careful balance here. Fear-based warnings—"Don't talk to anyone online or bad things will happen"—often backfire, breeding shame and secrecy. Instead, children should be armed with clear, practical guidelines about privacy, encouraged to trust their instincts, and reassured that they can approach their parents without fear of blame or punishment. Discussing age-appropriate real-life examples and reviewing safety settings together can help build both awareness and practical protective skills. When children understand they won't be judged, they are far more likely to disclose troubling experiences.

Digital misbehaviour also arises from the child's own choices: flouting family tech rules, seeking out inappropriate content, stretching screen time through deception, or even engaging in cyberbullying. While these require firm attention, they also offer moments to reinforce values, cultivate accountability, and strengthen the parent-child bond. The knee-jerk reaction might be to respond with punitive measures—bans, shaming, or swift discipline—but a gentler, reflective approach tends to bear better fruit.

Imagine a child caught watching videos beyond their age range. Instead of immediately revoking privileges, a parent might ask, "What drew you to that content?" or "How did it make you feel?" Such questions create space for the child to explore influences—curiosity, peer pressure, or emotional needs—and open a dialogue about shared values: why certain content isn't suitable, how it shapes thoughts or behaviour, and what healthier alternatives exist. Any consequences should aim to restore trust rather than instil fear—perhaps through setting new safeguards, agreeing on supervision, or collaboratively re-establishing boundaries.

Digital overload is another familiar concern. Both children and adults sometimes overindulge in screen time, especially during holidays, stressful spells, or when daily routines falter. Signs are often clear: disrupted sleep patterns, mood swings, listlessness, irritability. This should not be seen as failure but rather as a signal that balance requires adjustment. A "reset" might involve reintroducing screen-free routines, encouraging exercise, re-engaging with offline interests, or simply spending more quality time together, device-free.

Framing this reset positively—as a chance to recharge, reconnect, and feel better—helps children accept it more willingly. They may even develop their own insight. One family, for instance, noticed their teenage son habitually gaming through weekends, but after recognising he felt anxious and drained come Sunday evening, he voluntarily asked for limits. Such self-awareness is the fruit of a home environment where reflection is encouraged, not punished.

Yet, there are times when professional support is warranted. If a child's digital use significantly disrupts daily life or becomes compulsive, involving psychologists, therapists, or digital wellbeing specialists may be necessary. Similarly, if excessive screen time masks underlying emotional or developmental difficulties—like depression, ADHD, or social anxiety—then the digital habits should be viewed as symptoms, not root causes.

Schools and counsellors often serve as invaluable allies here. Teachers, who see children in academic settings, might notice behavioural issues linked to digital use: difficulty concentrating, assignment avoidance, or disruptive device use in class. Engaging them in dialogue can provide a fuller understanding and access to further support. The key is collaboration rather than blame: "We've noticed this pattern at home—have you observed anything similar at school?"

Ultimately, the objective in managing digital difficulties is not to prevent every mishap but to equip children with the tools and support to recover when things go awry. We don't expect a child to master cycling without falling now and then, so it's unrealistic to assume they'll navigate the digital world flawlessly. What truly matters is how parents respond. When mistakes invite guidance instead of punishment, children cultivate resilience. When support is steady and free of judgment, they feel safe enough to be open. And when boundaries are firm yet empathetic, parents become trusted partners in their child's digital growth.

This chapter delves into the practicalities of handling moments when screen use crosses boundaries—whether those lines involve behaviour, emotion, or safety. It offers strategies for addressing excessive use, guiding children through digital missteps, protecting them from harm, and resetting the balance when it falters. It also explores when professional help should be sought, and how to do so without casting stigma. The overarching message is one of realism and reassurance: digital parenting is less about perfection and more about showing up consistently, compassionately, and with adaptability.

Because when technology problems inevitably arise—as they will—children need more than punishment. They need presence. They need adults steady enough to uphold boundaries, wise enough to perceive deeper struggles, and humble enough to learn alongside them. In doing this, we do more than resolve the immediate crisis; we build the trust and skills that will sustain them far beyond any screen.

Addressing Screen Addiction

In today's digitised world, it is increasingly difficult to discern where healthy screen engagement ends and problematic overuse begins. Children are growing up surrounded by devices that are deeply integrated into their academic, social, and recreational lives. The challenge for parents is not simply managing time spent on screens, but recognising when digital habits cross a threshold into compulsive or harmful behaviour. Screen addiction, while not yet classified as a formal disorder in every diagnostic manual, is a real and growing concern. It describes a pattern of use where a child struggles to disengage, prioritises screen activities over real-world responsibilities, and shows signs of emotional distress or functional impairment when technology is limited or removed.

The first step in addressing potential screen addiction is to look beyond the number of hours and instead assess the *impact* of screen use on the child's well-being. Excessive digital engagement may manifest as disrupted sleep patterns, social withdrawal, irritability, falling academic performance, or avoidance of offline interests. Parents may notice their child becoming preoccupied with online activities to the point of neglecting hygiene, skipping meals, or resisting even short breaks from screens. When a child displays distress during transitions away from devices or when screen access becomes a point of persistent conflict, these are signs that intervention is warranted.

However, effective intervention requires more than abrupt restriction. Screens, particularly video games, social media platforms, and streaming content, are designed to be immersive and rewarding. They offer immediate feedback, variable reinforcement, and often a sense of control or escape that may be missing in a child's offline life. Simply removing access without addressing the underlying appeal—or the psychological needs being met—can exacerbate the problem and damage the parent-child relationship.

A more constructive approach begins with understanding. Parents should approach the child not with blame or interrogation, but with genuine curiosity. Asking open-ended questions such as, "What do you enjoy most about this game?" or "What makes it hard to stop watching videos?" opens a space for dialogue. Children are more likely to reflect on their habits when they feel heard rather than judged. These conversations can reveal important motivations—such as needing to feel competent, connected, or entertained—which can then inform how support is offered.

It is also essential to distinguish between compulsive use and purposeful engagement. A child who spends hours coding, editing videos, or designing digital art may appear addicted at first glance, but if their use is goal-oriented, creatively driven, and balanced with other life areas, it is likely more of an intense interest than a dependency. The concern arises when screen use becomes habitual, reactive, and emotionally avoidant—when the screen is no longer a tool, but a crutch.

Once concerns are clarified, the next step is to introduce structure—not through rigid control, but through co-created boundaries. Children are far more likely to comply with rules they've helped shape. Sit down together and outline a daily rhythm that includes screen use alongside offline activities—meals, outdoor play, reading, family time, and rest. The goal is not to eliminate screens, but to re-establish balance. For example, agreeing that gaming can happen after homework and before dinner creates predictability and frames screen time as one part of a broader, meaningful routine.

Importantly, this structure must be accompanied by empathy and consistency. If a child erupts in anger when it's time to stop playing, this should be seen as a signal of emotional dysregulation rather than wilful disobedience. Parents can help by naming the emotion—"It looks like stopping feels really frustrating right now"—while still holding the limit. Over time, children begin to internalise both the boundary and the emotional language, gaining tools for self-regulation.

In many families, screen addiction is not just a child's issue—it is embedded in family dynamics. Parents too may be tethered to devices, modelling compulsive checking or emotional withdrawal into screens. Addressing screen overuse in children must therefore include honest reflection from adults. Children are acutely aware of parental habits and often mirror what they see. When parents choose to put phones away during meals, step outside for breaks, or talk openly about their own digital limits, they reinforce the very behaviours they hope to instil.

Sometimes, screen addiction masks deeper issues. A child who compulsively scrolls or games for hours each day may be struggling with anxiety, depression, low self-esteem, or social rejection. In these cases, the screen provides relief—but not resolution. Parents should observe whether excessive screen time is accompanied by signs of emotional withdrawal, self-criticism, or hopelessness. If so, digital habits may be symptomatic of a broader mental health concern that requires professional support. Consulting with a therapist, school counsellor, or child psychologist can provide essential insight and offer strategies tailored to the child's emotional and developmental needs.

Technology itself can also be used to help mitigate problematic use. Many platforms now offer screen time reports, focus modes, or app timers that can be adjusted collaboratively. When a child sees a visual representation of how their time is being spent, it can prompt greater self-awareness. Rather than imposing a time cap, parents might say, "Let's look at your usage this week and talk about what you'd like to change." This approach respects the child's autonomy while still guiding behavioural shifts.

Supporting offline alternatives is another essential component. Children will not simply stop using screens because they are told to—they need meaningful replacements. Encouraging participation in sport, music, outdoor exploration, hands-on projects, or social activities provides the stimulation and satisfaction that screens often replace. These alternatives must be offered without coercion and should align with the child's interests. It is not enough to say "Go outside"—the question is, *what will they find there that captivates them, challenges them, or helps them feel alive?*

There will be setbacks. Digital habits, like any deeply entrenched behaviour, take time to rewire. Parents may see progress for a few days followed by regression. This is normal. The focus should remain on progress, not perfection. Celebrating small wins—choosing to take a break unprompted, stopping after one episode, or initiating an offline activity—builds the child's confidence and sense of agency.

Above all, addressing screen addiction requires patience and relational trust. Children need to know that their parents are not trying to punish or control them, but to help them thrive. This sense of safety allows for vulnerability, reflection, and cooperation. It turns digital discipline into a shared project rather than a battleground. The process is rarely quick or tidy—but it is profoundly worthwhile.

Because at its core, the goal is not simply to reduce screen time. It is to help children become aware of their needs, responsible for their choices, and capable of creating a life where technology serves their growth rather than stalling it. This is the essence of healthy digital development: not abstinence, but balance; not control, but connection; not restriction, but reflection. And when children learn this from the adults who love them most, they are far more likely to carry it into their adolescence, their relationships, and their futures.

Dealing with Online Strangers and Predators

The digital landscape offers children unprecedented access to knowledge, entertainment, and communication, but it also opens doors to risks that were unimaginable a generation ago. Among the most serious threats are interactions with online strangers and predators—individuals who exploit the anonymity and reach of the internet to deceive, manipulate, and harm. These encounters, though often invisible to adults, can have profound psychological and emotional consequences for young users. As digital natives spend increasing amounts of time online, it is critical that parents and caregivers understand how to protect them from digital threats without resorting to fearmongering or invasive control. Education, awareness, and open dialogue form the bedrock of a proactive defence.

Online predators are rarely the caricatured villains of sensational headlines. They often present as peers, build trust gradually, and use highly sophisticated strategies to blend into digital spaces frequented by children. From multiplayer gaming platforms and social media apps to private messaging services embedded within educational or creative tools, predators exploit environments that seem harmless on the surface. Their aim is to create emotional dependence, elicit personal information, or groom a child for inappropriate interactions. They often begin with flattery, shared interests, or sympathy—tactics designed to make a child feel seen and valued, particularly if they are experiencing loneliness or low self-esteem offline.

The challenge for parents is that these conversations often unfold in private digital spaces, far from the protective gaze of adults. Moreover, children may not immediately recognise the danger, especially if the contact feels friendly, validating, or exciting. They might even protect the secrecy of the interaction, fearing parental anger, the loss of privileges, or being misunderstood. This is why fostering an environment of openness and psychological safety is paramount. Children must know they can share anything—no matter how embarrassing, confusing, or serious—without being blamed or punished. The ability to report a concern, even after rules have been broken, could be the very thing that protects them from harm.

Establishing this trust begins long before any specific incident occurs. From a young age, parents can help children understand the concept of digital strangers by drawing parallels with real-world interactions. Just as we teach children not to follow a stranger in a shopping centre, we must help them recognise that not everyone online is who they claim to be. This education should not be built on fear but on empowerment—providing children with the tools to think critically, ask questions, and follow their instincts.

A child who receives a friend request from someone they do not know in real life should be encouraged to pause and reflect. Who is this person? What do they want? Why are they trying to connect? Encouraging children to bring such instances to a parent or trusted adult for discussion reinforces the idea that digital decision-making is not something they have to navigate alone. Parents can say, "Whenever someone reaches out online and you're not sure who they are, we'll look at it together," or "It's always okay to walk away from a chat that doesn't feel right." These conversations normalise caution without inducing anxiety.

It is also crucial to address the emotional tactics used by online predators. They may compliment a child excessively, offer gifts in gaming environments, or suggest that no one else understands them. In more concerning cases, they might threaten to share private images or messages if the child refuses to comply with requests. Helping children recognise manipulation tactics gives them language and perspective. Phrases like, "When someone online tries to make you feel special very quickly or asks you to keep secrets, that's a red flag," can be revisited and reinforced regularly.

Technology can support these efforts when used intentionally. Privacy settings, parental controls, and content filters provide a foundational level of protection, especially for younger children. However, they are not infallible. No technological barrier can replace the nuanced understanding that comes from regular conversations and guided exploration. Rather than banning specific apps or websites reactively, it is more effective to explore them together. Sitting alongside a child while they navigate a platform allows parents to understand the features, risks, and culture of that space. It also communicates a message of partnership: "I'm interested in your world and want to help you enjoy it safely."

A family might discover, for example, that a popular game includes live chat features where players can communicate with strangers. Rather than immediately forbidding the game, parents might explore whether those settings can be disabled, whether chat can be limited to known friends, or whether play can occur in a shared space where occasional supervision is possible. These collaborative decisions build digital literacy while respecting a child's autonomy.

Adolescents, in particular, require a different approach. Older children are more likely to seek privacy, to test boundaries, and to feel confident in their ability to navigate the online world. They may resist perceived interference or control, especially if it feels authoritarian or uninformed. With teens, the goal is less about direct supervision and more about influence through respect, education, and emotional availability. Parents can ask reflective questions: "What do you do when someone you don't know messages you?" or "How do you decide whether someone online is trustworthy?" These questions invite self-assessment rather than impose judgement.

If a child does encounter an online predator or finds themselves in a conversation that becomes inappropriate, the priority must be emotional containment and support. The child may feel confused, ashamed, or frightened. They may worry they are in trouble. It is essential that the adult respond with calm reassurance: "Thank you for telling me. You did the right thing. I'm here to help." This creates the conditions for recovery and learning, rather than secrecy and further risk.

Depending on the nature of the interaction, different responses may be appropriate. For minor incidents, blocking the contact, reporting the user through platform protocols, and reviewing safety settings may suffice. In more serious cases involving grooming, explicit content, or threats, it is important to contact relevant authorities, such as child protection services, school counsellors, or cybercrime units. Preserving evidence—screenshots, messages, usernames—

can aid investigations. While involving authorities can feel daunting, it reinforces to the child that their safety is paramount and that they are not alone in navigating complex situations.

Real-world examples help contextualise these ideas. Consider a twelve-year-old girl who, while using a drawing app, received repeated messages from someone claiming to be a fellow artist. The conversation began innocently, with compliments on her artwork, but gradually shifted into requests for personal photos. Fortunately, the child remembered a family conversation about online secrecy and told her parents. They responded supportively, reported the user, and used the incident as a catalyst for revisiting safety practices. Rather than shaming the child, they praised her discernment, reinforcing her confidence in setting boundaries.

In another case, a teenage boy found himself drawn into a friendship with someone he met in an online forum. The person claimed to be a few years older and offered mentorship on coding projects. Over time, the boy was asked to keep secrets, share more personal details, and isolate the relationship from others. This grooming dynamic became increasingly uncomfortable, and eventually the teen confided in a teacher. The school facilitated a conversation with the family, who responded with compassion and sought professional guidance. What could have been a deeply damaging experience instead became a turning point in the child's digital awareness and emotional maturity.

These stories underscore a key principle: when children are supported, informed, and believed, they are more likely to come forward. Prevention, then, is not about surveillance—it is about relationship. It is about creating a home environment where questions are welcomed, missteps are forgivable, and digital life is treated as a shared responsibility rather than a solitary venture.

Ultimately, protecting children from online strangers and predators is a continuous process. It evolves with age, with technology, and with the child's own developmental needs. It involves vigilance without fear, boundaries without rigidity, and communication without shame. Most of all, it involves a commitment to seeing the digital world not as a threat to childhood, but as part of its new terrain—a space that requires navigation, support, and courage. And when children are equipped with trust, knowledge, and agency, they are far more capable of recognising danger and choosing safety—even when no one is watching.

When Kids Break Digital Rules

In any household that engages with technology, boundaries are bound to be tested. Despite parents' best efforts to set thoughtful limits and encourage responsible digital behaviour, children will, on occasion, overstep the agreed rules. Whether it's secretly extending screen time late into the night, bypassing content restrictions, downloading unauthorised apps, or engaging in online conversations they've been advised to avoid, such moments are not evidence of parental failure or inherent defiance. They are developmental events—moments that signal growth, experimentation, and the very human tendency to test the contours of independence.

How parents respond to these transgressions profoundly shapes not only future behaviour but the overall relationship a child has with both their parents and their digital world. When the focus is purely on punishment, especially when it's abrupt or shaming, the risk is that children become more secretive, less reflective, and more resistant to adult guidance. However, when parents respond with clarity, empathy, and a desire to understand, the incident becomes an opportunity for learning and deeper connection.

The first step in responding to digital misbehaviour is to pause before reacting. A breach of rules can easily trigger frustration, especially if it follows a repeated conversation or seems calculated. Yet, reacting from anger—through confiscation, yelling, or threats—can overshadow the deeper issues that need addressing. When a parent instead takes a moment to breathe, gather their thoughts, and prepare for a constructive conversation, the dynamic shifts from adversarial to collaborative.

Consider the case of a ten-year-old boy who was discovered playing an online game well past the agreed time limit. His parents had noticed increased tiredness and irritability in the mornings, prompting them to investigate. Rather than confronting him with accusations, they sat down and asked open questions: "We've noticed you seem more tired lately—what's going on at bedtime?" This approach allowed the child to admit, somewhat sheepishly, that he had been sneaking extra game time. Rather than reacting with a device ban, the parents used the moment to talk about self-control, consequences of poor sleep, and why boundaries matter. Together, they renegotiated a screen-wind-down routine that included reading and dimmed lighting, restoring trust and balance.

Non-punitive responses do not mean avoiding consequences altogether. Natural and logical consequences—those that are directly related to the behaviour—are far more effective than arbitrary punishments. If a child misuses a device, it makes sense to temporarily adjust access to that device while working on the skills needed to rebuild trust. What matters is how this is framed. Saying, "We're going to take a break from the tablet this week to reset and talk more about respectful use," is vastly different from, "You've lost your iPad for a month because you can't be trusted."

Consequences should never be meted out in the heat of the moment. They should be part of a wider conversation in which the child is involved—not just to apologise, but to reflect on their choices, articulate what they were thinking or feeling, and contribute to a repair plan. This restores their agency and helps them integrate the experience as a lesson rather than a punishment. A child who feels heard is more likely to reflect than one who feels humiliated.

Digital misbehaviour is often a form of communication. A teenager who is caught creating a secret social media account may be expressing a need for autonomy, connection, or self-expression that they don't feel they can pursue openly. Rather than focusing solely on the deception, parents can ask, "What does this platform give you that you're not getting elsewhere?" or "What made it hard to come to us about this?" These questions invite dialogue about needs and boundaries, and they may even prompt parents to reconsider whether current rules are developmentally appropriate.

This doesn't mean compromising on safety or abandoning standards, but it does mean acknowledging that as children grow, so must the parameters around digital engagement. Adolescents in particular need increasing room to make decisions, even imperfect ones, within a framework of support. A parent who insists on complete control over every digital decision risks eroding the very skills they hope to instil—discernment, self-regulation, and ethical judgement.

In many cases, rule-breaking is not malicious but impulsive. Children may bypass a rule simply because they were curious, caught up in the moment, or unaware of the consequences. A twelve-year-old who downloads a prohibited app may not fully understand the risks associated with data sharing or online interactions. Rather than assuming ill intent, parents can use the incident to teach: "What do you think the risks of this app might be?" or "Why do you think we had concerns about that platform?" This approach builds critical thinking rather than compliance.

Another valuable practice is revisiting the family's digital agreement regularly. Just as children grow and technology evolves, so too should the family's approach to tech use. If a rule is consistently broken, it may be a sign that it needs to be revised, clarified, or communicated more collaboratively. Inviting children into this process reinforces that digital boundaries are not arbitrary impositions but shared commitments to wellbeing, respect, and trust.

Real-world consequences also help children connect behaviour to broader values. For example, a child who shares an unkind meme about a classmate might be asked to reflect on the impact of their actions, write a note of apology, or discuss online empathy with a trusted adult. These consequences focus on restoration and emotional growth, not shame or fear. They also reinforce that digital actions, though intangible, have very real effects.

Parents may also need to reflect on their own responses to digital misbehaviour. If a child lies about screen time, is the consequence of honesty too harsh? If a child hides their online activity, is there too much surveillance and not enough conversation? These are not questions of blame, but of calibration. Just as children are learning to navigate the digital world, so too are their caregivers. A culture of mutual reflection and adaptation helps foster a dynamic of respect rather than control.

The long-term goal of digital discipline is not merely to prevent misbehaviour, but to help children internalise values and practices that will guide their digital choices long after parental oversight has faded. It is to raise children who can pause before posting, consider the effects of their clicks, and take responsibility for their mistakes. These qualities are not born from fear but from practice—from repeated experiences of being held accountable with kindness, corrected with dignity, and taught with care.

When parents treat missteps as teaching moments rather than transgressions, they build something far more enduring than compliance. They build trust. They build resilience. And they build the foundation for a lifelong relationship with technology that is not only safe, but self-aware and grounded in integrity. Misbehaviour, then, becomes not a detour, but a necessary part of the path toward responsible digital maturity.

Helping Kids Recover from Digital Overload

In households across the world, digital overload has become an increasingly common concern. Children, often through no fault of their own, can find themselves caught in a loop of excessive screen use, leading to symptoms such as mental fatigue, irritability, disrupted sleep, reduced focus, and a general disconnection from their physical environment. Whether the cause is a particularly absorbing video game, a binge-worthy series, social media scrolling, or back-to-back video lessons, the signs of overload tend to present themselves in subtle yet profound ways. What once may have been a healthy balance can slowly slip into compulsion, leaving children feeling emotionally flat and physically depleted, and parents unsure of how to intervene effectively.

The first step in helping a child recover from digital overload is recognising that this state is not a moral failing or behavioural problem. It is, fundamentally, a regulatory imbalance—a mismatch between stimulation and restoration. The human brain, particularly in children and adolescents, is highly sensitive to novel stimuli. Screens provide constant novelty through sound, motion, colour, and interaction. While this can be engaging and educational in moderation, extended exposure overwhelms the brain's processing capacity, particularly when offline decompression time is lacking.

Parents often sense this imbalance instinctively: a child who was previously energetic and focused becomes withdrawn, resistant to offline play, or perpetually "wired" despite being exhausted. Their capacity for creative thinking may diminish, and their interest in previously enjoyed activities may decline. These changes can be disorienting, especially if digital use initially seemed harmless or beneficial. Understanding that recovery requires a reset—not just a temporary halt—enables parents to respond with greater clarity and compassion.

Initiating that reset begins with environment and rhythm. Instead of launching into a confrontation about screen use, parents can gently reintroduce routines that help the child reconnect with their body, mind, and surroundings. This might include reinstating consistent meal times, bedtimes, and periods of outdoor activity. These anchors serve to recalibrate the child's internal clock and provide a predictable structure around which balance can be restored. For instance, a parent might begin by re-establishing a screen-free morning ritual—waking up with music, a shared breakfast, or some light stretching—rather than rushing straight into digital content. The aim is to create moments of stillness and presence that signal to the nervous system that it can slow down.

Importantly, a digital reset is most successful when it is collaborative rather than imposed. Instead of announcing a screen ban, parents can sit down with their child and express genuine concern: "We've noticed you've been feeling a bit off lately—less energised, more frustrated. We think it might be helpful to take a break from screens and try some different things together for a while. What do you think would help you feel better?" This approach invites the child into the process and frames the reset as a path toward wellness, not a punishment.

Many children are initially resistant to the idea of unplugging. After all, screens often serve as emotional crutches—sources of comfort, identity, or distraction. If a child resists change, this should not be interpreted as defiance but as a signal that they may be using digital content to cope with something underlying. A teenager immersed in social media may be seeking social validation they feel is missing offline. A child who binges games might be compensating for stress or a lack of autonomy in other areas of life. Parents can use these cues to explore gently: "What do you like most about spending time online?" or "Is there something about being off screens that feels uncomfortable?" Such conversations help uncover unmet needs and provide direction for offering healthier alternatives.

As screen time is gradually reduced, the focus should shift to filling the vacuum with meaningful, embodied experiences. Children need alternatives that provide pleasure, challenge, or relaxation without digital mediation. These can be tailored to individual interests—drawing, building, music-making, storytelling, cooking, or physical movement. A child who enjoys design might work on a craft project.

A child who is drawn to strategy games might enjoy board games or puzzles. The key is not to replicate the digital experience, but to provide engagement that is tactile, relational, and self-paced.

These screen-free activities are not just distractions—they are mechanisms of re-regulation. Physical play, creative expression, and quiet reflection all help soothe the nervous system and reintroduce natural rhythms of attention and rest. When a child is given the opportunity to experience boredom, to wander outdoors, or to follow their imagination without a programmed agenda, their capacity for internal regulation begins to rebuild. They start to experience satisfaction that comes from within, rather than from the dopamine hits engineered by digital platforms.

There is also a role for shared experiences in this process. Family time—whether through cooking, conversation, walking, or playing together—helps re-establish emotional connection, which can sometimes erode under the isolating influence of screens. A family might take a weekend afternoon to visit a museum, try a new sport, or simply go for an unhurried walk. These moments serve as antidotes to digital fragmentation by fostering presence and togetherness. They remind the child that richness exists outside the digital world and that human connection remains the most profound source of meaning.

As the reset unfolds, parents should remain attuned to signs of withdrawal or frustration. These are not setbacks, but natural responses to behavioural change. A child who is used to immediate gratification and constant novelty may initially struggle with the slower pace of offline life. Parents can validate these feelings—"It makes sense that this feels hard"—while encouraging persistence: "Let's see how you feel after a few days. Your brain might need time to catch up." In doing so, they teach resilience and model emotional literacy.

Technology can be gently reintroduced when the child demonstrates readiness. This might be observed in their improved mood, increased flexibility, re-engagement with non-digital activities, and greater awareness of time. At this stage, parents can facilitate a conversation about intentional use: "Now that we're feeling a bit more balanced, how do you want to approach screen time moving forward?" Together, they can establish boundaries that are not only agreed upon but understood. This might include setting time limits, designating tech-free zones in the home, or creating shared digital rituals like co-viewing a show or taking turns on a game.

It is also important to discuss red flags with the child—those moments when screen use begins to feel compulsive or draining again. Parents can help the child develop internal cues: "How do you know when you've had enough?" or "What signs tell you that it's time to take a break?" These reflective skills are more sustainable than external controls. They equip the child to monitor their own wellbeing, a skill that becomes especially vital during adolescence and adulthood when parental oversight naturally recedes.

Throughout this process, parents must be prepared to reassess and adapt. What works for one child may not suit another. What was effective one month may need recalibrating the next. The goal is not perfection, but progress. A child who learns to recognise overload, to ask for a break, and to reset with support is far better equipped than one who adheres to rules out of fear or habit alone.

It is worth noting that digital overload can sometimes mirror broader family dynamics. If screen use has become excessive across the household, a collective reset may be necessary. Parents who model balanced screen habits—by putting away phones during meals, limiting background noise, and engaging fully in family life—send a powerful message. They show that screen management is not a child's responsibility alone, but a shared commitment to wellbeing.

Helping children recover from digital overload is not a one-off intervention; it is an ongoing practice. It requires parents to observe without judgement, to guide without control, and to respond with both firmness and flexibility. It is not merely about taking devices away, but about reintroducing the child to themselves—their sensations, curiosities, and capacity for engagement beyond the screen.

With thoughtful support, children can learn to self-correct, to recognise when they are digitally saturated, and to choose activities that restore their sense of balance. They come to understand that screens are powerful tools, but not substitutes for real experience. And in that understanding, they are not only protected from the risks of overload but empowered to build a life where technology supports rather than supplants their humanity.

Seeking Professional Help for Digital Struggles

As children become increasingly immersed in the digital world, the lines between typical screen use and problematic digital behaviour can sometimes blur. While most children will, at some point, overindulge in screens or resist limits, there are occasions when digital struggles indicate deeper issues—patterns of behaviour that extend beyond the capacity of even the most mindful and involved parents to address alone. In such cases, seeking professional help is not a sign of failure, but an act of foresight and care. Just as one would consult a doctor for persistent physical symptoms, turning to a therapist, educator, or digital specialist for ongoing technology-related challenges can offer both insight and intervention.

Knowing when to involve a professional can be difficult, particularly in a culture where high screen usage is often normalised. Many children appear to be online constantly—communicating, learning, gaming, or consuming content—making it hard to discern when use becomes genuinely problematic. However, there are certain behavioural indicators that suggest a need for external support. These include significant emotional distress linked to screen time, sharp declines in academic performance, marked changes in mood or sleep, withdrawal from offline activities, and persistent conflict within the family over digital habits. If a child becomes irritable, anxious, or even aggressive when access to devices is limited, or if screen use begins to replace vital aspects of life such as relationships, exercise, and creative play, it is worth considering a professional perspective.

It is also important to pay attention to the emotional tone surrounding digital use. A child who consistently uses screens to avoid uncomfortable feelings—such as loneliness, boredom, sadness, or stress—may be developing a dependency that masks rather than resolves emotional difficulties. This is especially true if digital habits are paired with signs of low self-esteem, apathy, or social anxiety. In such instances, a mental health professional can help distinguish whether the screen is the problem itself or a symptom of an underlying emotional need that has yet to be met in healthier ways.

Therapists, particularly those who specialise in child and adolescent psychology, are well-positioned to explore these dynamics. They can help children identify what draws them to digital content, what feelings it may be soothing or avoiding, and how to develop alternative coping strategies. For example, a young teen spending hours scrolling through social media might be seeking validation or a sense of connection. A therapist could work with that child to build emotional awareness and self-worth, helping them form real-world connections and internalise a more resilient sense of identity. Through structured reflection and emotional skill-building, children begin to reclaim their relationship with technology rather than feel consumed by it.

Educators, too, have a crucial role to play. Teachers are often among the first to notice when digital behaviour begins to interfere with learning. They may observe declining attention spans, incomplete assignments, or excessive fatigue during class. In some cases, students might engage in inappropriate digital behaviour at school, such as accessing restricted sites or using devices during lessons. Involving teachers or school counsellors in early conversations provides valuable context and allows for consistency between home and school. Collaborative plans—such as limiting screen time before homework, providing offline alternatives, or building digital literacy lessons into the curriculum—can support the child more holistically.

Importantly, engaging educators need not wait until problems emerge. Many schools have wellbeing teams or digital citizenship initiatives that offer resources and preventive support. A parent concerned about their child's screen habits might arrange a meeting with a teacher to ask, "What do you observe about my child's engagement in class? Have you noticed any patterns related to their technology use?" These discussions open up a broader understanding and show the child that the adults in their life are communicating and unified in their support.

There are also times when highly specialised input is needed—particularly in cases involving online exploitation, cyberbullying, digital trauma, or compulsive behaviours that resemble addiction. When a child becomes deeply distressed due to online interactions—such as receiving threats, being shamed on social media, or falling victim to grooming tactics—professional intervention becomes essential. These experiences can have significant psychological impacts, including anxiety, shame, or post-traumatic symptoms. In these situations, therapists trained in trauma-informed care can help children process their experiences, rebuild trust, and regain a sense of safety. They also help families navigate next steps, whether that involves school involvement, legal reporting, or platform-based action.

Similarly, if a child exhibits behaviours consistent with technology addiction—such as lying about use, losing interest in offline life, experiencing withdrawal symptoms, or repeatedly failing to cut back despite negative consequences—a consultation with a psychologist or behavioural therapist trained in compulsive behaviours is critical. These professionals use evidence-based strategies, such as cognitive behavioural therapy (CBT), to help children understand the triggers behind their usage, identify distorted beliefs (such as "I'm only valuable when I'm online"), and develop healthier patterns. Such interventions are most effective when integrated with family support, ensuring that home dynamics align with the therapeutic work.

In some cases, parents may also benefit from working with a digital parenting coach or technology consultant. These experts provide guidance on setting up healthy digital ecosystems at home, choosing age-appropriate tools, and establishing collaborative tech agreements. A family struggling with device management might consult a specialist to redesign household screen policies or troubleshoot recurring conflicts. These professionals help bridge the gap between technical know-how and psychological insight, ensuring that the family's digital habits align with its broader values and goals.

One parent, for example, sought help after her eleven-year-old son began staying up all night playing online games, resulting in deteriorating school performance and constant meltdowns. After several failed attempts to impose strict time limits, she worked with a behavioural specialist who helped her design a tiered re-engagement plan. The child was involved in rebuilding his schedule, with clearly defined digital use windows, rest periods, and offline rewards. Over time, he regained control of his usage and began sleeping regularly, without the cycle of conflict that had previously defined their relationship.

Another family faced a different challenge: their teenage daughter was experiencing online harassment after a peer group posted manipulated photos of her. The situation had spiralled, and despite attempts to manage it internally, the emotional toll was severe. A child psychotherapist helped the teen rebuild her confidence, process the betrayal, and reframe her relationship with social media. At the same time, the school worked with the family to enforce digital conduct guidelines and provide a structured support plan. The coordinated response proved far more effective than any single disciplinary measure.

Ultimately, deciding to seek professional help requires courage. It means admitting that a situation is complex enough to need outside perspective—and that can feel vulnerable. Yet it is also an act of strength. It communicates to the child that their wellbeing matters so much that the family is willing to engage extra support. It models healthy help-seeking behaviour and fosters a culture in which struggles are met with problem-solving, not silence or blame.

For parents navigating the digital world alongside their children, this awareness is vital: you do not have to do it alone. Whether the concern is mild or acute, occasional or chronic, there is no shame in asking for assistance. Professionals bring a depth of experience, objectivity, and training that can illuminate patterns, suggest new strategies, and offer reassurance. More importantly, they help restore a sense of forward motion when families feel stuck.

As digital life continues to expand and evolve, so too must our willingness to adapt, reflect, and respond. Children deserve not only access to technology, but the guidance to use it well—and the support to heal when it harms. Seeking professional help is one of the many ways we honour that responsibility. It is a reminder that while digital challenges may be complex, they are not insurmountable—and that with the right tools and allies, we can help our children thrive in a connected world with clarity, resilience, and humanity.

Chapter 10
The Future of Digital Parenting: Adapting to a Changing World

The digital realm is not merely growing—it's accelerating at a pace that reshapes nearly every corner of our existence: how we live, work, learn, and connect with one another. As artificial intelligence gains sophistication, virtual and augmented realities enter everyday life, and automated systems redefine industries, today's children find themselves not simply surrounded by technology but moulded by it in ways their parents could hardly have envisioned. For those raising the next generation, this presents a complex mix of challenge and opportunity: to equip children not just to endure this digital world but to flourish within it, recognising that fluency with technology has become essential, and that the ethical, intellectual, and emotional demands it places on them will only grow.

This chapter grapples with what it means to parent with an eye firmly on the future—to nurture children not solely for today's realities but for the unpredictable digital landscapes they will inherit. Much of the current conversation around digital parenting rightly focuses on mitigating risk, enforcing boundaries, and fostering healthy habits. Yet, equally vital is the task of cultivating the skills, attitudes, and moral frameworks that enable children to engage with emerging technologies in thoughtful, creative, and responsible ways. Parenting in this domain must shift from being reactive—merely managing or restricting screen time—to becoming an active, deliberate cultivation of curiosity, resilience, and ethical awareness.

Consider, for example, the rapid rise of artificial intelligence and automation. AI quietly powers a vast array of daily experiences, from voice-activated assistants and personalised recommendations to facial recognition and generative content. For children, these technologies are often invisible, embedded so seamlessly into the platforms they use that they barely register. But the stakes are significant: AI shapes what children see, how they think, and even what they value, frequently without their conscious awareness. Parents have a crucial role in demystifying AI—not as an arcane, futuristic force but as a human-created system with both strengths and blind spots.

Helping children grasp how AI operates—what it can do well, where it stumbles, and how it mirrors the biases and data it ingests—is an essential step towards meaningful digital literacy. No one expects parents to become machine learning experts overnight. Yet even casual remarks—"Have you noticed how your video suggestions shift after you watch something?" or "Why do you think your search results look different from mine?"—can provoke thoughtful reflection about the algorithms shaping their digital experience. These questions sow the seeds of critical thinking and invite deeper conversations about bias, privacy, and personal agency.

Meanwhile, virtual and augmented reality are redefining how children learn, play, and socialise. Schools are beginning to use VR for immersive history lessons, scientific explorations, and creative storytelling. At the same time, digital spaces like the metaverse offer new arenas for identity-building and exploration. But these innovations bring fresh developmental questions to the fore. How does a child's sense of reality shift when virtual experiences become indistinguishable from the real? What becomes of empathy and focus when face-to-face interaction yields to avatars?

For parents, engagement must go beyond mere content monitoring to encompass the broader context. Participating in, or at least observing, children's activities within virtual spaces allows parents to grasp the cognitive demands and emotional undercurrents these environments evoke. It is here that social norms are forged and values contested. Rather than seeking to shield children from these realms outright, parents should aim to help them interpret their experiences through reflection, ethical understanding, and emotional insight.

Preparing children for a future shaped by digitisation, automation, and global connectivity also means equipping them with skills that may be unfamiliar to today's parents. The roles children will eventually fill might not even exist yet, but the competencies needed—adaptability, creative problem-solving, data literacy, intercultural communication, and ethical judgement—are becoming increasingly clear. Thus, parents should think not only about limiting screen time but about leveraging technology to foster learning, collaboration, and meaningful contribution.

Real-life examples abound: youngsters learning coding and game design through platforms like Scratch or Roblox Studio, joining online communities devoted to science or creative writing, or launching small online ventures to explore entrepreneurship. Far from mere pastime, these activities build confidence, initiative, and a fluency with digital tools that can translate into future vocational success. Encouraged thoughtfully, such engagement nurtures a mindset focused on creation rather than passive consumption—a mindset of shaping the digital world, not simply being shaped by it.

However, greater technological capability brings with it heightened ethical responsibility. One of the most important tasks for parents today is fostering their children's moral compass within the digital realm. As AI increasingly makes decisions on our behalf, as data turns into a valuable commodity, and as online interactions replace many face-to-face moments, children must develop frameworks for ethical reflection. This includes grappling with issues like surveillance, consent, misinformation, digital identity, and the environmental impact of technology production.

Ethical conversations need not be reserved for adolescence or formal schooling. Even young children can start to understand fairness, privacy, and consequences. Parents might ask, "How would you feel if someone shared your photo without asking?" or "Why is it important to check if something you see online is true?" These dialogues help embed digital ethics early and reinforce that technology is never value-neutral—it reflects human decisions.

As the digital terrain continues to evolve, lifelong learning becomes less a lofty ideal and more a practical necessity. While no parent can predict every technological twist their child will face, they can instil a mindset of curiosity, humility, and critical inquiry. Teaching children how to question, verify, and adapt equips them with the resilience to remain literate in a world of constant change.

Modelling this approach matters just as much. Parents who show genuine curiosity about new apps, admit when they don't fully understand a tool, and learn alongside their children cultivate an environment where adaptation is seen as natural rather than intimidating. This shared journey strengthens bonds and demonstrates that true competence lies not in having all the answers but in the willingness to explore, reflect, and grow.

Above all, this chapter offers a message of hope: technology, complex and sometimes overwhelming though it may be, is not inherently threatening. It is a tool—a powerful one, capable of enriching lives, fostering creativity, and connecting people. Used thoughtfully, it can deepen relationships, open doors, and support a child's development in myriad ways. To achieve this, parents must resist extremes: neither blindly embracing every new gadget nor rejecting technology out of fear. Instead, they must engage thoughtfully, purposefully, and with an openness to change.

The future of digital parenting does not rest on stricter rules or looser control but on deeper presence. It flourishes through evolving conversations, enduring values, and a commitment not just to digital skills but to digital wisdom. By doing so, we prepare children not merely to use technology, but to make wise choices with it—and ultimately, to grow into the thoughtful, capable people they are meant to be.

How Emerging Tech Will Shape the Next Generation

The rapid evolution of digital technology is not simply altering how children learn, play, and socialise—it is reshaping the architecture of childhood itself. Artificial intelligence, virtual and augmented reality, blockchain-based systems, and increasingly intelligent automation are no longer speculative features of a futuristic world; they are part of a living ecosystem that influences a child's development from the moment they pick up a tablet, engage with a smart assistant, or immerse themselves in a digital environment. Understanding how these emerging technologies are likely to influence the next generation is not just a theoretical exercise for educators or futurists—it is a practical imperative for parents, who are tasked with preparing their children for a reality defined by constant digital innovation.

Artificial intelligence, in particular, is swiftly becoming an ambient force in children's lives. Once confined to science fiction, AI now powers the recommendation engines behind YouTube Kids, personalises learning platforms used in classrooms, filters content on social media, and even generates text and images with minimal human input. These tools are capable of extraordinary benefits—offering tailored educational content, streamlining communication, and enhancing creativity. Yet they also raise fundamental questions about autonomy, agency, and influence. When an algorithm decides what a child sees, hears, or plays next, it subtly shapes their attention, preferences, and even aspirations.

What's more, AI systems learn from the data they are fed, which often reflects historical biases and unexamined assumptions. A child interacting with AI-generated stories or image-based search results may unknowingly absorb skewed representations of gender, ethnicity, or intelligence. If left unexamined, these biases can calcify into belief systems. Thus, it becomes essential not only to monitor *what* children are consuming through AI but also to teach them *how* these systems function. Even at a young age, children can begin to grasp that machines make decisions based on patterns—not wisdom—and that these patterns are only as fair as the data from which they are drawn.

Virtual and augmented reality are further transforming the boundaries between experience and simulation. Immersive VR environments allow children to step inside a cell, travel through ancient Rome, or walk through the rings of Saturn. These experiences hold immense potential for cognitive and emotional learning, offering a depth of engagement far beyond static texts or two-dimensional screens. Yet their very intensity raises concerns about overstimulation, emotional detachment, and the blurring of fantasy and reality.

Take, for instance, the case of children using VR for social interaction—whether in multiplayer games or in more expansive virtual worlds. The avatars they create, the roles they adopt, and the behaviours they exhibit can feel vivid and absorbing, especially for those who may struggle with offline confidence or social anxiety. While this can be liberating, it also risks becoming escapist, particularly when the virtual self is experienced as more valid or successful than the real one. Parents must pay attention not only to the content of these interactions but to their emotional residue: Is the child energised, emotionally regulated, and socially enriched after VR use, or withdrawn, dysregulated, and disconnected?

Equally significant is the way these technologies shift attention spans and sensory processing. Virtual and augmented realities present stimuli in high definition, surround sound, and real-time responsiveness, creating deeply absorbing experiences that can make the physical world feel dull by comparison. This can influence how children engage with reality, potentially reducing their capacity to tolerate boredom, delay gratification, or engage in sustained, unstructured play. To mitigate this, parents and educators must ensure that digital immersion is balanced with opportunities for real-world exploration, tactile learning, and emotional presence.

Beyond AI and VR, the broader digital landscape is evolving toward greater integration of decentralised systems, data-driven environments, and personalised experiences. Smart toys, wearables, and connected home devices now create a constant feedback loop between child behaviour and machine learning. On the one hand, this can enable safer, more customised environments. On the other, it introduces new layers of surveillance, commercialisation, and dependency. The fact that many children now grow up with their data being collected from infancy raises profound ethical questions about consent, privacy, and the commodification of childhood.

Children today are not merely using technology; they are becoming the subjects of technological systems that learn, predict, and respond in ways that can feel seamless yet remain opaque. The predictive text that finishes their sentences, the app that anticipates their interests, the smart speaker that knows their favourite song—these tools are remarkable in their utility but subtle in their encroachment. Over time, they may condition children to expect frictionless experiences, immediate answers, and curated realities—traits that are at odds with the messiness, uncertainty, and complexity of real life.

This creates a developmental paradox. Emerging technologies can offer children more power, more access, and more expression than ever before—but only if they are accompanied by the critical capacities to use them wisely. Without intentional guidance, these tools may instead foster passivity, entitlement, or susceptibility to manipulation. The antidote is not abstinence, but education—teaching children to question, reflect, and navigate. Helping them understand, for instance, that an AI-generated answer is not necessarily correct, that a virtual experience is constructed rather than spontaneous, or that a smart device remembers more than it reveals.

Real-world applications of this approach are already visible in forward-thinking classrooms and homes. Children are being introduced to coding not just as a technical skill, but as a form of digital authorship. They are being taught to analyse the news with an awareness of algorithmic curation. Some schools now incorporate digital ethics into their curriculum, prompting students to consider what fairness, consent, and justice mean in a digital context. These are early steps toward a more literate generation—one that does not merely consume digital content but interrogates and contributes to it with intelligence and integrity.

For parents, staying abreast of these changes can feel overwhelming, especially when the pace of innovation often exceeds the capacity for oversight. But it is less important to master the technicalities than to stay relationally present. A parent who is curious, open to dialogue, and willing to learn alongside their child models the very adaptability the digital age requires. Asking questions such as "How does that work?" or "What do you think about what that AI just said?" signals to the child that their thinking matters—and that technology is not a fixed authority, but a space for exploration and critique.

It is also vital to maintain spaces for digital rest. Just as children need sleep to consolidate memory and learning, they need time away from the algorithmically mediated world to develop a stable sense of self. Time in nature, unstructured play, creative experimentation, and face-to-face conversations provide the counterbalance to digital acceleration. These experiences root children in embodiment, empathy, and presence—qualities that no algorithm can replicate.

Ultimately, emerging technologies will not only shape how children learn and play; they will influence how they define reality, identity, and meaning. They will grow up in a world where machines can write essays, simulate emotion, and predict behaviour. But it will be their capacity for judgement, imagination, and ethical reflection that determines how these tools are used—and whether they amplify our shared humanity or erode it.

The next generation does not need to be shielded from technology—they need to be prepared to shape it. That preparation begins at home, with conversations that foster curiosity and caution, freedom and responsibility, creativity and critique. When parents engage with technology not as a threat but as a field of shared inquiry, they empower their children to meet the future with confidence—not because they have all the answers, but because they have been taught how to think deeply, question bravely, and lead wisely in a world that is still being built.

Preparing Kids for Digital Careers

The world of work is undergoing a seismic shift. The proliferation of artificial intelligence, robotics, blockchain technology, and intelligent automation is not simply augmenting human labour—it is redefining what labour looks like altogether. The skills that once served as cornerstones of employability are evolving, and new competencies are emerging that were virtually unknown a generation ago. As this transformation gathers pace, parents are faced with an essential task: not only to guide their children through the digital present but to prepare them for professional futures that will be increasingly shaped by digital innovation.

Digital careers no longer reside solely within the confines of traditional tech roles. While coding, data science, and cybersecurity remain essential, the influence of technology has expanded into nearly every sector—healthcare, education, law, finance, agriculture, design, entertainment, and social impact. A marketing executive today is expected to understand analytics dashboards and machine learning-driven customer segmentation. A journalist must navigate content algorithms and audience engagement tools. Even artists and musicians increasingly rely on digital platforms for creation, distribution, and monetisation. This means that digital literacy is no longer a niche skill—it is a foundational fluency.

For children to thrive in this environment, education must go beyond technical proficiency. The ability to write clean code or use design software is valuable, but it is not sufficient. What distinguishes resilient and forward-thinking professionals is the capacity to learn continuously, solve novel problems, collaborate across cultures and disciplines, and adapt ethically to shifting landscapes. These meta-skills—often termed "21st-century skills"—are the connective tissue of tomorrow's job market.

One of the most critical areas is computational thinking, which encompasses the ability to break down complex problems, recognise patterns, and develop logical sequences. Children exposed to basic programming languages like Scratch or Python learn far more than syntax—they internalise a way of thinking that underpins not only computer science but also engineering, architecture, finance, and logistics. More importantly, these skills teach persistence, strategic iteration, and the understanding that failure is a temporary phase on the path to innovation.

Creative problem-solving is another essential capability. As automation handles repetitive and rule-based tasks, human contribution will increasingly centre around innovation, improvisation, and originality. A child who can design a new product, reimagine a flawed system, or invent a more inclusive user experience will be far more adaptable in a digital economy than one who has memorised facts or mastered rote operations. Parents can nurture this creativity by encouraging open-ended play, hands-on tinkering, and interdisciplinary curiosity. A child who codes a game, builds a robot, writes a blog, or invents a new way to recycle at home is already participating in the kind of imaginative thinking that defines digital leadership.

Equally vital is an understanding of digital communication and collaboration. Many careers now take place in distributed or hybrid environments, where employees interact through video conferencing, shared documents, asynchronous platforms, and AI-enhanced tools. Children who learn how to contribute respectfully in online communities, give and receive feedback constructively, and manage their digital presence with intention are already developing the soft skills that employers consistently identify as indispensable. These are not innate talents—they are teachable habits, reinforced by parental modelling, structured digital projects, and positive screen experiences.

Data literacy is another cornerstone of future-readiness. In an age where data drives decision-making across industries, children must be able to interpret charts, understand basic statistics, and evaluate claims based on evidence. More broadly, they need to learn how data is collected, what it represents, and how it can be misused. A teenager analysing the metrics of their YouTube channel, reviewing traffic to a family-run Etsy store, or exploring public datasets on climate change is practising skills that will be relevant in fields as diverse as epidemiology, urban planning, policy-making, and investment banking.

Of course, digital fluency is not only about output but also about judgement. Ethical thinking must run parallel to technical training. As children encounter AI tools, facial recognition software, deepfakes, and surveillance technologies, they need to be able to ask nuanced questions: Who built this system? What biases might it reflect? Who is affected by its outcomes? Teaching digital ethics at home—through discussions about privacy, digital rights, misinformation, and accountability—prepares children not just to use tools, but to shape them responsibly.

Real-world applications of this philosophy are already visible in forward-thinking educational programmes. In Estonia, for example, children begin learning coding in primary school—not to become programmers, necessarily, but to understand the logic behind the systems that shape their world. In the United Kingdom, computing is now part of the national curriculum, integrating algorithms, data representation, and online safety from an early age. Beyond formal schooling, countless informal avenues—such as hackathons, coding clubs, digital storytelling camps, and open-source collaborations—provide children with experiential learning that blends technical expertise with personal expression.

Parents can reinforce these efforts by embracing a mindset of co-learning. Rather than positioning themselves as digital outsiders, they can explore tools, platforms, and innovations alongside their children. Watching a documentary on AI ethics, building a family website, trying out a 3D printing project, or experimenting with game development software together can transform digital skills from abstract obligations into shared adventures. This approach not only deepens family bonds but models a lifelong learning attitude that children will carry into their careers.

Preparing children for digital careers also means broadening their awareness of what is possible. Many young people limit their aspirations based on narrow representations of work—thinking that tech means only software engineering or that digital careers are confined to Silicon Valley. Parents can expand their children's horizons by exposing them to diverse role models—female data scientists, disabled VR developers, Indigenous technologists working on climate resilience. Highlighting social impact tech projects or creative technology applications shows children that digital work is not just about profit or prestige but about solving real-world problems and contributing to the public good.

Importantly, not every child will become a tech specialist—and that's perfectly acceptable. The objective is not to produce a generation of coders, but to raise a generation that is fluent, critical, and empowered in digital environments. A future teacher will use data dashboards to support personalised learning. A future nurse may use augmented reality to visualise patient anatomy. A future lawyer will engage with AI-assisted research. In every case, the professional will need not only technical tools but the judgement to use them wisely.

The most enduring preparation, then, is not technical training alone but the cultivation of adaptability, curiosity, and ethical clarity. These are the attributes that will allow children to pivot between roles, integrate new technologies into their work, and continue learning as the digital landscape evolves. As parents, we do not need to predict the future of work in precise detail—but we do need to plant the intellectual and emotional seeds that will allow our children to flourish within it.

Preparing kids for digital careers is less about teaching them *what* to do and more about teaching them *how* to think, explore, and create. It means helping them see technology not as something to passively consume, but as a space in which they can build, question, and contribute. It means fostering both competence and conscience, so they can lead not just with skill but with vision. And above all, it means believing that their digital future is not something to fear—but something they are ready to help shape.

The Ethical Side of Technology

As technology increasingly weaves itself into every dimension of childhood, from the apps they use to communicate to the algorithms that influence what they see and learn, conversations about digital ethics can no longer be considered optional or premature. In a world where children interact with artificial intelligence, generate and share vast amounts of personal data, and navigate digital spaces that are often surveilled and commercialised, the need for ethical literacy is not just timely—it is urgent. Parents must help their children think beyond convenience and entertainment, and begin to explore what it means to be responsible, fair, and humane in an interconnected digital world.

Artificial intelligence represents one of the most profound technological shifts confronting this generation. From voice assistants and recommendation systems to facial recognition and generative AI models, children are being introduced to technologies that appear intelligent, capable, and even authoritative. However, what lies beneath this apparent intelligence are vast data sets, statistical models, and design decisions made by human programmers—decisions that embed cultural assumptions, historical biases, and commercial motives. When a child asks Siri a question or uses a generative chatbot for homework, they are not just receiving a neutral answer; they are engaging with a tool that prioritises certain kinds of knowledge, language, and behaviour over others.

Parents and educators must help children deconstruct these experiences. A simple query like "Why do you think the chatbot answered that way?" or "Do you think another tool would give a different answer?" can spark a discussion about how AI systems are trained and why their outputs must be questioned. Children should understand that AI is not inherently fair or objective. For example, studies have shown that facial recognition software often performs less accurately on individuals with darker skin tones due to unbalanced training data. Similarly, recommendation algorithms on platforms like YouTube or TikTok may lead users toward increasingly extreme content because sensational material drives engagement.

These are not abstract concerns—they directly affect how children perceive themselves and others. If a child searches for "smart people" and the image results predominantly feature one race or gender, that child absorbs a powerful message about who belongs in certain intellectual spaces. If their content feed subtly reinforces stereotypes or isolates them in ideological bubbles, it shapes their worldview in ways they may not recognise. Teaching children to interrogate these systems is part of helping them think ethically: to consider whose voices are amplified, whose experiences are marginalised, and what consequences arise from these patterns.

Surveillance is another critical area of ethical concern. Children today grow up under a level of observation that previous generations would find unimaginable. Their activities are tracked by apps, educational platforms, social media sites, and even toys connected to the internet. While some of this surveillance is marketed as safety—location sharing for parental peace of mind, or monitoring software to protect against harmful content—it raises deeper questions about autonomy, consent, and the right to privacy.

Children have a right to understand who is collecting their data, why it is being collected, and what is being done with it. Parents can begin by explaining how digital footprints work: how clicks, likes, and searches contribute to user profiles that are bought, sold, and used to target advertisements or personalise content. These are not scare tactics, but empowering knowledge. A child who knows their app history affects what they see tomorrow is more likely to pause and reflect before engaging impulsively. Moreover, such understanding encourages children to think about their own data choices and how those choices affect others.

For instance, when children post photos of friends without asking, or share someone's location in a group chat, they are engaging in ethical decisions about visibility and consent. Parents can help them consider these actions in broader terms: "Would you want that shared if the roles were reversed?" or "How do we decide what's OK to post about someone else?" These conversations teach children that digital responsibility includes respecting the boundaries and dignity of others—even in casual, everyday interactions.

The ethical use of technology is also about intent and consequence. When children use generative AI tools to complete assignments, copy code, or replicate artwork, the question is not simply whether it's allowed—it's whether it's fair, honest, and aligned with their values. Digital ethics includes understanding the importance of original work, the responsibilities of attribution, and the implications of outsourcing thinking to machines. A child who relies on AI to complete their homework may produce a passable result, but they also miss the opportunity to engage critically, to wrestle with the material, and to develop their voice. Parents can use such situations not to punish, but to prompt reflection: "What part of this work did you feel confident doing on your own?" or "How could AI support your learning without replacing it?"

Ethics in the digital world also includes recognising the environmental impact of our technologies. Data centres that power cloud computing and AI require enormous energy, and the production of devices depends on rare earth minerals and complex supply chains. Children do not need to become experts in environmental science, but they should be introduced to the idea that digital choices have physical consequences. Turning off autoplay, reducing redundant downloads, or extending the life of devices are all simple habits that reflect a deeper awareness of digital sustainability. Framing technology as part of a shared planetary system rather than an abstract, limitless resource fosters a sense of stewardship and interdependence.

Perhaps the most powerful ethical lesson, however, comes from modelling. Children learn most effectively not from lectures, but from lived experience. When parents show curiosity about technology's implications, set boundaries around their own screen use, ask critical questions about the apps they use, and admit when they don't have all the answers, they are showing that ethical engagement is an ongoing process. They are teaching that being digitally responsible is not about having perfect control, but about staying conscious, informed, and compassionate.

Consider the case of a parent who discovers their child has used an AI image generator to alter a classmate's photo and share it as a joke. Rather than reacting with anger or blanket bans, the parent chooses to explore the deeper impact. Together, they discuss how the image might affect the classmate's reputation, what it feels like to be made fun of online, and why digital tools amplify these effects. They talk about humour, harm, and what it means to have power at the click of a button. The parent might involve the school, facilitate an apology, and help the child find ways to repair trust. This becomes a defining moment not just in discipline, but in ethical growth.

Such scenarios are increasingly common, and they illustrate that digital responsibility is not static—it evolves as technologies evolve, and as children encounter new capabilities and new dilemmas. The aim is not to create children who always do the right thing, but who know *how* to think about what the right thing might be. It is about cultivating discernment, empathy, and accountability.

In the end, the ethical side of technology is not merely a set of rules—it is a way of seeing the world. It involves recognising that every click, share, and interaction is part of a broader ecosystem of impact. When children are taught to consider that impact—not only on themselves, but on others, on society, and on the environment—they develop the kind of moral imagination that is indispensable in the digital age.

These conversations may begin simply, but their implications are profound. They prepare children not only to navigate technology, but to shape it. And in doing so, they equip the next generation with what truly matters: not just the skills to use digital tools, but the wisdom to wield them with care.

Lifelong Digital Literacy

As technology continues to evolve at an unprecedented pace, one thing becomes increasingly clear: digital literacy can no longer be viewed as a fixed body of knowledge to be mastered in childhood and left behind. Rather, it must be understood as a lifelong competency—one that enables individuals to adapt, evaluate, and thrive in a world where technological fluency is as vital as reading or numeracy. For today's children, growing up with screens, smart devices, and algorithmically curated content is not a novelty—it is a default. But familiarity with digital tools does not necessarily translate into wisdom, critical awareness, or adaptability. Raising children who are truly digitally literate requires far more than ensuring they know how to use a tablet or navigate a search engine. It requires cultivating a mindset that remains curious, ethical, and resilient across decades of digital transformation.

At its core, digital literacy involves more than technical skill. It encompasses the ability to critically assess digital content, understand the socio-political implications of technology, interact ethically and respectfully online, and stay agile in the face of constant change. In practice, this means teaching children to question what they see, understand how information is structured and presented, and navigate digital ecosystems without being overwhelmed or manipulated. It also means nurturing the flexibility to learn new tools as they emerge—an ability that has become essential in virtually every profession and facet of adult life.

Consider the speed at which technological norms have shifted in just the last two decades. The tools that dominated early internet culture—basic websites, email, instant messaging—have been eclipsed by streaming platforms, virtual classrooms, immersive gaming environments, social networks, and machine-learning driven services. Children today are interacting with AI-powered tutors, creating videos that reach global audiences, and accessing information through voice-controlled interfaces. Within the next decade, they will likely be navigating technologies that we cannot yet fully imagine, from neural interfaces to quantum-powered systems. This pace of change means that static instruction is insufficient. Instead, children must learn how to *learn* technology—how to approach new systems with confidence, evaluate their implications, and determine their relevance to their lives.

This process begins with critical thinking. A digitally literate child does not accept online content at face value but asks, "Who created this? Why was it made? What is it trying to persuade me to believe or do?" These questions are essential for resisting misinformation, understanding bias, and making informed decisions in a world where content is often shaped more by algorithms than editorial boards. For example, when a young person watches a seemingly innocent video that subtly promotes harmful stereotypes, or when they encounter a viral post containing distorted facts, their ability to dissect these messages becomes a form of intellectual self-defence.

Yet critical thinking must be balanced with creative engagement. Digital literacy is not only about scepticism; it is also about expression. Children should be encouraged to use digital tools to create—whether they're coding a game, composing digital music, curating a blog, or editing a short film. These acts of creation teach children that technology is not merely something to consume but a medium through which they can shape ideas, influence culture, and solve real problems. Moreover, such experiences build confidence. A child who learns how to build a basic website or contribute to an open-source project is more likely to approach future technologies with a sense of capability, rather than intimidation.

The challenge for parents and educators is to support this kind of engagement without falling into either of two traps: passive permissiveness or rigid control. Overregulation can stifle exploration and breed secrecy, while unchecked access can leave children vulnerable to exploitation and dependency. Instead, the goal should be co-learning. Adults don't need to have all the answers, but they do need to model curiosity, self-reflection, and ethical awareness. When a parent says, "Let's figure out how this app works together," or, "I wonder what happens to our data when we use this platform," they are demonstrating that digital literacy is an ongoing process, one that continues into adulthood.

The importance of digital adaptability is perhaps most evident in the workplace. Many of the careers that today's children will pursue are likely to be shaped—or even created—by technologies that are still in development. This means that vocational success will depend not only on qualifications but on the ability to learn new systems quickly, collaborate across digital platforms, and navigate the ethical dilemmas posed by emerging tools. A future healthcare worker may need to interpret data from AI-assisted diagnostics. A future teacher might conduct hybrid lessons across virtual environments. Even roles that seem unrelated to tech today may require digital dexterity, from farmers using drone analytics to artists selling NFTs.

Therefore, cultivating lifelong digital literacy must also include emotional resilience. Children need to be prepared not just for technological complexity but for the psychological toll of life lived partially online. They must learn how to manage screen-related fatigue, resist the lure of constant comparison, and maintain a healthy sense of self in digital environments that are often engineered for persuasion and engagement rather than wellbeing.

This means helping children recognise when they need a break, build habits of intentional use, and develop an internal compass that is not swayed by the metrics of likes, followers, or algorithmic visibility.

It also requires teaching children to navigate digital relationships with empathy and accountability. In an era of anonymous comments, viral outrage, and performative content, it's easy for young users to lose sight of the fact that there are real people on the other side of the screen. A digitally literate child understands that online behaviour carries consequences, and that kindness, consent, and boundaries are just as vital in digital interactions as they are offline. These are not abstract ideals—they can be taught through real-time conversations about group chats, gaming etiquette, or the sharing of images and stories.

Schools play a vital role in this ecosystem. While many educational systems have made strides in integrating technology, the emphasis is often on functionality rather than fluency. It is not enough for students to know how to submit assignments through a learning management system or use collaborative documents. They need structured opportunities to reflect on digital identity, explore the implications of surveillance technologies, understand the economics of data, and participate in meaningful digital citizenship projects. When schools partner with families in fostering these competencies, children receive consistent messages that help them build a cohesive understanding of their digital environment.

Real-world examples can bring these principles to life. A secondary school in Denmark invites students to design their own apps that solve local problems, encouraging both technical skill and civic engagement. In New Zealand, some primary schools incorporate digital storytelling projects that combine Māori oral tradition with multimedia tools, blending cultural heritage with technological fluency. In Singapore, coding bootcamps for young girls address gender imbalances in tech and build confidence through mentorship and peer collaboration. These initiatives exemplify how digital literacy can be culturally responsive, socially embedded, and emotionally enriching.

At home, similar practices can be introduced in age-appropriate ways. A family might create a shared digital calendar to teach time management and planning. They might discuss a documentary about deepfakes or AI bias to stimulate ethical reflection. Or they might co-create a video to share with relatives, discussing together what makes content respectful, meaningful, and authentic. These practices are not about mastering specific tools—they are about forming habits of thoughtful interaction with technology that will serve children well, no matter what the future holds.

Ultimately, lifelong digital literacy is about equipping children not just to keep up with the world, but to shape it. It is about raising individuals who can respond to new technologies not with passive acceptance or reactive fear, but with informed curiosity, critical discernment, and grounded values. These children will not only be capable users of technology—they will be active participants in its direction, advocates for its ethical development, and builders of inclusive, humane digital futures. And that, perhaps more than any technical skill, is what true digital literacy demands.

Final Thoughts – Parenting with Confidence in the Digital Age

Parenting has never been a static role. Across centuries and cultures, mothers, fathers, and caregivers have constantly adapted to the shifting social, cultural, and technological realities of their time. Yet the digital age presents a unique set of challenges and opportunities, not only because of the sheer speed at which technology evolves, but because it reshapes the very fabric of childhood and adolescence. Screens are no longer confined to the living room; they are in our children's pockets, classrooms, bedrooms, and even in their toys. Amid this transformation, many parents understandably feel overwhelmed—unsure whether to welcome new tools with open arms or to push back with protective force. But confidence in digital parenting does not require certainty or technical mastery. It begins with reframing technology not as an adversary, but as a tool—one that, when used thoughtfully, can support growth, connection, and lifelong learning.

For many, the instinctive response to digital change is caution. Horror stories about online predators, cyberbullying, screen addiction, and algorithmic manipulation dominate headlines and social media feeds. These concerns are not without merit. The digital world *does* pose risks, and children are especially vulnerable to its exploitative corners. But fear alone does not prepare children to thrive. Nor does shielding them from technology indefinitely. What builds competence—for both parents and children—is informed engagement. It's about approaching digital life with discernment, curiosity, and a willingness to learn together.

A parent who embraces this mindset might not know how an AI image generator works, but they will ask, "How did it come up with that result?" They might not understand every detail of blockchain, but they will recognise its relevance to emerging online economies. Most importantly, they will invite their children into open conversations—not just about *what* technology does, but about *why* and *how* it matters. This approach models humility and adaptability—two essential qualities in a world where no one, not even the experts, can fully predict what's coming next.

Confidence also grows through relational presence. One of the most valuable assets any parent has in the digital age is their emotional connection to their child. Algorithms may personalise content, but they do not love. Platforms may be engaging, but they do not nurture trust. Children who feel anchored in strong relationships are better equipped to evaluate digital experiences, recover from online disappointments, and seek help when they encounter distress. A child who knows they can speak openly to their parents about what they've seen, felt, or done online—without fear of punishment or dismissal—is far more likely to develop resilience and ethical awareness.

This does not mean avoiding boundaries. It means replacing rigid control with collaborative guidance. Instead of imposing arbitrary screen time limits, parents can co-create family agreements that reflect mutual understanding and shared values. For example, rather than declaring that "no phones are allowed at dinner," a parent might explain, "Dinner is our time to be fully present with each other. Let's all put our devices away so we can really connect." This reframing invites participation rather than resistance. It also models respect—something children are more likely to reciprocate when making their own digital choices.

There are countless examples of parents using technology not just as a management issue, but as an opportunity for bonding and learning. One mother in Toronto began playing the same online multiplayer game as her son—not to monitor him, but to better understand what drew him to the experience. Their shared gameplay became a point of connection, leading to richer conversations about teamwork, fairness, and online conduct. Another father in Bangalore used YouTube tutorials to learn basic animation with his daughter, resulting in a short film they created together about their family's migration story. These moments illustrate that screens, when approached mindfully, can foster creativity, collaboration, and storytelling across generations.

Technology can also support family life in more subtle ways. Shared digital calendars help coordinate busy schedules. Video calls connect relatives across continents. Meditation apps support wellbeing. Digital scrapbooks preserve memories. Even simple voice notes can maintain connection during long workdays. These tools are not inherently harmful—they reflect how digital systems, when purposefully integrated, can complement rather than compete with human relationships.

Of course, no tool is neutral. Every technology reflects the priorities of its creators and the cultures in which it is used. That's why raising digitally literate children also involves raising socially aware children. Parents can prompt reflection by asking questions such as, "Why do you think this app is free? How does it make money?" or "What kinds of people do you see represented in this video—and who's missing?" These discussions teach children to move beyond passive consumption and begin to interrogate the power structures behind their digital worlds.

Confidence also involves recognising when to seek support. Parents are not expected to navigate every digital dilemma alone. Teachers, school counsellors, digital literacy organisations, and child psychologists can all offer guidance and perspective. Joining parent groups, attending workshops, or reading trusted resources provides not only knowledge, but a sense of community—reminding caregivers that their concerns are shared and their questions valid.

Equally important is allowing space for failure and repair. Children will make mistakes online. They will share things they later regret, follow misleading content, or overstep boundaries. But each of these missteps is an opportunity for growth. A child who accidentally stumbles into inappropriate content can be helped to understand context, reflect on emotion, and develop strategies for future encounters. A teenager who breaks a screen rule can be invited into a conversation about consequences—not as punishment, but as a path to rebuilding trust.

What matters most in these moments is the parental response. Shame closes doors; empathy opens them. A parent who reacts with curiosity rather than accusation sends a powerful message: "Your digital life matters to me. Not because I want to control it, but because I care about *you*—your integrity, your safety, your wellbeing."

Over time, this foundation enables children to become self-aware digital citizens. They begin to anticipate consequences, question intent, manage impulses, and reflect on their digital habits. They also become more capable of resisting peer pressure, disengaging from toxic spaces, and building healthier online relationships. These are the hallmarks of maturity—and they are developed not through prohibition, but through consistent guidance and mutual respect.

Ultimately, parenting with confidence in the digital age does not mean knowing everything. It means being willing to ask questions, stay engaged, and model the values we hope our children will carry forward. It means understanding that technology is not an enemy to be defeated, but a terrain to be explored—a terrain where families can learn, play, build, and grow together. By shifting from fear to curiosity, from control to collaboration, and from rules to relationships, we empower our children not just to survive the digital world—but to shape it with wisdom, creativity, and care.

About the Author

Anika Vermeer is a parenting and education researcher with a deep interest in the intersection of child psychology, technology, and modern family dynamics. With years of experience advising schools and families across Europe and Asia, she brings a global perspective to the challenges of raising emotionally intelligent, digitally aware children. Her work blends scientific insight with practical tools, empowering parents to foster resilience, empathy, and healthy screen habits in a fast-moving digital world. Digital Parenting: Raising Balanced Kids in a Screen-Filled World is her latest contribution to equipping modern parents for an age of constant connection.

www.ingramcontent.com/pod-product-compliance
Lightning Source LLC
Chambersburg PA
CBHW031339230926
51848CB00002B/309
9789371349666